Subcontinental Drift

South Asia in World Affairs Series
T. V. Paul, Series Editor

Titles in the Series

Pakistan's Pathway to the Bomb: Ambitions, Politics, and Rivalries
Mansoor Ahmed

Afghan Endgames: Strategy and Policy Choices for America's Longest War
Hy Rothstein and John Arquilla, Editors

The China-India Rivalry in the Globalization Era
T. V. Paul, Editor

The Engagement of India: Strategies and Responses
Ian Hall, Editor

Globalization and India's Economic Integration
Baldev Raj Nayar

India and Nuclear Asia: Forces, Doctrine, and Dangers
Yogesh Joshi and Frank O'Donnell

India's Rise as an Asian Power: Nation, Neighborhood, and Region
Sandy Gordon

The Indian Ocean and US Grand Strategy: Ensuring Access and Promoting Security
Andrew C. Winner and Peter Dombrowski, Editors

Pakistan's Counterterrorism Challenge
Moeed Yusuf, Editor

Pakistan's Political Parties: Surviving between Dictatorship and Democracy
Mariam Mufti, Sahar Shafqat, and Niloufer Siddiqui, Editors

Vying for Allah's Vote: Understanding Islamic Parties, Political Violence, and Extremism in Pakistan
Haroon K. Ullah

Subcontinental Drift

Domestic Politics and India's Foreign Policy

Rajesh Basrur

Georgetown University Press / Washington, DC

Library of Congress Cataloging-in-Publication Data

Names: Basrur, Rajesh M., author.
Title: Subcontinental drift : domestic politics and India's foreign policy / Rajesh Basrur.
Other titles: South Asia in world affairs series.
Description: Washington, DC : Georgetown University Press, [2023] | Series: South Asia in world affairs series | Includes bibliographical references and index.
Identifiers: LCCN 2022001377 (print) | LCCN 2022001378 (ebook) | ISBN 9781647122850 (paperback) | ISBN 9781647122843 (hardcover) | ISBN 9781647122867 (ebook)
Subjects: LCSH: India—Foreign relations—1984-
Classification: LCC DS449 .B373 2022 (print) | LCC DS449 (ebook) | DDC 327.54—dc23/eng/20220712
LC record available at https://lccn.loc.gov/2022001377
LC ebook record available at https://lccn.loc.gov/2022001378

This paper meets the requirements of ANSI/NISO Z39.48-1992 (Permanence of Paper).

24 23 9 8 7 6 5 4 3 2 First printing

Printed in the United States of America

Cover design by Erin Kirk
Interior design by Paul Hotvedt, Blue Heron Typesetters, LLC

To

Swati

CONTENTS

TABLES

PREFACE

This book has been a decade in the making, perhaps necessarily so, because it reflects my efforts over time to grapple with numerous tensions in the academic analysis of international relations. Three tensions in particular stimulated my writing on these pages. At the most elementary level, it is driven by a desire to investigate the contradiction between India's quest for power and status and the limitations of its policies and policymakers, most recently visible in the struggle to manage the COVID-19 pandemic. Many works address this issue, but I try to explain the contradiction in ways that I do not think have been done before through the lens of theory-driven analysis. In the process, I have felt it necessary to wrestle with the limitations of theory itself and to try to modify it in a way that brings in what I think are vital elements missing from the current theoretical enterprise.

Over the decades, I have also been struck by the gulf between studies on India's external relationships and cutting-edge theory (with a few exceptions). However, this is rapidly being bridged by younger scholars, many of whom are cited in this work. This concern, in conjunction with my sense that India faces serious constraints in seeking to attain the international prominence it has been pursuing, persuaded me to look more closely at neoclassical realism, which has done much to bring rigor to the analysis of foreign policy. Neoclassical realism spans the external and domestic realms, and it highlights the ways in which policymakers are often confounded by the political environment in which they function or the methods they choose. To my mind, they are also hobbled by their own shortcomings, particularly by their neglect of their responsibility to act morally, but this aspect has been somewhat neglected by scholars working on India and by theoreticians generally (again, with exceptions). My effort in these pages is to build on the rich research in neoclassical realism and examine the tensions between the India that is an increasingly influential "rising power" and the India that from time to time seems to lack the capacity to marshal its resources optimally and translate its policy objectives into effective action. Herein lies my attention to policy drift, a phenomenon that to my mind has not been adequately explained by neoclassical realists or indeed by adherents of other schools of thought.

Finally, this book reflects my concern about the materialist/normative divide in academia. This apparent dichotomy appears to have sharpened as scholars around the world have tended to focus more and more on their perception of empirical study—often watered down to quantitative analysis—while normative scholarship struggles to be heard outside its own subsect. If, as my professors used to say, the purpose of academic study is ultimately normative—to make the world a better place—then why are we bogged down in narrowly conceived empirics and why do we not pay more attention to normative questions like responsibility and accountability? In this book I seek to do just this, insisting that the empirical and the moral are closely bound and that key realities of international political life cannot be properly grasped if we neglect the latter. Its primary thrust is to show that, in important respects, the moral *is* the empirical when accountability is neglected in making policy.

The long, slow process of working on the book has been a stimulating and enjoyable journey that has taken me far and wide. Putting it all together has been exacting, at least as much for those around me as for myself. I hope that the reader will find it less so.

ACKNOWLEDGMENTS

No writer travels alone or without the wisdom of others. The numerous drafts that went into the making of this book and presentations on it have been read, heard, and commented on over the years. I have benefited enormously from all of them. I have so many people to thank that I cannot possibly name them all. Prominent among them are Bhumitra Chakma and colleagues at the University of Hull; Bhavna Dave and colleagues at the SOAS University of London; Kate Sullivan de Estrada and colleagues and students at the University of Oxford; Ian Hall of Griffith University; T. V. Paul and colleagues and students at McGill University; Pascal Vennesson and colleagues at the S. Rajaratnam School of International Studies at Nanyang Technological University in Singapore; and my good friend and Rajaratnam School colleague, Anit Mukherjee, who has offered his discerning comments on much of what I have written over the past decade. Papers that contributed to the book received excellent feedback from a number of presentations at conferences held by the British International Studies Association and the International Studies Association. If I have inadvertently overlooked someone, I hope I will be forgiven.

Enriching conversations with many knowledgeable individuals gave me much food for thought over the years. I learned a great deal from Vappala Balachandran, Shekhar Dutt, Lawrence Freedman, Sumit Ganguly, Happymon Jacob, Manoj Joshi, Yogesh Joshi, Prakash Menon, M. K. Narayanan, Arun Prakash, P. S. Raghavan, Rajesh Rajagopalan, Satish Sahney, Ashley Tellis, Jayadeva Uyangoda, and Nicholas Wheeler. There were also several others who cannot be named. I owe them individually and collectively an enormous intellectual debt.

I must make a special mention of four individuals who have critiqued the entire manuscript and provided invaluable suggestions and criticisms. Two anonymous reviewers plowed through the manuscript with great acuity and helped enormously to make me ponder over and rethink my ideas and the way I had organized them, in several instances zeroing in on areas that needed further investigation or refinement. One of them I can name because he agreed to reveal his identity after reviewing the manuscript:

Nicolas Blarel, a young scholar who has produced wonderful theoretically grounded work on the relationship between India's foreign policy and its domestic politics. Donald Jacobs at Georgetown University Press gave me the benefit of his insights as well as the infinite patience that only a great editor can offer, and I cannot say how much I appreciate these. I owe an enormous debt to my friend and series editor T. V. Paul, who never let me lose sight of the end and played such an influential role in shepherding me to it both intellectually and psychologically.

The Library at the Rajaratnam School was immensely helpful. Many thanks to Chong Yee Ming, Jean Lai, and Sharifah Nazila for their ever-smiling assistance.

Finally, this book would not have been possible without the unceasing support, endurance, and love of my wife, Swati, who bore my transgressions and diversions in her inimitable style, propelled me forward in my weakest moments, and gave me the intellectual energy that seeing through a monumental project like this requires.

1

RISING INDIA AND POLICY DRIFT

On July 18, 2005, Indian prime minister Manmohan Singh and US president George W. Bush announced an agreement on civil nuclear cooperation that would be the cornerstone of what has become a strategic partnership of global significance. Three years later, the expected agreement, which had undergone a prolonged delay in finalization involving unpredictable twists and turns, nearly collapsed under the weight of India's domestic politics before squeaking through after a domestic political deal to save it. This book is an attempt to explain why such uncertainty and indecisiveness have periodically afflicted India's foreign policy in areas of critical importance to its national security.

Aside from the India-US case, three others are examined at length. A second example of policy drift was the Indian government's inability to follow through on its desire to help Sri Lanka defeat the Liberation Tigers of Tamil Eelam (LTTE), which had assassinated the former Indian prime minister, Rajiv Gandhi, and threatened the regional order and India's security. But Indian leaders were unable to make much headway toward fulfilling this goal as they struggled for years to override strong pressure from regional parties in India's Tamil Nadu state that threatened to bring down the ruling coalition in New Delhi. In a third instance, India in 1998 declared itself a nuclear-armed state and proclaimed a strategy of minimum deterrence but soon deviated considerably from its stated preference and continues to lack direction more than two decades later. In the fourth example studied here, policy drift was starkly underscored when a commando-style attack by a small team of ten terrorists on Mumbai in November 2008 killed 160 persons and held the country in thrall for four days before it ended with the capture of one of the attackers and the killing of the rest. The episode reflected a long-standing inability on the part of the Indian state to respond effectively to a constant threat to Mumbai, at least as old as 1993, emanating from neighboring Pakistan.

Other examples abound. India has been unable to consolidate a growing friendship with Bangladesh because policymakers have judged it politically risky to come to an agreement on the vexed question of sharing river waters. Most recently, India's efforts to attain high global status by projecting itself as the provider of vaccines for the world have stumbled owing to domestic mismanagement of the crisis. These events and processes are symptoms of a problem that has dogged India on critical occasions over the years: the lack of decisive policymaking and the tendency of important policies to drift uncertainly.

In this book, I try to explain why policymakers, consciously responding to systemic incentives, often find their policy initiatives caught up in prolonged and meandering pathways in trying to attain their objectives. A number of analytical tools are available for those attempting to explain why this happens. Most useful is the theoretical school known as "neoclassical realism" (NCR), which spotlights the domestic political reasons for the slip between the cup and the lip on so many policy questions. However, NCR's focus on the material sources of the problem presents, to my mind, an incomplete picture. I attribute the recurrent lack of policy decisiveness to two very different causes: first, the material distribution of domestic political power, for instance the distribution of seats in legislatures, which determines whether a government's power is firm and self-supporting or dependent on coalition partners; and second, the leadership's willingness or—in the cases studied here, the lack of it—to meet the obligations of political responsibility and accountability. As I show in the book, the two kinds of explanations are not sharply distinct: the state's normative failings are themselves an empirical phenomenon—akin to material reality—that exacerbates sustained policy drift.

The question of why India is susceptible to policy drift on key strategic issues is important for a number of reasons. First, there is the obvious matter of national interests, which may be set back if policy is not properly formulated or implemented. There are always costs—human, political, and economic—that arise from the state's inability to carry out its tasks optimally. The examples given above show this in very different ways. Let me elaborate on two of them. The potential cost of failure in the India-US case was considerable. In a post–Cold War world, where India was relatively isolated and under growing pressure from the nuclear nonproliferation regime, the failure of the nuclear entente would have left India a nuclear outsider struggling to meet its security needs in response to two nuclear-armed adversaries, China and Pakistan. The cost in the Mumbai case was more immediate and dramatic: the toll in dead bodies. But there was also a longer-term implication. If the Indian security establishment could not prevent a small band of ten terrorists from running amok for four days, the prospect of repeat occurrences—with their attendant costs in fatalities and severe injuries—was very real. The other two instances, as I show in the chapters below, are of similar importance.

A more general question that concerns scholars and analysts of international politics is about what such failings imply for India's capacity as a rising power with claims to being a major player in world politics. It is not unreasonable to doubt that a state unable to respond effectively to opportunities that affect its vital interests is capable of becoming a "leading power," as its key policymakers have asserted (Jaishankar 2015; see also Tellis 2016, 3).

The thread running through this book is about India's thrust to become a major power and the internal obstacles that have dogged its path, more specifically, the problem of policy drift that has appeared repeatedly in the India story. This is not to say that there are no serious external obstacles to India's push for higher power status. In the aftermath of its breakthrough nuclear agreement with the United States and the Nuclear Suppliers Group, India expected to become a member of the group, but—till the time of writing (late October 2021)—was thwarted by opposition from some members, chiefly China. Nevertheless, the fact is that China was not instrumental in nearly derailing the India-US nuclear deal; the process was nearly stymied by domestic politics. India's rise and its potential to become a major player in global strategic politics did not hinge entirely on the successful execution of the deal; but it would almost certainly have left the country vulnerable to future pressure from the nonproliferation regime and hence somewhat uncertain and less than self-confident in pursuing its ambition.

A nation hobbled by its internal disabilities is bound to lose momentum in striving to meet its objectives and to lose something of its image both in its own estimation and in that of others. It behooves us, therefore, to tackle the problem of policy uncertainty that has been India's constant companion in important ways. Some of these are well known, as with most of the instances mentioned above; others are less widely recognized.

RISING INDIA AND POLICY DRIFT

Despite early optimism after India obtained independence in 1947, India's capacity to deliver on its own expectations that it was bound to be a significant player in global politics was severely constrained by its slow growth. In the twenty-five-year period (1966–91) preceding India's shift to a liberalized economy, its gross domestic product grew (in 2010 constant US dollars) by 191.38 percent; in contrast, Brazil's gross domestic product rose by a much higher 276.59 percent, and China's, which had been slightly below that of India in 1966, by 511 percent during the same period (calculated from World Bank n.d.) In this sense, the experience of drift that has received much attention since the turn of the millennium is not new. But the present is supposed to be different: India is widely viewed as having "emerged" economically from decades of somnolence and is said to be ready for a bigger role in international politics. There is good reason for this higher expectation.

The end of the Cold War marked a watershed of sorts for India's *weltansicht* (Ganguly and Pardesi 2009; Kale 2009; Nayar and Paul 2003; Raja Mohan 2003) from a defensive and inward-looking to a more confident and outwardly oriented state. Two exogenous shocks were responsible. First, the core of its foreign policy paradigm—nonalignment—became irrelevant since there was no longer a predominantly two-bloc Cold War world from which India could stand apart. Besides, the Soviet Union—its chief source of ballast in terms of military hardware, oblique balancing of China, and reliable support on the thorny issue of Kashmir—had dissolved. Its successor state, Russia, was weak and at that time westward-leaning. In short, India stood isolated and insecure, confronting strategic adversaries, China and Pakistan, on two sides and simultaneously under pressure from the United States to freeze and roll back its fledgling and covert nuclear weapons program. The Indian leadership, having taken stock of a discomfiting environment, chose to turn to the United States. The process was marked by considerable hesitancy, both because of the baggage of history and because the American approach toward India was at the time ambivalent, viewing it as an emerging economy but also as a recalcitrant nuclear proliferator.

The second shock was economic. The Indian economy, weighed down by a prolonged and unsuccessful effort aimed at self-sufficiency, accumulated a high level of debt that propelled it into a serious balance-of-payments crisis in 1991. India was compelled to turn to the International Monetary Fund to tide over the crisis, which meant it had to undertake "structural adjustment" and loosen its restrictive controls over investment, trade, and manufacturing (Mukherji 2014, 63–107). Prime Minister P. V. Narasimha Rao and Finance Minister Manmohan Singh took the bull by the horns and initiated a more far-reaching liberalization program than the IMF had demanded. Rapid economic integration with the global system and a consequential spurt in growth brought India the label of an "emerging economy" and sparked a new interest in Washington and elsewhere. Nevertheless, the world did not yet view India as a future great power. That began to happen as the consequence of a different shock—one administered by India itself.

In the summer of 1998, deeply uncomfortable with the intensifying pressure being applied by the US-led nuclear nonproliferation regime, India under Prime Minister Atal Bihari Vajpayee broke out of its covert nuclear weapons status by carrying out a series of tests (Saksena 2006). It had tested a nuclear weapon once back in 1974 but refrained from building an arsenal at that time. Later, India began building an arsenal circa 1989 but refrained from testing. In 1998 it did both, explicitly declaring that it was a nuclear-armed state and that there was no going back. Anger in Washington, Tokyo, and elsewhere, followed by a spate of sanctions, was short-lived. The new American leadership under George W. Bush reversed the view that India was a problem state and began to treat it as an opportunity. The new label for India was "rising power."

To be sure, there was debate over India's capacities. In one view, which reflected the Bush administration's perspective, India was becoming a key player in international politics at the *global* level. With China's rise, Asia was now the new center of world power. To counter China, the United States and India would become partners—not allies—in the central strategic triangle that would dominate the global power structure (Blank 2007). Against this, it was arguable that India's capacities were limited. Its power to say no was amply demonstrated in a number of instances: its refusal to toe the nonproliferation line; its rejection of the developed countries' approach to the international trade regime; and its resistance to efforts to counter climate change that tended in its view to ignore the historical responsibility of industrialized nations. Beyond that, it could not be an active shaper of global institutions and processes. In short, it had the power to resist, but not to drive change in the world (Perkovich 2003–4). Nevertheless, the accelerated rapid growth of India's postliberalization economy from $471.46 billion in 1991 to $1.76 trillion in 2011 (in constant 2010 dollars) and the accompanying expansion of its military capabilities, both conventional and nuclear, underlined its potential as a major power (World Bank n.d.–c).

But doubts began to appear as growth slowed down from a high of 10.26 percent in 2010 to much lower single-digit rates thereafter (World Bank n.d.–c), and the euphoria of the preceding period receded. The United Progressive Alliance, a coalition led by the Congress Party under Manmohan Singh (2004–14), fell from grace in the public eye. It was during the later years of the Singh government that the term "drift" came increasingly into use to lament the lack of vibrancy, primarily in economic policy but also in foreign policy generally. Vajpayee's Bharatiya Janata Party (BJP) attacked Singh's Congress for its "uninspiring" performance, particularly its failure to push economic reforms forward at a time of faltering growth (*Indian Express* 2013b). Corporate India expressed a similar view, holding the United Progressive Alliance's leadership responsible for the slowdown in economic reforms, inefficiency, cronyism, corruption, and poor handling of the public sector (Kundra 2014). Singh, widely viewed as a weak leader, seemed hesitant on both domestic and external fronts and was derided for his "missteps on economic policy" and for "maladroit diplomacy and wishful strategic thinking" (Raja Mohan 2014; see also Pant 2009; Sridharan 2013). There was a vigorous debate about India's prospects as a potential major power. Optimists pointed to the spurt in its economic and military growth (Baru 2006; Bergenwall 2016; Blank 2007; Giridharadas 2008; Poddar and Yi 2007; PwC 2017; Kapur 2006; Ladwig 2010). Pessimists objected that India was weighed down by a plethora of problems, ranging from weak infrastructure to organizational incapacity, corruption, and political turbulence (DeVotta 2003; Ganguly 2008, 2012; Lee 2010; Markey 2009; Mitra 2003). One observer characterized it as a "flailing state" (Pritchett 2009).

This criticism of the government's indecision and lack of purpose was hardly new. It had also been made for earlier periods and in diverse contexts (Chari 2012; Reich and Bowonder 1992; Smith 1994; Wariavwalla 1989). Considerable attention to the domestic dimension problem has also been given more recently (e.g., Agarwal and Somanathan 2005; Sharma,

Unnikrishnan, and Sharma 2015). Looking outside the present analytical framework pertaining to India, the concept of drift in the sense utilized here has appeared in such varied fields as interstate political and economic relations (Matthijs 2016; Nye 2000), the making of foreign policy (Rumer 2000); social policy (Béland, Rocco, and Waddan 2016); biological weapons policy (Balmer 1997); and the study of diplomatic history (McCormick 1982). None of these explicitly defines drift, though all imply stagnation and uncertainty.

The *Oxford Dictionary* gives us a wide range of meanings for "drift." The relevant ones for this book convey a sense of slow and aimless movement, indecision, and deviation from an expected path (*Oxford Living Dictionaries* n.d.). One cannot a priori provide a general rule for identifying policy drift precisely. As this book's four empirical chapters show, the sense of loss of direction and pace is different in each case. But the important point is that the only standard for identifying drift is that set by policymakers themselves (broadly in line with realist expectations) in all cases. Policymakers sought a quick sealing of the India-US nuclear deal, consolidation of relations with Sri Lanka through substantial military assistance, a minimalist deterrence strategy and posture for optimal security, and a strongly organized counterterrorism apparatus. None of these was achieved efficaciously or speedily. On the contrary, the nuclear deal meandered through a tortuous process over several years; military aid to Colombo was limited and hence overtaken by China; nuclear strategy became subject to a creeping, open-ended expansion of capabilities; and counterterrorist policy failed to implement a host of necessary organizational and physical security measures identified by the government itself.

Some writings focusing explicitly on policy drift relate it to change in the operation or effects of policies arising from incremental and cumulative alterations in institutional environments (Béland and Powell 2016; Mahoney and Thelen 2010; van der Heijden 2010). This is not the case here. In the present analysis, policy drift does not occur because of the external environment but arises from factors operating at home. The metaphor that comes to mind is a boat that moves erratically and uncertainly in difficult waters, either because there are too many hands pulling at the steering in different directions (a material problem) or because the hands that *can* steer it lack the motivation or sense of responsibility to do so effectively (a normative problem). Sometimes, the term "policy paralysis" is used to describe this lack of drive (*Times of India* 2013; *Indian Express* 2013b). But policy drift is not policy paralysis. Paralysis occurs when there is no movement. In the present context, there is movement, but it is erratic, slow, and uncertain. It does not involve purposelessness, but rather a deviation from purpose. And it is not meant to imply complete failure or an absence of policy. Policy drift, as opposed to policy paralysis, may be defined as consisting of doing something (but not enough), as opposed to doing nothing; and engaging in at least a modicum of visible action, not displaying substantial inaction.

The meaning I utilize here, to be precise, is that of a policy process that is neither wholly purposeful nor wholly aimless, but rather *movement that is initiated purposefully but is greatly impeded by intervening factor*s. There is a rich literature on policy "failure," and many of its aspects are relevant here (Bovens and 't Hart 2016; FitzGerald, O'Malley, and Ó Broin 2019; McConnell 2016, 2017). However, apart from the lack of clarity in what exactly is meant by failure and who is to define it, the literature does not adequately incorporate the temporal aspect. The present study is precisely about this: why delays, often prolonged, and uncertainties dog certain policies. Moreover, it clarifies a critical aspect about the relevance of control in shaping how policies turn out.

As will become clear shortly, policy drift might be the result of forces beyond the control of policymakers (and therefore involuntary) or, where policymakers do have control, a form of self-inflicted constraint (for want of a better contrasting term, I employ the term "voluntary"). The distinction is central to the analytical framework of this book and to our understanding of how and why policy drift appears on important issues.

INVOLUNTARY AND VOLUNTARY DRIFT

The key to differentiating involuntary from voluntary drift is the notion of control. This may vary according to the structure of the political system. Executive autonomy is greater in the Westminster parliamentary system and in semipresidential systems (where the president is independent of parliament, but the prime minister is not); it is less in the presidential system and in the coalitional parliamentary systems (where there is proportional representation) (Elman 2000). But in a Westminster system with a coalition government, especially an unstable one, the executive's power is curtailed, which is apparent in India's recent political history (Blarel 2017).

As shown below in chapters 2 and 3, this is the main reason why India's national policymakers found themselves constantly in difficulty.

To the extent that political leaders are unable to exercise a substantial degree of control over the making and implementation of policy, there is "involuntary drift." For instance, a weak coalition government may lack the capacity to extract support from key members whose interests diverge from those of the executive. This means that some members of the coalition may act as veto players and resist the formulation and/or implementation of a specific policy. Policymakers are then confronted with a Hobson's choice: compromise on policy or risk the fall of the government. In practice, they often try to defuse the problem by offering a deal to the naysayers or adjusting the content of policy to make it more palatable to them. The fate of the policy is then determined by a bargaining process. In the realm of foreign policy, this means policymakers are enmeshed in a "two-level game" that requires them to bargain simultaneously with their domestic constituency and with an external interlocutor (Putnam 1988). The bargaining process may go through a series of twists and turns, or simply be characterized by unyielding adversarial relations (within or without the state or at both levels), which in effect produce drift.

This book explores two such bargaining processes, one involving India's relations with the United States, a large and powerful state; and the other shaping its relationship with Sri Lanka, a small and weak neighboring state. In both cases, a fragile coalition government in New Delhi ran into stiff opposition from its own members or allied parties and faced enormous difficulty in carrying out a desired policy. Involuntary drift has been a constant domestic structural problem in a fragmented political system, where the distribution of domestic political power is such that the executive lacks sufficient control over the making of foreign policy.

In the two other cases analyzed here, important policies have wandered uncertainly or lost momentum for very different reasons. This is visible in India's inconsistent adoption of a nuclear weapons strategy of minimum deterrence and its inability to safeguard the homeland from cross-border terrorist attacks. In both cases, we find the existence of policy drift despite the absence of serious material constraints—that is, the structure of domestic politics is not a significant factor holding policy back. There are certainly *some* material factors at work, and these even appear to fit into well-known, materially based theoretical frameworks. For instance, the division of power between civilian and military office holders is the source of much that is suboptimal in military strategy generally. Similarly, the distribution of power between the central and state governments does hamper policymaking with respect to counterterrorist action. But material explanations simply do not work beyond a point, as will be shown.

The critical point is that, in sharp contrast to the first two cases, there is no serious difficulty with regard to control. Policymakers have been—and in both cases continue to be—unable to produce effective policies, despite exercising substantial control over the levers of policy. And because they do have control—but fail to exercise it responsibly—policymakers are the chief source of what I call "voluntary drift." In contrast to involuntary drift, they do have the capacity to make choices. But they often choose options that avoid difficult and costly action, in part because the political cost of inadequate action is not severe, and sometimes because responsibility for a lack of decisive action can be transferred to other agents. But ultimately, because choices *are* available to policymakers, the responsibility for making the wrong choices, and hence for policy drift, lies with them. Hence, the gap between policy expectations and performance is attributable to a "responsibility deficit" arising from a lack of political commitment.

To be sure, domestic politics is not the only source of difficulty causing policy drift. Sometimes, domestic politics may not hinder effective policymaking. Policies can work quite well because there is neither a structural problem arising from opposition by veto players nor a serious deficiency in political commitment—and hence no responsibility deficit. In contrast to the four cases of visible drift, there are instances where the source of drift is in large part external. Three examples will be presented to make this point. First, India's inability to resolve its enduring rivalry with Pakistan has been a function primarily of the hostile dynamic between them. Second, India's policy toward China in the post–Cold War period has similarly been shaped by external factors driving varying degrees of competition and cooperation between them. And third, India's pursuit of status in the hierarchical society of states has maintained a reasonably successful course but has been hampered in important respects by external obstacles. In all three cases, domestic politics and choices have been relatively free of both involuntary and voluntary drift. Yet policy has been constrained, I will show, because of systemic factors at work.

THEORIZING DOMESTIC POLITICS AND POLICY DRIFT

The recent upsurge of interest in the linkage between domestic politics and foreign policy is arguably a reaction against the preoccupation of international relations as a discipline with systemic sources of state behavior. Starting in the 1970s, realists such as Kenneth Waltz held that two features, which they identified as the structure of the interstate system, explained the essence of state behavior: anarchy (the absence of a sovereign regulator) and the distribution of power (Waltz 1979; see also Mearsheimer 2001). Reacting to the state-centric analysis of structural realism (widely labeled "neorealism"), liberal scholars such as Robert Keohane and Joseph Nye pointed to other systemic features—notably, economic interdependence and international institutions—that undermined the autonomy of states (thus inviting the marque of neoliberalism); while the emerging school of constructivists, led by Alexander Wendt, showed that intersubjective beliefs drive the world as we know and understand it (Kaarbo 2015, 193; Keohane and Nye 1977; Wendt 1999). This predominantly systemic perspective was in time followed by a return to the much older understanding that domestic factors play a central role in shaping the way states interact with other states. In the late 1990s, James Fearon's survey of a single leading journal, *International Organization*, found that more than a third of its published papers linked domestic politics to external policy (Fearon 1998, 290).

The tradition of linking domestic politics and foreign policy is an old one. Early realists did so even while drawing attention to systemic effects on state behavior. Kenneth Schultz (2013) notes that Thucydides, widely viewed as a founding father of realism and best known for his emphasis on anarchy and the distribution of power, did in fact recognize that the domestic features of the state were intrinsic to relative power. The same point is made by scholars with regard to Machiavelli and others (Doyle 1997). Likewise, the quintessential realist treatise from ancient India, Kautilya's *Arthashastra*, highlighted the importance of domestic governance in determining state power (Kautilya 1992; Mitra and Liebic 2017, 98–103). Post–World War II "classical" realists like Hans Morgenthau (2006) similarly focused on national characteristics as determinants of national power and its optimal employment.

Postwar scholars of international relations separated inquiry into levels of analysis (Waltz 1959; Singer 1961). These were primarily three: the international system, the state, and the individual (including small groups). For present purposes, the latter two can be combined into a single category—the subsystemic, or simply the state level. Studies highlighting the influence of state-level factors in international politics are legion (e.g., Bueno de Mesquita 2002; Carlsnaes 2013; Gourevitch 2002; Kaarbo 2015; Schultz 2013). Prominent variables include regime types, party systems, interest groups, public opinion, strategic culture, ideology, bureaucratic politics, and leaders' perceptions and personalities. Although much of this is not explicitly theoretical, it could be said to fall within the province of liberal theory—excluding, of course, the systemic approach mentioned above (Moravcsik 1997). Scholars of foreign policy analysis have tried to carve out an independent domain (Hudson 2007; Kaarbo 2015), but their claim to a separate identity rests on areas of focus (especially, close attention to psychology and decision-making) that fall within the state level. A substantial literature has developed on state capacity, or the state's ability to extract resources, optimize policy coordination, and obtain compliance to policies (Berwick and Christia 2018; Paul 2010b; Weiss 2018). Though of immense value, this approach tends to focus heavily on material factors, which—I will show—are insufficient to explain the cases examined in chapters 4 and 5. Constructivism (again, leaving aside the systemic variety) also overlaps with other groups, but is more distinctive because it prioritizes the ideational—as opposed to the material—sources of state behavior and focuses on norms, culture, identity, discourses, and roles in influencing foreign policy (Finnemore 1996; Legro 2005; Onuf 1989; Wendt 1999). None of these approaches provides a thorough overarching approach combining material and normative factors in the way I have tried to do in this volume.

The foreign policy–domestic policy linkage is by no means new to the study of India's foreign policy and continues to attract much attention (Appadorai 1981; Bajpai and Chong 2019; Bandhyopadhyaya 2003; Betz 2010; Blarel 2017, 2019; Blarel and Van Willigen 2021; Hall 2019; Malone, Raja Mohan, and Raghavan 2015). The literature is large, and only a few examples are noted here. Well-known works on individual leadership as the source of foreign policy have analyzed the preferences of Jawaharlal Nehru, Indira Gandhi, and Narendra Modi (Bandyopadhyaya 2003; Mansingh 1984; Tremblay and Kapur 2017). Recent analyses that have focused on state-level domestic factors and their interplay with the politics of the international system have examined economic interests (Betz 2012; Betz and Hanif 2010); ethnicity and culture (Schmidt 2017); federal relations (Mattoo and Jacob 2010; Kumar 2013; Plagemann and Destradi 2015; Singh and Misra 2012); ideas (Miller and de Estrada 2017); identity (Singh 2013); interest groups (Ramanna 2004); religion (Ganguly 2015); and state capacity (Ganguly and Thompson 2016; Paul 2010a). Barring a handful, few authors adopt a clear theoretical framework (exceptions include Das 2015; Hansel, Khan, and Levaillant 2017; and Singh 2013—as well as the neoclassical realists discussed below). As in the general literature cited in the preceding paragraph, many of these writings tend to focus on material factors and do not pay much attention to normative questions of responsibility and accountability.

In this book, I draw extensively from neoclassical realism, a reframed version of realism that acknowledges the importance of the structure of the international system but brings in domestic politics as a critical determinant of what states actually do. This effort to link the two levels of analysis was a reaction to the limitations of neorealism. As the discipline recognized, neorealism was rigorous in its explanation of basic patterns of state behavior, but it could not explain recurrent variations and unexpected patterns in the ways that states interact with others. Waltz, it hardly escapes notice, was primarily concerned with producing a *scientific* theory of international politics that was parsimonious and elegant, seeking to overcome the difficulties confronting Morgenthau's claim to scientific theorizing, which was inconsistent (e.g., in its Hobbesian assumptions about human nature) and incorporated a multitude of variables. Inevitably, neorealism said something important about the system as a whole, but not much about the specifics of the behavior of its chief components—that is, states. Its very simplicity also left very little beyond basic patterns to be said about state behavior from within its own analytical boundaries (Schweller 2006, 313).

Consequently, realists found themselves at something of an explanatory dead end, the more so in a post–Cold War world wherein balance-of-power politics seemed to have receded and there was, particularly in the United States, a sense that the world was far more complex than their disciplinary forebears had imagined. The challenge came from different directions. A leading historian castigated international relations theorists for failing (despite its claims to be scientific) to anticipate a watershed event like the end of the Cold War (Gaddis 1992–93). Constructivist scholars led a disciplinary charge against the realist worldview, attacked the notion that anarchy invariably produces a power-centric system, and initiated a major debate on the utility of realism (Lapid 1989; Wendt 1992, 1999). Liberals joined in the fray and wondered why anyone should remain a realist in a rapidly changing world (Legro and Moravcsik 1999). One scholar argued that, strictly speaking, a systemic theory like that of Waltz was also a theory of foreign policy: "By saying that systemic IR [international relations] theories explain how states 'behave'—which surely refers to their foreign policies—Waltz has to be granting that systemic international relations theories are theories of foreign policy in the core sense" (Fearon 1998, 297). Realists had to respond in a way that explained variations in state behavior, which they could only do by accommodating the diversifying effects of domestic politics. And they had to do it without entirely jettisoning the core of their paradigm. The result was "neoclassical realism," which quickly picked up a substantial and diverse group of scholars (Lobell, Ripsman, and Taliaferro 2009; Rathbun 2008; Ripsman, Taliaferro, and Lobell 2016; Rose 1998; Schweller 2006; Wivel 2005).

Neoclassical Realism

Neoclassical realism has evolved over time, from explaining state behavior that is unexpected (from the neorealist standpoint) to accounting more broadly for foreign policy outcomes and more recently to an approach that additionally shows how state-level factors make an impact on the system and its characteristics. The first two approaches, conceptually clarified by Fearon (1998), have been more extensively amplified, along with the third, by Ripsman, Taliaferro, and Lobell (2016). In their formulation, there are three classes of NCR theory. Type I theories explain anomalies and puzzles where states do not adopt policies in sync with systemic incentives. A typical case is that of "underbalancing," where states do not respond adequately to threats by balancing against them (Schweller 2006). This class of NCR theories is "a theory of sub-optimality or pathology to explain what are only understood to be infrequent deviations from structural realist expectations" (Ripsman, Taliaferro, and Lobell 2016, 28).

Type II theories have a broader explanatory value: they explain why states, in responding to systemic incentives, make specific choices from a range of options available to them. This type of NCR theory is thus "more about foreign policy choices than about pathologies" and facilitates a "theory of foreign policy in its own right" (Ripsman, Taliaferro, and Lobell 2016, 28, 31). The degree of variation from optimal, structurally driven policy in this category relates to the degree of threat at the time the choice is made. Under threat, states exhibit structurally driven behavior; when the threat is not immediate, domestic factors play a significant role in determining choices (Ripsman, Taliaferro, and Lobell 2016, 28, 52–56). For instance, Mark Brawley (2009) shows how Britain, France, and the Soviet Union responded to the rise of Germany in different ways, a good part of their policies being driven by domestic politics.

Finally, Type III theories—the major contribution of the volume by Ripsman, Taliaferro, and Lobell (2016, 80–98)—show how the choices produced by domestic politics may have an impact on systemic process as well as systemic structure. With regard to the latter, as Ripsman and his colleagues point out, Deng Xiao Ping's decision to undertake major economic reform set China on the path to rapid growth and thus an altered structural position (Ripsman, Taliaferro, and Lobell 2016, 87). The same can be said about the restructuring of India's economy after 1991, which would not have accelerated as it did if the leadership at the time had not made a deliberate decision to liberalize beyond the conditions required by the IMF.

NCR has produced a growing literature on a diverse range of countries, many of them in Asia. Type I theory has influenced studies on differing missile defense policies in Japan and South Korea (Yoo 2012); China's nuclear doctrine (Rosa and Foradori 2017); and Iran's "squandered opportunity," in its inability to expand its influence despite favorable systemic conditions (Juneau 2015). The literature on Type II is more extensive and encompasses a variety of states and topics, such as the domestic sources of uncertainty in China's foreign policy (Sørensen 2013); status and perceptions in Russian foreign policy (Kropatcheva 2012); the interplay of environmental and domestic factors in the reorientation of Japanese foreign policy (Saltzman 2015); the role of leadership preferences in shaping UK prime minister Tony Blair's proclivity for overseas intervention (Dyson 2009); the manipulation of domestic debates by Australian foreign policy elites (McLean 2016); and the role of leaders' perceptions and economic interests in determining United States–China relations (He 2017). Explicitly Type III approaches are relatively rare, though many of the writings on the other two types do have analytical space to show an impact on systemic processes, which is to be expected because all foreign policies, including those shaped by domestic politics, are by their nature bound to have an impact on others. Exceptions that argue explicitly for a significant systemic impact are Cha's (2000) study of how Japan–South Korea relations are affected by their separate perceptions of the United States and Verma's (2017) comparative study of how domestic factors influence the competitive drives of China and India for oil resources.

On Indian foreign policy, a well-known Type I analysis is Jacob's (2010) paper on the influence of domestic politics on India's relations with Sri Lanka—a subject I explore in depth in chapter 3. Another example (not elaborated on in this volume) is of Prime Minister Manmohan Singh's inability to carry out his side of a proposed deal on river water sharing with Bangladesh as a consequence of the weakness of the coalition over which he presided. Opposition from the state of West Bengal, which represented a small yet significant component of his coalition, blocked his policy (Kumar 2013). Among Type II explanations, one rests on strategic culture: despite the significant threat India faced after China's 1964 nuclear test, the building of the Indian nuclear arsenal was retarded by normative leadership preference until a more immediate threat—from Pakistan—led Prime Minister Rajiv Gandhi to order the making of the bomb a quarter of a century later (Basrur 2001). Another shows how elite perceptions and public opinion influence Japanese policy toward India (Tuke 2011). The only Type III analysis on India I have encountered is Raj Verma's study cited above. An interesting one might be attempted on India's reluctance to abandon its unproductive policy of economic autarky even as the world—and especially China—was letting go of a similar preference and the consequent impact on India's structural position, that is, its economic weakening relative to China.

This book—because it focuses on the problem of drift in Indian foreign policy—almost naturally falls into the Type I category. Though Ripsman, Taliaferro, and Lobell (2016) argue that Type III analyses are more powerful because of their wider explanatory utility, I demonstrate in the chapters below that a Type I approach focusing on India's policy drift can be just as powerful. Chapter 2 shows how Indian domestic factors induced significant changes in American policy on the India-US nuclear agreement; chapter 3 highlights China's structural gain vis-à-vis India as a result of Indian policy drift vis-à-vis Sri Lanka; chapter 4 draws attention to the strategic uncertainty resulting from India's doctrinal confusions; and chapter 5 underlines how India's weak response to cross-border terrorism has helped sustain Pakistan's asymmetric warfare strategy.

However, there is a further complexity that NCR has as yet to accommodate, owing to its inherent limitations. In the four cases examined here, policymakers failed to pursue an effective policy in response to systemic incentives. Instead, the policy response was uncertain and indecisive, owing to factors that are readily identifiable as domestic. But these factors were of very different types. In the first two cases, which I have classified as involuntary drift, where policymakers suffered from insufficient control over the policy process, the distribution of domestic political power generated policy uncertainty. In the remaining two, labelled voluntary drift, where policymakers did have control, none of the variables hitherto identified by NCR—leader images, strategic culture, state–society relations, and domestic institutions—apply. Instead, I draw on normative theory to explain why the state underperformed (and continues to do so). The most appropriate explanation for policy drift in these two cases lies in the unwillingness, not the inability, of policymakers to act in accordance with the principle of accountability attached to their holding of public office and hence in the "responsibility deficit" they have displayed as officeholders.

Ripsman, Taliaferro, and Lobell (2016, 80–90) have also specified time frames and their influences on decision-making. In their view, in the short term (from days to months), states necessarily respond in line with immediate structural concerns (notably, crises), which does not normally produce significant structural outcomes (as the authors imply rather than explicitly state). The longer the time frame, the greater their ability to exercise choices and, one may infer, the greater the possibility of structural impact because their strategic choices interact with structural factors in shaping systemic outcomes such as war and peace. Domestic choices also produce structural changes: "Growth rates are largely determined by strategic economic and political choices these states make over time as part of their foreign policy and grand strategic planning. Consequently, structural change has its roots in the individual investment decisions of the great powers, their decisions to pursue a grand strategy of restraint or one of overextension, and the particular domestic constraints and opportunities of particular great powers" (Ripsman, Taliaferro, and Lobell 2016, 86–87).

The authors' discussion of their typologies of NCR theories and of time frames is separate and, though the thrust of the argument seems to be that Type I behavior has limited effect on systemic outcomes (Ripsman, Taliaferro, and Lobell 2016, 82, figure 4.2), the two are not clearly integrated. Crisis decisions, arguably, can have important systemic outcomes: the Cuban Missile Crisis produced two major systemic effects. At the process level (interstate relations), it led to a major effort directed at controlling the arms race between the Soviet Union and the United States. At the structural level, it demonstrated—counterintuitively, for realists—that the distribution of military power between nuclear-armed states was no longer meaningful because the apparent imbalance in US-Soviet nuclear capabilities did not significantly affect the outcome of the crisis, which was essentially a compromise.

This volume demonstrates that "pathological" policies apply to time frames that vary from the short to medium terms to the long term. Policy drift in the India-US instance was exhibited over a period of about three years. With respect to India–Sri Lanka relations, the focus is on a three-year time frame, but the problem of drift was visible, I show, for a much longer period. Both the cases of voluntary drift have spanned much longer periods and are still discernible. The problem with nuclear strategy is already well over two decades old, while policy on cross-border terrorism has drifted for still longer.

All these cases have produced systemic effects. The effect of the slow movement and near derailment of the India-US nuclear deal was process-related: it demonstrated the limits to the relationship arising from Indian domestic preferences and center–state politics. With respect to India–Sri Lanka relations, the long-term impact was on process: the government in Colombo was encouraged to look to other sources for the succor India did not provide, which adversely affected relations with New Delhi; and the short-term impact was in an important sense structural: China stepped in to aid Sri Lanka, and India's position was weakened as a result. India's inconsistent strategy of "minimum" deterrence had the systemic impact of exacerbating rising tensions with China and Pakistan, but did not alter the structure with respect to either dyad. And, finally, India's failure to respond effectively to cross-border terrorism emanating from Pakistan encouraged the latter to persist with that same policy, which in turn resulted in sustained tensions between them—in short, a process effect, not a structural one.

The NCR view—that the impact of system structure on national policy is strong when there is a high-threat or highly enticing environment; and that, conversely, domestic politics has more room to manifest itself when the threats and incentives are less immediate (Ripsman, Taliaferro, and Lobell 2016, 52–56, 94–95)—needs also to be qualified with a little nuance. It depends, of course, on what one means by the imminence of the threat or opportunity. On a continuum between immediacy and an open-ended time frame, three of the cases involved choices that were high-consequence and fairly short-term. An isolated India needed to turn around its relationship with the United States quickly, both because of the China threat and because of the need to overcome the tightening pressure applied by the United States–led nuclear nonproliferation regime. On Sri Lanka, the possibility of a strong Chinese presence there if India did not assist it, though not producing a crisis-like situation, was for Indian policymakers a major short-term threat. On cross-border terrorism, the repeated occurrence of terrorist attacks in Mumbai alone was a constant "clear and present danger," and not one where there was the luxury of time to respond. In other words, though it may be true that domestic politics comes to the fore in a relatively less urgent situation, it can nevertheless seriously inhibit policymaking in a strategic environment that has potential effects of magnitude in a relatively short time frame.

In the first two of these examples, structural domestic inhibitors played an important role in constraining policy. In the third, the lack of political commitment and, as we will see, the ability to get away with lackadaisical action, have been important in shaping an ineffective policy. Only in the remaining instance of nuclear strategy—where policy lethargy has not thus far produced visible negative results—is there a direct correspondence between the relatively low level of threat and the primacy of domestic politics. I will also show that, on the contrary, there have been unexpected and substantial side benefits arising from policy inconsistency, which has helped sustain a policy that has subverted its own claims to being optimal.

NCR has been subjected to a number of criticisms, of which three are particularly important. First, the liberal argument claims that domestic politics rather than the system deserves analytical priority because "the state is not an actor but a representative institution constantly subject to capture and recapture, construction and reconstruction by coalitions of social actors" (Moravcsik 1997, 518). In other words, if inputs from the system are constant, variations in domestic preferences produce varying foreign policy outcomes. Lacking in this standpoint is the recognition that, for the most part, the policymaking executive plays a dominant role in formulating and implementing foreign policy. And if we find that this executive, regardless of its composition and the domestic political environment generally, regularly exhibits policy preferences that conform to realist expectations, then it is reasonable to view the system as analytically prior. In all the cases explored in this book, we find that, regardless of changes in leadership, parties in power, and the status of center–state relations, the preferences of makers of foreign policy do in fact correspond to what a realist analysis might expect. It is only subsequently—once an initial preference has been exercised—that policies begin to drift.

Second, NCR is criticized for incorporating an ever-growing number of variables, which requires us to accept that "everything matters" (Narizny 2017, 178). As Narizny observes (2017, 178): "As each new piece of neoclassical research was published, the amount of variance in state behavior explained by domestic politics would expand. How long, then, would neoclassical realists be able to claim that systemic pressures matter more than domestic factors? In the long run, therefore, neoclassical realism is self-defeating."

This criticism is inappropriate. NCR clearly specifies the conditions under which its intervening variables are likely to apply (i.e., nonthreatening environments). It does not hold that domestic factors are determinants in all situations. The argument seems to be more about the large number of variables incorporated into NCR. The latest exposition on NCR shows an awareness of this and attempts to reduce the number of intervening variables to just the four identified above. This book perhaps aggravates Narizny's complaint by adding a normative dimension. But the criticism is in any case off the mark. First, preoccupation with the number of variables reflects an old bias in favor of parsimony and elegance in the construction of scientific theory. The problem, as has been more than evident for some time, is that neorealism, which says just a few big things (and not always accurately), is the only theory that can claim to be parsimonious. Liberalism is open to the same criticism as NCR: too many variables. So is the constructivist approach. If one starts with the aim of explaining phenomena rather than constructing neat theory, an expansion in the number of variables is not inherently an obstacle to theoretical analysis. Indeed, there is arguably no such thing as a truly scientific paradigm in international relations—the notion being borrowed with limited success from the natural sciences—and it is explanatory power that attracts adherents to this or that school of thought or tradition (Sterling-Folker 2009, 191–95).

That the admission of a substantial number of variables is inherently problematic is more difficult to counter because it raises a question about the boundaries between NCR and other theoretical approaches. But this criticism does not apply here because the prioritization of the system in policymaking is not from the scholar's standpoint. It is clearly shown that, in every case examined here, the initial response by policymakers was realist in its reaction to systemic pressures—that is, directly in tune with standard realist expectations. It is only later that the drift began to be manifest as domestic factors kicked in.

A third critical contention, aimed squarely at Type I theories, is that there is no such thing as an "objective" correct response relative to which deviation can be identified (Sears 2017, 25–26). In a sense, the "objective" standard from which states may stray is the scholar's standard as used in the literature. One might counter that there is nothing wrong in this because it is consistent with the assumptions of realist theory. My position is somewhat different. As pointed out in the preceding paragraph, I show that policymakers have in every instance initially responded in accordance with the expectations of realist theory and demonstrated their preference through broad changes in policy. The deviation that has occurred has been relative not only to the expectations of realist theory but equally in relation to the preferences of policymakers themselves. Here, it is important to underscore the NCR contention that nonrealist critics often fail to acknowledge the centrality of the foreign policy executive in the making of policy. This is precisely what is clearly visible in every case examined here.

The approach I adopt also conforms to that of NCR with regard to the much-debated issue of how to transcend the levels-of-analysis divide (Dessler 1989; Mahoney and Snyder 1999; Wendt 1987; Wight 2006). There are different ways of looking at the relationship. At a simple level, structure is viewed as a constraint rather than a determinant—that is, it sets negative limits to what a state can do but does not determine what it *can* do (Stein 2006). Constructivists hold that structures can be transcended—a logical extension of their view that anarchy is what states make of it (i.e., it is fundamentally a human construct)—and that structures are not independent things; rather, agency and structure are mutually constitutive (Wendt 1987, 1992). NCR rejects the notion that structures can be transcended and asserts that structures are an objective reality. The system of states exists independent of states and "delimits the range of possible strategies any actor can pursue, as well as the range of possible bargaining outcomes among those actors" (Ripsman, Taliaferro, and Lobell 2016, 174). But it moves somewhat closer to the constructivist approach by showing that, within limits, the system and its units (states) are co-constitutive—that is, there is a two-way interaction between states and structure that can also alter the system, though not transcend it. Priority (as the analytical starting point) is given to structure, but NCR stresses that structure not only constrains states' foreign policies but is also, under certain conditions, shaped by them.

The analysis presented in this book is in tune with this limited, co-constitutive perspective. In each of the four cases, I show, Indian foreign policy moves to make major changes in accordance with systemic pressures and constraints. In every case, too, foreign policy drift has a systemic impact: the India-US relationship is hobbled; India–Sri Lanka relations are strained; nuclear arms racing with Pakistan is stimulated; and strategic tensions with Pakistan are exacerbated. In the second case, there is also a structural effect, with respect to relative power vis-à-vis China, not in the sense of the distribution of economic or military capabilities but certainly in the sense that China's strategic reach is significantly enhanced at India's cost. This aspect of the study, however, is an intellectual by-product: the chief aim is to show why foreign policy outcomes deviating from the realist expectations of policymakers have occurred.

The Normative Dimension

Agent–structure relations are critical to understanding outcomes in international relations. And yet the role of agents as drivers of outcomes cannot be fully understood without bringing in the normative dimension. The distinction between involuntary and voluntary drift makes this plain. In the former, policymakers are *unable* to carry out preferred policies because they lack sufficient control over the policy process; in the latter, control is not at issue: policy drift occurs because policymakers are *unwilling* to carry out stated objectives. What I do here is not only identify what should have been done but was not (with reference to policymakers' preferences) but also identify the empirical gap between what should have been done and what was or has been actually done, which itself becomes the *cause* of sustained policy drift. Also, this centers on the normative gap between the principle of responsibility and its practice. This is, strictly speaking, not what is generally conceived of as normative theory, which is concerned with "answering questions about *what we should do* in global political life: what ends we should pursue, what rules we should obey, and what institutions we should build and support" (emphasis in the original; Hurrell and Macdonald 2013). Rather, the norms of "national interest" and "national security" are taken as understood from the standpoint of realist expectations about optimal and morally guided policymaking and, to underscore their relevance, from the preferences expressed through the initial policy formulation undertaken by policymakers themselves. The concern here is not so much with what should be done but with deviation from norms—that is, what was not done and how this exacerbated policy drift.

A useful starting point is to connect with the moral component of classical realist theory, which—contrary to its reputation for an amoral approach to national security—is deeply moral with respect to the relationship between society and the state. The apparent prioritization of reasons of state and national interest over moral principle by classical realists like Morgenthau gave the impression that they had abandoned morality in their approach to international politics. Subsequently, the desire to fashion a scientific theory of international politics seemed to take this further, given that morality did not have a place in seminal writing like that of Waltz, which focused on *what is* and not on what *ought to be*. But the sharp distinction usually made between them is unhelpful. A focus on the latter can and does regularly shape the former, as in the ban on land mines and chemical and biological weapons, or action taken against war crimes and ethnic cleansing.

In any case, major realist writers do carry a strong moral content in their writings. This is unambiguous in the work of Hans Morgenthau, the towering figure in post–World War II realism (Bain 2000; Cozette 2008; Williams 2005). Morgenthau was a realist, in that he focused on the practical difficulty of being moral in the world of sovereign states; but he held that, though national interest must come first, it must be constrained by moral limitations (Murray 1996). As he put it: "In the absence of an integrated international society, the attainment of a modicum of order and the realization of a minimum of moral values are predicated upon the existence of national communities capable of preserving order and realizing moral values within the limits of their power" (Morgenthau 1962, 38). From a practical standpoint, therefore, he held that the national interest must be given priority because the state must give overriding preference to "the moral principle of national survival" (Morgenthau 2006, 12). There is an important limitation here on the exercise of violence by the state. As Michael Williams points out, for Morgenthau, the legitimacy of the state and its use of violence as an instrument rest ultimately on the security it offers its people and is "limited to the defense of that order" (Williams 2004, 648). For the realist, moreover, the national interest must represent the interests of the people, not those of an elite (Gilpin 1984, 303).

This central point—that the state's legitimacy derives from its promise to ensure the security of its people—is embedded in the idea of the social contract: the agreement by which the people give away much of their individual freedom to the state so that the latter might preserve their lives and protect their interests (Boucher and Kelly 1994; Heyman 1991). The contract, of course, is an implicit rather than a historical one (Huemer 2013, 20–58). This goes to the heart of the argument in this book: a state that fails to protect its people violates the social contract and can be held accountable for its actions or inaction. Moreover, as I will show, this failure to abide by the terms of the social contract has practical consequences, in that it makes a significant impact on the existing and future security of the people.

In using the term "state," I risk muddying the question of responsibility. Ultimately, the proper question is: who is responsible for a specific event or occurrence? Moral responsibility for acts carried out in the name of the state must lie (to varying degrees) with those who act on its behalf, that is, its "responsible agents" (Vargas 2010). However, we must acknowledge that an agent of the state can only be held responsible for an act to the extent that he or she has control over the situation and over what is done in a specific policy context. Control may be broadly defined as "the capacity to bring about a certain result or make something happen, or, alternatively, to preclude something from happening" (Walton 1974, 163). Control may be full or partial, and the latter may exist when control is exercised by more than one individual (Walton 1974, 166). In the context of the state and its responsibility, the meaning of control is slightly complicated because it is not always clear who is to be held responsible for the acts of a lower-level functionary since that functionary is accountable to and supervised by an official at the next higher level, who is in turn accountable to the next higher level, and so on, all the way to the top. There is inherently a tension between the individual and the collective as to where responsibility is located (Erskine 2008, 701–2). But that difficulty does not allow us to bypass the question of responsibility.

"Systemic failure" is often the explanation for catastrophic events when there are many points of malfunction (which is the case with the response to the terrorist attack on Mumbai, as we shall see in chapter 5). However, this is really an evasion of the sometimes-difficult task of finding one or more persons who are accountable. In addition, the general slackening of a system in which no one is held responsible tends to create a pervasive sense that it is defective and that no one is responsible, which further encourages a reluctance to take on responsibility (Sajó 1992, 1119–20). Nevertheless, someone *is* responsible, and it becomes important for a system—in this case, the state—to acknowledge where the buck stops. Morgenthau's ethics of responsibility, drawing from Weber, centers on this: "an intention consequence dissonance, which, given the assertion of moral responsibility, must be taken into account in the formulation and evaluation of action" (Murray 1996, 99). Following from the argument above, the existence of a "responsibility deficit" (Sajó 1992, 1107), or a gap between expectations (or stated intentions) and implementation, has two related aspects: the failure of policymakers to meet their own realist expectations, and the moral responsibility for this failure. The practical consequences of this responsibility deficit can be severe, as we will see, in its human and economic costs, which is why it is important to investigate it.

We need to distinguish between ex ante and post facto judgments with regard to moral responsibility. The former relate to acts that ought to be performed, which are about obligation and duty; and the latter relate to acts that should have been performed but were not, which pertain to accountability and responsibility (Erskine 2008, 700–701). In this study, the focus is on the latter. In chapter 4, which is on nuclear strategy, as well as in chapter 5, on policy response to cross-border terrorism, the problem is primarily one of failure of responsibility.

There are two ways of looking at responsibility. I draw here from Robert Gregory's (1998) critical paper on responsibility with respect to the collapse of a viewing platform at Cave Creek in a New Zealand wilderness area in 1995. Owing to faulty construction of the platform, fourteen persons standing on it fell more than a hundred feet and were killed, while others were seriously injured. Drawing from Bovens and 't Hart (1996), Gregory argues that there are two ways to conceive of assigning responsibility in this case: forward-mapping and backward-mapping. As outlined by Gregory (1998, 520–21), "The former starts from the policy conception stage and traces events through to implementation 'on the ground,' highlighting any mismatch between intentions and outcomes. The latter . . . also identifies any such mismatches, but focuses on how problems faced at the implementation stage might have their origins earlier in the policy process."

In short, forward-mapping highlights failures before or at the time of a catastrophe or crisis, whereas backward-mapping traces the problem back to the conditions created earlier, under which the event in question occurred. This approach avoids the loose conception of "systemic failure" (also used in the New Zealand case). A "systemic failure," Gregory (1998, 527–29) notes, is usually said to occur when a system of controls is (1) faulty in design; (2) is not implemented; or (3) is not put into place at all. The first may be excusable, but moral responsibility must apply to the other two. In this book, I utilize the conception of forward- and backward-mapping to assess the responsibility issue with respect to both the inadequacies of nuclear strategy and the poor preparation for and response to the terrorist attack on Mumbai. Though the former case does not involve a catastrophe, Gregory's analysis can nevertheless be productively applied for the attribution of responsibility.

There is also the related problem of "agency loss," which, in the context of the social contract, occurs "when the agent gets a bit of extra slack from the principal to pursue its own interests rather than the principal's" (Gailmard 2014, 92). Agency loss is common enough because much of the stuff of foreign policy is not within the grasp of—or for that matter of much interest to—the general public, and India is no exception. As Mark Warren (2014, 44) observes, "Scale, distance and complexity increase the opaqueness of organizations and citizens, increasing the costs of accountability to such an extent that it is hard to imagine that any citizen (or group of citizens) could marshal the information necessary for close and thorough monitoring." Nonetheless, in a democracy, there is always a point beyond which the responsibility of the principal is also to *itself*: "any democracy is a system of accountabilities: of representatives to the people they represent, of officials for the public trust they hold, and even of the people to themselves for past and future decisions" (Warren 2014, 39). In chapter 5, this becomes plainly manifest.

Might the responsibility deficit be adequately explained by assessing the extent to which an "accountability environment" is conducive to the meeting of decision-makers' obligations (Narang and Staniland 2018)? The innovative approach taken by Narang and Staniland shows that the extent to which leaders "devote political effort and resources to foreign policy issues" is determined by two factors: (1) the degree to which an issue is salient; and (2) the degree of clarity of responsibility applying to it (Narang and Staniland 2018, 2). By salience, they mean "how much the voter cares"; while "clarity of responsibility" is about "how easily elected officials can be held responsible" (Narang and Staniland 2018, 7). Conceptually, this is a useful but still incomplete explanation in the context of the two cases of voluntary deficit examined here. The accountability environment is useful as an intermediate variable because it tells us something important about why leaders do, or do not, exercise responsibility where they have control over the levers of a policy. But it tends to shift the onus of responsibility away from policymakers and onto the "environment" wherein they function. If policy drifts, we want to know precisely why, and the mere existence of a specific accountability environment—as with "systemic failure"—tends to divert our attention away from where the responsibility buck stops.

In chapter 4, my analysis complements the accountability environment argument. Nuclear strategy is not an issue of high salience for the Indian public; nor is there clarity of responsibility, because the crafting of strategy is a task not clearly allocated to either civilian or military authority. But this in itself says nothing about the outcome—that is, about why policy drift is visible over two decades, which is traceable to the choices made by the political leadership. Indeed, the making of wrong choices in such conditions is due not to the accountability environment but to the muddle-headed thinking of the leadership, as I will show, and to the lack of effort to make choices that are logically consistent with the declared doctrinal preferences of those same leaders. In chapter 5, the inadequacy of the theory is even more evident: the failings of counterterrorism strategy are visible in an accountability environment where there is high salience as well as clarity of responsibility. For the Indian public, the high cost of recurring cross-border terrorist attacks was all too visible, and there was no second opinion that the government of the day was responsible for outcomes. An apparently strong accountability environment did not produce a sound policy because someone—in this case, both the agent and the principal—was not exercising responsibility.

Hence, it is not the accountability environment that explains suboptimal policy but the failure to exercise responsibility. It bears repetition that my focus on the normative aspect transcends the empirical/normative divide. It is not so much about what *should be done* as about what *should have been done* and about the practical consequences of the latter for understanding why a specific outcome occurs. In sum, if foreign policy decision-makers' inability to optimize policy is attributable to factors beyond their control (in the present case, the distribution of domestic power), it is proper to say that, when they do have control, their failure to produce optimal policy may be ascribed (at least in the cases explored here) to a responsibility deficit.

THE ARGUMENT

The four cases of policy drift examined here all relate to the central concerns of Indian national security strategy. The first two relate to involuntary drift. In the first case, the India-US nuclear agreement was pivotal to a wider revamping of Indian grand strategy that was designed to lean toward the United States for material gain, both military and economic. The drift that was displayed, though by no means entirely internally caused, was in large measure produced by the distribution of domestic political power. This was a case of opportunity nearly missed, for a failure to sign the nuclear agreement would have seriously constrained the thrust of India's strategy. In the second case, India's inability to provide substantial military assistance to the Sri Lankan government in its campaign to destroy the LTTE did prove to be a missed opportunity because it prevented the development of a long-term strategic relationship between the two countries.

This also had a threat-inducing effect as China filled the gap left by India and became a major weapons supplier to Sri Lanka, thereby quickly enhancing its influence with that country.

The two cases of voluntary drift—which are still continuing—have similarly added to India's security problems and produced an additional layer of threat. In the third case, the lack of clarity in India's nuclear doctrine and the resultant inconsistency in its nuclear weapons development and conventional deployment programs have led to a cost-ineffective posture that has stimulated arms racing with Pakistan and generated risks that span the thin divide between nuclear and conventional weapons and war, again with Pakistan, but also vis-à-vis China. Finally, in the fourth case, India's lopsided response to cross-border terrorism emanating from Pakistan, having failed to pressurize the latter to abandon its strategy of asymmetric warfare, has enabled Islamabad to sustain that strategy—at considerable cost in the form of casualties inflicted on the Indian public.

The four instances of policy drift range across diverse types of India's strategic relationships: the involuntary ones with two relatively friendly states, the United States and Sri Lanka; and the voluntary ones with major adversaries, China and Pakistan. Of India's four interlocutors, two (the United States and China) are large and powerful states by virtue of their military as well as economic capabilities; one is a militarily powerful but economically struggling middle-level state (Pakistan); and the last (Sri Lanka) is a small and weak state in every respect. Other cases might have been selected, but they were inappropriate for one reason or another. India–Bangladesh relations could have fit well into the involuntary drift framework, but the drift in this particular relationship is of lesser magnitude than it is in the ones chosen for this analysis. The India–ASEAN (Association of Southeast Asian Nations) Free Trade Agreement, which took considerable time to fructify from its initial signing in 2003 to the final agreement in 2009—and hence evoked considerable impatience from India's future partners—was certainly an important case of policy drift, but my concern here is with the realm of national security in a fairly narrow sense, which means that economic relationships are not germane in this particular instance.

I do, however, endeavor to strengthen my argument by examining—albeit somewhat briefly—three cases where the appearance of policy drift is not generated by domestic politics. The India–Pakistan and India–China strategic relationships are two instances of military ups and downs wherein the source of uncertainty lies not so much within the Indian state as with external factors and the competitive dynamic between India and its two main strategic rivals. A third area of drift is with respect to India's quest for major power status, which it has pursued with considerable vigor but limited success. The latter is partly due to domestic political constraints, primarily state capacity, given India's economic limitations. But, this said, Indian strategy has not been adversely affected by domestic politics because Indian policymakers have been mindful of potential costs and have evaded them with not a little political acumen. External constraints, I will show, have been the chief determinants of the limited progress that is visible thus far.

I have also taken care to consider alternative sources of policy drift in each of the four major cases studied here. An important potential source of the slowing down of policy, as noted above, is systemic. This is most evident in the negotiations over the India-US nuclear agreement. Washington, facing its own domestic constraints, tried to bargain for an agreement that would make no more than limited concessions to New Delhi before agreeing to bypass the restrictions imposed by its domestic law as well as the nonproliferation regime on civil nuclear commerce with India. But it ended up making substantial concessions to New Delhi because of its own structural priority—the desire to build a partnership with India against a rising China. On India–Sri Lanka strategic relations, there was no external factor at work to delay Indian defense support for Colombo, which would have been happy to obtain it. With regard to nuclear strategy, there was no external pressure that drove India off its minimum deterrence track (though an erroneous response to apparent systemic incentives is identified in chapter 4). Only with respect to cross-border terrorism was there a major external inhibitor to action: India could not respond militarily to pressure from Pakistan because the latter possessed nuclear weapons. But, as I show, an important reason for policy drift lay—and still lies—in the domestic realm, for domestic preparedness has been well below the expectations aroused by the government's policy initiatives.

On the domestic side, other factors do have a role to play. First, governmental politics—other than the distribution of domestic political power, on which I focus in the two cases of involuntary drift—impinges significantly on policymaking. The civil/military divide affects the making of military strategy and doctrine; and the constitutionally mandated center–state (i.e., federal–provincial) relationship places limits on the center's capacities for responding to terrorist threats. But in neither instance, it will be apparent, have these limitations been critical in weakening the capacities of the state to the extent that decisive policy is not possible.

Second, bureaucratic politics does play a part in obstructing efficient policymaking. The role of the technical bureaucracy in holding up the Indian side of the nuclear agreement with the United States was substantial; but I show that this bureaucratic intervention in the bargaining process was only a subsidiary factor: it was indeed facilitated by the distribution of domestic political power and would not have been possible beyond a limited extent otherwise. On counterterrorism policy, bureaucratic pathologies have been evident—a reality of which the government has been made aware from time to time. But I show in chapter 5 that these have not been the chief source of indecisive policy, for which the responsibility lies squarely with the political leadership.

A third domestic factor is the role of party-based political preferences. One can certainly observe sizable differences in the political leanings of the two main political parties, the Congress and the BJP. As we will see, in the domestic negotiations over the India-US nuclear agreement, the BJP opposed the deal not because its preferences diverged significantly from those of the Congress, but because it saw an opportunity to bring a weak government down. Party preferences did have an impact, in the sense that the Communist Party of India–Marxist was ideologically opposed to the nuclear deal and strong opposition to a pro-Colombo policy came from Tamil parties in India, which emphasized kinship with the LTTE. But the influence of these parties' preferences in causing policy drift was only possible because of the distribution of domestic political power.

Fourth, the same applies to the role of leadership preferences. The BJP leadership opposed the nuclear deal despite having initiated a decisive foreign policy turn toward the United States; it is clear that its motives on this issue were instrumentalist in nature. In the remaining cases, diverse leaders responded similarly under varying circumstances. Fifth and finally, public opinion has set outer limits on what policymakers can do, but there is no real evidence that it has played a key role in shaping any of the policy processes, with respect to drift or otherwise, other than in the most general way.

I argue that the relative domestic costs associated with a foreign policy action tend to determine the choices that policymakers make and the degree of opposition they face. Policy drift occurs when the costs of appropriate action outweigh those of limited action. This applies both to general policy frameworks and to specific policies. However, the likelihood of drift is greater with respect to the latter. Policy drift is less likely to occur when general policies are introduced because the effects of such policies are diffuse and not immediate and therefore opposition or internal (to the policymakers themselves) resistance does not manifest itself. When specific policies—key active components of general policy frameworks—are introduced, the prospect of immediate cost galvanizes oppositional interests, often with diverse sources of opposition making common cause against the policy. Where internal braking effects are concerned, much the same happens: the prospect of high cost attached to a specific policy generates an unwillingness to follow it through to completion and a readiness to be content with limited action. However, I must clarify that this does not amount to a cost/benefit analysis. In particular, I do not believe that the cost/benefit calculations of policymakers undercut my argument about responsibility. On the contrary, they *explain* the abdication of responsibility: when policymakers face costly decisions to act responsibly, they often take the easier way out and neglect responsibility.

Exogenous shocks from the international system affecting India's national security have produced broad policy responses in accord with realist expectations. The changes introduced in foreign policy have sometimes (but not always) evoked resistance and criticism from the realm of domestic politics, but the opposition has not greatly hobbled the foreign policy executive. This applies to all the cases discussed here, regardless of variations in the actual power of the ruling party and its leadership. Why do such dramatic reorientations produce relatively little adverse reaction? First, public opinion may not react negatively to the policy shift. Indeed, in every case examined here, public opinion was generally supportive or acquiescent. The warming of India-US relations did not invite much public criticism, though there was resistance from left-leaning intellectuals and elements of the bureaucracy that were habitually wary of American power. India's new closeness to Sri Lanka starting in the mid-1990s was also accepted widely, with the exception of Tamil Nadu state, which had a population that was barely a twentieth of India's. India's 1998 nuclear tests and its proclamation of nuclear-armed status were welcomed by most that cared to react. And the decision to revamp the security structure in order to strengthen counterterrorism policy was expectedly unopposed. Whatever grumbling and uneasiness there was was insufficient to galvanize opposition to policies that were broad and did not provide focal points for diverse interests to come together.

For policymakers, the broad changes they introduced in each case did incur some costs: it was not easy, for instance, to shift away from the long-standing policy of keeping aloof from the United States, or to break through long-standing restraint and publicly cross the nuclear weapons threshold. Nevertheless, the cost of inaction was clearly greater than that of transformative policy action. With regard to India-US relations, the potential cost of change (the risk of losing much-cherished autonomy; the difficulty of virtually abandoning nonalignment) was less than that of continuity (navigating a strategic environment where India would be isolated and under pressure from three sources: China, Pakistan, and the United States–led nonproliferation regime). The calculus in the India–Sri Lanka case was also clear. There was no significant cost accompanying change toward a pro-Colombo policy in a situation where there was much public anger against the LTTE for the assassination of former prime minister Rajiv Gandhi (though, as it turned out, the degree of resistance from Tamil Nadu was clearly not anticipated). Against this, the cost of not making the change was potentially large because a victory for the LTTE was not in India's interests (it might have raised the risk of Tamil unification across the Palk Strait) and defeat of the LTTE without Indian assistance would have necessitated an unwelcome role for China and Pakistan in enhancing the capacity of the Sri Lankan military. But, though Tamil parties were critical of New Delhi's growing closeness with Colombo, there was no focal point around which their antipathy could be energized into all-out opposition.

On nuclear strategy, India's nuclear coming out in 1998 brought immediate costs in the form of sanctions imposed by several countries, notably Japan and the United States. Indeed, at least one previous plan to test nuclear weapons (by Prime Minister Narasimha Rao in 1995) had been abandoned to avoid just such an international reaction. But this was considered a considerably lower cost than the security risk arising from strategic isolation, given the growing post–Cold War pressure from the United States for India to roll back its covert nuclear weapons program. With regard to cross-border terrorism, the rising tide of terrorist activity originating in Pakistan, especially starting in the 1990s, exacted a high cost, to which India had to respond by means of a multipronged strategy that would tighten domestic security and exert increased pressure on Pakistan both bilaterally and through multilateral means. Unsurprisingly, there was no serious domestic opposition to a revamped counterterrorism policy, though critics did object to some aspects of the form it took, for instance, by concentrating power in the hands of the state and its antiterrorist forces.

But, though none of these general policy approaches faced serious opposition, specific policies that fell within a general policy framework came to be characterized by policy drift because of a change in the weight of potential costs and benefits, to the detriment of the latter. This does not mean that rising costs alienated the public at large. In none of the cases examined here did this happen. Yet policy drift did occur: the India-US nuclear agreement stalled; military aid to Sri Lanka was sharply curtailed; nuclear strategy displayed serious cracks; and counterterrorist policy was ineffective because of internal anomalies. In the first two, which involved involuntary drift, active opposition was roused as otherwise-disparate opposition groups came together to contest policy and to threaten the survival of the government of the day. In the other two, involving voluntary drift, the prospect of rising costs associated with carrying a policy through impeded decisive action.

Involuntary drift—where policymakers are severely constrained by the distribution of power—has been a constant phenomenon in India since the late 1980s. The Congress Party, which had dominated the national political structure during the early decades after India's independence, began to decline. In its place emerged an increasingly decentralized system, in which regional parties became the new power holders in many states. Between 1989 and 2004, the proportion of seats held by regional parties grew from 15.5 to 24.6 percent (Chakravarty 2008, 166, table 1). Simultaneously, the BJP, an offshoot of the Bharatiya Jana Sangh representing the Hindu right, came to the forefront as a new party with an India-wide ambit. As a result, after 1989, no party was able to obtain a majority by itself in Parliament until 2014.

Coalition governments struggled to stay afloat in a sea of intense political bargaining over the terms of power sharing among the two big parties—the Congress and the BJP—and a large number of small parties. After the short-lived tenure (1989–91) of a coalition government stitched together by the Janata Dal, a small party with national pretensions, the Congress-led

Narasimha Rao government lasted a full five-year term, until 1996. Under Rao, Indian policies underwent the first phase of their post–Cold war reversals in foreign strategic and economic relations. The subsequent period from 1996 onward saw the rise and fall of several coalition governments as parties struggled with the formation of alliances and party politics became fiercely competitive. Coalitions became large and unwieldy, and governments were unstable (Sridharan 2018).

Patchy coalitions often depended on support from nonmembers. Leaving aside supporting outsiders, coalition governments themselves became larger and larger. The Janata Dal coalition of 1989 consisted of five parties; the coalition that formed a government in 1996, also led by the Janata Dal, had nine; the BJP-led one of 1998 had eleven; the next one (1999) also led by it had twelve. The United Progressive Alliance's 2004 coalition topped them all, with seventeen; but it became relatively stable in 2009, when it formed a government with ten parties, though it still required outside support from a dozen members of the Lok Sabha (the lower house of Parliament). The capacities of governments were severely challenged by this fragmentation and the constantly shifting competitive politics it produced. One brief episode saw a coalition cobbled together by the BJP in 1996 last all of thirteen days. Between 1989 and 1999, there were as many as six general elections to a Parliament whose full term is five years. As a result, government policies became vulnerable to the vicissitudes of political uncertainty, and small players began to exercise unprecedented influence in shaping national policies. In this unstable environment, governments found it hard to push through policies that aroused opposition from sectional interests.

ORGANIZATION OF THIS BOOK

The four empirically grounded chapters of this book begin with a short introduction to the specific case being analyzed, followed by historical background covering Indian policy on that particular policy area. The main analytical portion then begins with a discussion of change in the broad policy area and why there was no significant difficulty in achieving it. This is followed by a review and an analysis of the policy drift that comes to the fore when specific policies are devised within the overall framework of change. A brief conclusion then sums up the findings and significance of the case.

Chapter 2 shows how a weak coalition headed by Prime Minister Manmohan Singh faced enormous pressure to radically alter the terms of, or abandon altogether, a proposed agreement on civilian nuclear cooperation with the United States. Whereas India's grand-strategic tilt toward the United States had stirred relatively little protest, the impending nuclear agreement, announced in 2005, brought together a number of disparate interests in opposition to the nuclear agreement: ideologically upset parties prepared to withdraw their support for the coalition from outside, opposition parties bent on overthrowing the government, and bureaucrats determined to protect their turf. The result was a prolonged period of uncertainty that came to a head three years later and a final confrontation that Singh's government barely managed to survive.

In chapter 3, the story was fundamentally similar but was played out through a different mechanism. There had been no significant opposition to the warming of India–Sri Lanka relations, which had led to the signing of a free trade agreement (1998) and talks on defense cooperation. As noted above, there was considerable prospect of strategic benefit from assisting Sri Lanka in its civil war with the LTTE. The cost/benefit balance, however, was upended when the question of actual security aid and the prospect of an LTTE defeat loomed larger. Opposition to India's involvement in the civil war in Sri Lanka coalesced among Tamil Nadu's competing parties, of which one or the other was a member of different coalitions that formed the central government, and each of which found itself shackled by its coalition partners and forced to water down its policy.

The volatility of Indian politics partly contributed to voluntary drift because political leaders were preoccupied with coalition politics. As chapter 4 demonstrates, the Indian state's general shift from covert to overt nuclear deterrence in 1998 was not internally problematic, but policy drift soon appeared as successive governments failed to adhere to the stated preference for a minimalist strategy and because the leadership's inability to comprehend the linkage between the nuclear and conventional dimensions of strategy laid the foundations of greater strategic instability in India's relationship with its adversaries. The failure to correct these anomalies, and the resultant lack of direction in overall military-political strategy, is explained by the state's reluctance to tackle a domestic disability: the civil/military divide. But as I show, the so-called civil/military bargain in Indian defense policy does not constitute a structural impedance to optimal nuclear strategy. Rather, it is a self-imposed barrier that the state has not exhibited the political will to surmount.

Chapter 5, which is in part an extension of the preceding chapter, focuses on critical flaws in India's policy response to cross-border terrorism originating across the Pakistan border. The general policy response—aimed at stemming the flow of terrorists by means of a policy overhaul—was unexceptionable and largely unopposed. But the failure of the Indian state to put in place the specifics of an optimal policy has been evident for a considerable length of time. In this chapter, I focus on the Mumbai terrorist attack of November 2008 as an emblematic manifestation of the Indian state's ragged counterterrorism policy. The two elements of a realist response to an external threat are external and internal. As will be seen, Indian policy has concentrated heavily and futilely on the external dimension and has neglected the internal one, leaving India open to recurrent attacks that have exacted a costly toll on its people. The failure to focus adequately on internal balancing by way of tightened security has left the Indian public vulnerable to repeated attacks of cross-border terrorism. There is no significant explanation for this, other than a responsibility deficit exhibited by the state and, once again, its failure to meet its fundamental obligation of providing security to its citizenry.

Chapter 6 looks at cases of policy drift that do not arise from domestic politics: the lack of substantial improvement in India–Pakistan and India–China strategic relations, in the latter case, despite remarkable growth in economic cooperation; and the limited achievements of India's drive for status over the quarter-century since it began to think of itself seriously as a rising power. All three are instances where the constraints have been external. With respect to India–Pakistan relations, the problem may to a large extent be attributed to the Pakistani state's revisionist policies. In the India-China case, trade and investment relations have risen concomitantly with strategic tensions, belying the expectations of liberals. Although domestic politics is certainly significant, it has not been a serious obstacle to a détente between the two countries. In the third case, India has obtained a significant degree of recognition as a "rising power," but not the enhanced role one might expect with respect to major international institutions, whether formal or not—for example, international organizations and multilateral forums on major international disputes. Again, domestic constraints have certainly been present, most visibly with respect to India's muddled response to the second phase of the COVID-19 pandemic. But in other respects, India's strategy has been prudent. The possibility of high costs arising from a more proactive military role overseas has constrained India from taking on this attribute of major powers—a calculation that did not inhibit its strategic policies during the 1970s and 1980s.

THE SIGNIFICANCE OF THIS STUDY

This study lays claim to be of value in a number of ways. First, it clarifies the nature of policy drift by differentiating its two distinct dimensions: involuntary and voluntary. This distinction is key to understanding the conditions that produce the phenomenon of drift and hence helps us better comprehend the extent to which we can anticipate drift and consider what might—or might not—be done about it. If the constraints on effective policymaking are addressed, this opens up possibilities for optimizing policymaking by addressing the factors that tend to hamper it. Although this book examines the problem only in the context of Indian foreign policy, its findings can also apply to other cases of drift—that is, to other specific states and to the policies of states generally. Specifically, for instance, it helps explain why states fail to tackle long-standing issues such as drug and human trafficking and why they build weapons capabilities that are far beyond their optimal requirements.

Second, from the standpoint of strategic planning, the ability to anticipate the sources of drift will assist policymakers, scholars, and analysts in assessing India's prospects as a rising power. Particularly relevant here is the distinction between what is structurally hard to do (which connects to involuntary drift) and what is not (which relates to responsibility). Third, from the perspective of analytical lucidity, this work helps refine the theoretical lenses through which we view the world and investigate it. It is particularly important to broaden and strengthen neoclassical realism—and, more generally, the materialist approach—by infusing it with the normative dimension, without which it is unable to provide comprehensive explanations for serious policy problems.

Part I

MATERIAL CONSTRAINTS

2

THE INDIA-US NUCLEAR AGREEMENT

The India–United States nuclear agreement, which bypassed the rules of the nuclear nonproliferation regime to allow civilian nuclear commerce with India, was a pivotal moment in the bilateral relationship between the two countries. It was also an indication of India's shift from the margins of the central dynamics of the international system to a key position in its strategic politics. To be sure, there is room for debate over the degree to which India has been able to influence the system; but it is a reasonable argument that the "nuclear deal," as it is widely called, highlighted an important ongoing shift in the structure of the international system. The deal underscored India's arrival as a significant player, even if still secondary, on center stage, not unlike China's position vis-à-vis the US-Soviet relationship during the early 1970s (Chanda 2007; Hasan 2012). Yet between the initiation of the deal in 2005 and its fruition in 2008 lay a tale of twists and turns that brought it—and the government itself—to the brink of collapse. Although there was certainly a tug-of-war in American politics over the deal, it was in the internal politics of India that its fate hung in the balance till the eleventh hour. The stakes were huge for India, which stood to gain both greater security and higher status from the agreement. But domestic political resistance mired the agreement in a classic case of policy drift and nearly scuppered it.

In this chapter, I begin by placing the India-US nuclear agreement within the context of India's position in the structure of the international system and the way this shaped its policy framework. In its early post-independence period, Indian foreign policy vis-à-vis the global system was typical of relatively weak states. But gradually, by the 1980s, it emerged as a regional power and, by 1998, stood on the cusp of becoming a major player in the global strategic landscape. The signing of the agreement represented a critically important bargain that would enable India to strengthen its position by means of a strong strategic linkage with the United States. The process of developing a closer relationship had already begun in the early post–Cold War days, but with New Delhi long viewed by Washington as an obdurate proliferator of nuclear weapons—the more so after the 1998 tests—and New Delhi unwavering in its commitment to nuclear autonomy, both needed the deal to begin building a true strategic partnership.

In the pages that follow, I first trace the substantive shift in India's relationship with the United States starting in the early 1990s. As outlined in chapter 1, a discernible pattern emerged. The change in India's foreign policy strategy did bring considerable disquiet within sections of the Indian policy elite, but there was little serious opposition when a strategic partnership began to take shape. Once the intention to work toward a nuclear agreement was announced in 2005, it became the focal point around which disparate opposition forces formed a powerful coalition determined to derail the negotiating process. As is shown below, the effort almost succeeded after a prolonged period of internal contestation, even as external bargaining with the United States went on. The chief source of the drift, as might be expected from an argument drawing on the early formulation of neoclassical realism, was the domestic political structure—that is, the distribution of power in the Indian state—which hampered policymakers' ability to extract domestic political support. Policymakers were not greatly impeded by resistance to the broad shift in policy toward the United States, but they were almost foiled on the specific issue of the nuclear agreement as oppositional forces coalesced.

The next section discusses the background to Indian policy toward the United States in the first decades after independence in 1947 and the structural and other causes for its post–Cold War about-face. In the subsequent section, I highlight the positive turn in India-US strategic relations and consider the reasons why there was relatively light opposition to the shift. Thereafter, I examine the India-US agreement on civil nuclear trade, growing domestic opposition to the deal, and its uncertain path to conclusion. The internal contest underwent two phases. In the first, policymakers led by the prime minister wrestled with an alliance of the nuclear bureaucracy and diversely motivated political parties opposing the deal. The second phase was a straight fight between the government and the informal but powerful opposition party alliance. I conclude with a summation and highlight the theoretical significance of the analysis.

FROM WEAK TO RISING PLAYER: THE STRUCTURAL DYNAMICS OF INDIA'S RISE

Considerable research has been done on the period after India's independence and the divergence of interests between an India focused on postcolonial autonomy and a US preoccupied with the Cold War, which inclined the latter to lean toward a more accommodating Pakistan (e.g., Ali 1999; Kux 1993; McGarr 2013; McMahon 1988, 1994; Chaudhuri 2014). For the most part, this is cast in the historian's ideographic mold, highlighting differences in strategic priorities and consequent policy preferences. From the standpoint of international relations theory, a structural perspective provides a more general pattern showing continuities over time and spanning diverse leaderships.

Aside from the characteristic behavioral symptoms displayed by states in the realist's world—primarily competition and balancing, but periodically also bandwagoning—it is possible to discern fairly typical policies followed by strong, middling, and weak states—that is, policy approaches congruent with how states stand in relation to their counterparts in the international system. In particular, though middling states (neither strong, nor weak) tend to vary in the policy positions they adopt, strong and weak states tend to show broadly predictable tendencies (Mandelbaum 1988). Strong states usually (1) seek policy acquiescence from weak ones by leveraging their power advantage, that is, by offering carrots and sometimes brandishing the stick; (2) favor close economic (and often) cultural relationships with the weak in order to induce the latter's dependence; and (3) insist on tackling disputes bilaterally, again to reinforce their inherent power advantage. In contrast, weak states tend to (1) devise ways of strategic moat building in order to avoid vulnerability to major powers (though they may lean on them when threatened by other states); (2) avoid close economic and cultural relationships with big players—since this leaves them vulnerable to bigger powers' nonmilitary strengths—and instead attempt strategies of economic and cultural distancing to keep them at arm's length; and (3) seek strength through numbers, prefer multilateral approaches to their relationships with major powers.

India's position in the global structure after independence was that of a weak state—doubtless, one with potential to grow significantly, but at that time a country mired in poverty. More than a decade after independence, its gross domestic product (GDP) in 1960, $13.5 billion, was only 6.72 percent of the United States' GDP, $54.3 billion. In contrast, in 2017 the proportion had almost doubled, to 13.3 percent, with India's GDP at $2.5 trillion and that of the United States at $19.3 trillion (World Bank n.d.–b). Unsurprisingly, India's worldview and policy orientation during the postcolonial period were typical of many weak states.

After independence, Prime Minister Jawaharlal Nehru's preference for an autonomous position in international affairs corresponded broadly to this pattern. Politically, he opted for a distancing policy from the Cold War alliance systems and adopted a policy of nonalignment to maximize India's autonomy. Nonmembership of an alliance meant avoidance of dependency on an alliance leader, while simultaneously enabling Nehru to play off both the United States and the Soviet Union to a degree and to obtain significant benefits from both sides (Rana 1976). During the Cold War era, India was able to obtain substantial assistance from the United States in agricultural development and from the Soviet Union in the development of heavy industry and infrastructure through public-sector investment.

In the realm of economics, Nehru opted for an autarkic policy that sought to avoid dependence on the powerful capitalist economies in what he and his advisers felt was a structurally problematic world economy; one in which India, as a weak member of the South countries, was subject to unequal terms of trade skewed to the advantage of the developed countries of the North. Accordingly, Indian policy emphasized protective tariffs and minimal foreign direct investment. In this respect, India was hardly exceptional—most developed countries have historically done the same before their economies have taken off. Indeed, the United States had adopted similar protectionist policies when its economy was in its developing phase (Tickner 1987, 183–99). India had no major disputes with the United States. But the two had serious differences on major global issues, ranging from decolonization to interstate conflict, disarmament, and the terms of trade. Unsurprisingly, India's approach on these issues focused on multilateralism, seeking to foster change through the United Nations and the Group of Seventy-Seven developing countries.

But the strategy adopted by Nehru and continued by his daughter Indira Gandhi and her successors had serious limitations. Most important, India was unable to build its material strength significantly, which compelled it to seek military aid from the great powers when its security position was shaky. In 1962, after experiencing a severe military setback at the hands of China, Nehru sought military aid from the United States. But because he still refused to join the American alliance system, that source was restricted, particularly since Pakistan, which had been at loggerheads with India since 1947, was a US ally. Eventually, India came to depend on the Soviet Union for its military wherewithal and for balancing China, to which end Indira Gandhi signed the Indo-Soviet Treaty of 1971—ostensibly a "friendship" treaty, but one that was carefully designed to counter a common adversary, China, while avoiding the deeper commitments of an alliance relationship. Euphemistically put, the treaty "signified that the stronger version of non-alignment was no longer sustainable" (Krishna 1984, 286). After 1962 the Indian state focused on building up its armed forces, largely through imported weapons, which were primarily—but not only—from the Soviet Union. By the 1970s it had built up a formidable conventional military and, despite a long-standing rejection of nuclear weapons, tested the bomb (in 1974), though it refrained from actively pursuing the nuclear weapons path until much later.

Meanwhile, autarky had not fared well. The focus on self-sufficiency and the burgeoning red tape in a controlled economy that came derisively to be called the "license-permit raj" brought stagnation and corruption. As noted in chapter 1, India was experiencing slow growth and falling behind other developing countries like Brazil. With the oil crises of the 1970s, its import bill ballooned, resulting ultimately in ever larger balance-of-payment deficits. The hopes for a New International Economic Order through enhanced "South–South" economic relations faded as developing country debt piled up and the notion of Third World solidarity dissipated (Harris 1987). India was no exception. But serious reform was not forthcoming and, despite some minor adjustments, the old ways of doing things persisted until India was galvanized by two major external shocks into reordering its foreign policy framework.

The first was a financial emergency. Though there had been some increase in growth rates during the 1980s, the economy was fragile and overly reliant on external borrowing, which resulted in a balance-of-payments crisis in 1991 (Acharya 2002; Panagariya 2004). The Indian government not only had to approach the World Bank and the International Monetary Fund for succor, but was compelled to pledge physical stocks of gold with the Bank of England and the Bank of Japan as collateral for loans amounting to $400 million and to sell 20 metric tonnes to UBS Bank of Switzerland for an additional $200 million. This came as a humiliating shock to a country that places an inordinately high value on the possession of gold (Vikraman 2017).

The structural adjustment—essentially, deregulation—that was introduced owing to the crisis brought a significant change in the economy. Growth rates climbed: annual GDP growth, which had been a dismal 1.07 percent in 1991, went up steadily, with high points in 1995 (7.57 percent), 2007 (9.80 percent), and 2010 (10.26 percent) (World Bank, n.d.–b). Foreign investment began pouring in, and the new economic dynamism brought an attendant mood of confidence. India's self-image as well as its image overseas became more positive. It was now widely viewed as an "emerging economy."

The second external shock, which occurred at roughly the same time as the economic crisis, was the end of the Cold War. The collapse of the Soviet Union in 1991 meant that India was now deprived of its main source of strategic support for arms supplies and for countering the Chinese threat. Moreover, nonalignment, the bedrock of Indian foreign policy, had now become superfluous. Worse, as the United States and China seemed to be coming to terms with each other, India was acutely conscious of its isolation, particularly when both large states began to coordinate their nonproliferation policies and apply pressure on India to roll back its covert nuclear arsenal (Bhatia 2012, 91).

India responded to this combination of isolation and uncertainty with a radical strategic shift. In the summer of 1998, it carried out a series of five nuclear tests and declared itself a nuclear power. The tests had the effect of freeing India from its sense of isolation in the post–Cold War world and altered its self-image and its profile in the international system. It faced a period of intense pressure as the United States, Japan, and other countries applied sanctions against it, but these did not last. Conversely, as Prime Minister Atal Bihari Vajpayee put it, "The greatest meaning of the tests is that they have given India shakti [= power], they have given India strength, they have given India self-confidence" (quoted by Chawla 1998). Externally, the effect of the tests was to alter the way the world outside began to view India. For all its shortcomings with respect to social and economic development, India now acquired the label of "rising power."

INDIA'S BROAD POLICY SHIFT: SMOOTH SAILING

The transformation of the India-US relationship was propelled by structural factors. The perspective of both states was reshaped by new power configurations emerging after the end of the Cold War. For the United States, the collapse of one adversary, the Soviet Union, was followed—after a brief interregnum—by the rise of another. Relations with China had begun to fray. Once the euphoria of the "unipolar moment" had faded, Washington was disposed to look for new friends to hedge against the rise of Beijing (Mandelbaum 2010; see also Gelb 2009; Kennedy 2009; Layne 2012). The American elections of 2000 brought to power an administration that was less inclined than its predecessor to worry about India's newfound nuclear status. On the contrary, the United States under George W. Bush saw India as a potential partner in a broad sense—as Under Secretary of State R. Nicholas Burns (2007, 138) put it, "We see India as a stabilizing force in an often violent and unstable part of the world." American and Indian interests coincided in many ways: on responding to the rise of China, countering terrorism, curtailing the spread of weapons of mass destruction, establishing energy stability, and sustaining the liberal economic order (Blackwill 2005; Burns 2007; Carter 2006; Tellis 2013). Washington came to terms with New Delhi, retracted sanctions, and decided that India, as an emerging power with both economic and military potential, could become a major player in global politics and hence a useful friend against the possibility of a recalcitrant China.

The one big obstacle after the 1998 tests was labeling India a "proliferator" because it had refused to sign the Nuclear Non-Proliferation Treaty (NPT) and was subject to a long-standing set of American-led sanctions set in motion by its 1974 tests. India's nuclear capability was not in itself considered a threat; on the contrary, its democratic character meant that US policymakers did not directly "securitize" it (Hayes 2013). But particularly after its 1974 test, India's stand had complicated American efforts to curb the proliferation of nuclear weapons. President Bush, however, was not overly concerned about India's impact on the nonproliferation regime and was more inclined to view it as a potential partner because of their common values. Much before he became president, he had expressed his fascination with India to a friend (and a future ambassador to India), Robert Blackwill: "A billion people in a functioning democracy. Isn't that something? Isn't that something?" (quoted by Raja Mohan 2006, 92). According to Condoleezza Rice, then his national security adviser and later secretary of state, Bush saw India as "a natural fit for US strategic interests," and both were keen on dismantling the sanctions, though they were aware they would meet resistance from the nonproliferation "high priests" in the US Congress and bureaucracy (Rice 2011, 129).

Moreover, India's nuclear coming out made it an attractive potential partner for countering the rise of China—a balancing game that Australia, Japan, Singapore, and other countries were soon to emulate in varying degrees. US leaders were careful not to stress the strategic implications of India's nuclear capability, but the subliminal message was there. As Rice told the US Senate Foreign Relations Committee, "India is a rising global power and a pillar of stability in a rapidly changing Asia. India will continue to possess *sophisticated military forces* that, just like our own, remain strongly committed to the principle of civilian control, and will in the future help to promote peace in Asia and across the world" (emphasis added; quoted by Das 2015, 227).

The concord between Indian and American strategic interests was reflected in a Joint Study Group Report chaired by Blackwill and Naresh Chandra (2011), a senior Indian bureaucrat. It encompassed countering the spread of weapons of mass destruction, reducing the international terrorist threat, "maintaining a balance of power in Asia and in Europe," promoting global energy security, managing the global economy, and addressing the problem of climate change (Blackwill and Chandra 2011, 1–2). There was no question of a future alliance. Indeed, there were significant differences between the two countries on a variety of issues, such as Iran's suspected nuclear proliferation, Pakistan's support for terrorist groups attacking Indian targets, and the rules of international trade and intellectual property rights. Nevertheless, there was keen interest in fostering a stronger security relationship on both sides.

These systemically driven developments provided incentives to which Indian leaders responded in a realist vein. The leadership during the watershed period—chiefly, Prime Minister Narasimha Rao, Finance Minister Manmohan Singh, and a handful of senior bureaucrats—grasped the nettle and turned the economic crisis into an opportunity to bring about a series of fundamental reforms and transform the domestic economic environment. Like Russia's Gorbachev, they introduced changes from which there was no stepping back and which unleashed an accelerating process of economic and strategic transformation. Unlike Gorbachev, they required a crisis to set the process of change in motion. As we have seen, a sense of dissatisfaction in the leadership had not been sufficient to trigger change. Yet it would be an exaggeration to attribute the change entirely to systemic pressure. Though Gorbachev chose to introduce change where he need not have, Rao and his colleagues had virtually no option but to alter the framework of Indian foreign policy. However, it is also true that they chose to go the distance and place the Indian economy on an altogether new trajectory (Mukherji 2014). Continuing the trend, Bharatiya Janata Party (BJP) Prime Minister Vajpayee and his colleagues shed their preference for "swadeshi" (= autarky) and instead rode the wave of liberalization.

On nuclear testing, Vajpayee chose to tread where Rao had feared to. Rao had ordered a test in 1995 but pulled back upon receiving a warning from the United States (*Indian Express* 2013a). Vajpayee anticipated the US reaction, calculated the potential risk, and went ahead regardless in 1998. Was he driven by an offensive realist approach to international politics? It is easy enough to trot out the "Hindu nationalist" image of the BJP to underline such a claim. But, in fact, Vajpayee as a leader had always been more complex than the label implies. Back in the 1970s, as minister for external affairs, he had *opposed* the development of nuclear weapons (Subrahmanyam 2004b). And as a poet, he had wondered whether history would ever forgive those who produced the bomb (BBC News 2002).

Nevertheless, it is evident that Indian policymakers were responding in accord with realist expectations to systemic incentives. Having failed to gain from autarky, India shifted to economic liberalization, as had most developing countries by then. Having lost one balancing partner vis-à-vis China, India was looking for another (Kapur and Ganguly 2007; Raghavan 2018; Chaudhuri 2014; Schaffer 2009; van de Wetering 2016). And fearing the loss of its nuclear option, it decided to test.

The increasing convergence between India and the United States led to the flowering of a strategic partnership and growing cooperation in defense and other areas (Ladwig and Mukherjee 2019; R. Mukherjee 2020; Pant 2008, 19–37). The defense relationship began to pick up with the so-called Kicklighter proposals (1991), named after General Claude Kicklighter, who headed the US Pacific Command at the time. The proposals recommended strategic dialogue, training, and other exchanges between the two militaries. This was followed by an agreement in 1995 to initiate a program of regular military exercises. India's testing of nuclear weapons in 1998 stalled the process, but this was soon revived after a series of one-to-one talks between Indian foreign minister Jaswant Singh and US deputy secretary of state Strobe Talbott from June 1998 to September 2000 that cleared the air between them (Talbott 2004).

Yet India had not fully arrived, as it were. The one big hurdle that remained between India and the United States—one that more generally hampered the accommodation of India as a rising power—was the nuclear issue. The public position taken by Indian leaders (and echoed by their American counterparts) was focused on the rising Indian economy's need for energy, but the reality was that nuclear energy accounted for a marginal proportion of India's needs. Notably, in its pursuit of the nuclear deal, India did not present a position paper outlining its energy requirements and the role of nuclear energy therein (Hasan 2012, 8–9). As one insightful analyst remarks, "The US-India dispute over India's right to nuclear weapons and nuclear technology became a defining point in US-India relations. The lack of cooperation on civil nuclear power became symbolic of the estrangement of India and the United States. This symbolism took on an importance out of proportion to the role that civil nuclear power might play in ameliorating the electrical power deficiencies of India" (Vickery 2011, 52).

India remained an outsider to the US-led nonproliferation regime, which rankled the Indian elite. It was also an issue of technology denial, because India's access to dual-use technologies and materials in civil nuclear energy, space, computing, and other areas was restricted, owing to the sanctions imposed by the United States and by the regime. For a country acutely conscious of its history of colonial subjection, this was no small matter. It was inextricably bound up with its deeply felt need for strategic autonomy and its self-consciousness as a rising power.

Indian policymakers were realistically aware that, without the support of the United States, their strategic priorities would be hard to meet. Manmohan Singh, on becoming prime minister in 2004, was conscious of the enormous tasks before him: he wanted to push for extensive land reform, enhance economic growth, stabilize relationships with India's two nuclear adversaries, and tackle corruption (Power 2004). Shivshankar Menon, who as foreign secretary helped finalize the nuclear agreement, acknowledges that India needed American support to pursue these objectives, for "the United States could be either spoiler or enabler for India to achieve its goals" (Menon 2016, 37–38). Moreover, with respect to the nuclear agreement, as Menon's predecessor Shyam Saran notes, "We could not attain this objective without the US taking the lead on our behalf," and—specifically with regard to getting the Nuclear Suppliers Group (NSG) to agree to accommodate India—"no other friendly country which is a member of the NSG had the necessary standing to lead the process of opening up the existing multilateral regime to accommodate India" (Saran 2017, 223–24). In short, their goals fell broadly in the realist mold: the leadership, responding to the incentives of the evolving structure of the international system, wanted to draw strategically closer to the United States, despite past difficulties with it.

There was some opposition to the warming of India-US relations and national debates over the issue revealed the substantial hostility that was prominent among diverse groups ranging from the left parties to the domestic policy–oriented "neonationalists" in the Congress (Ollapally and Rajagopalan 2012, 33–38). The chief cause of this reluctance to strengthen links with the United States arose from a concern that the United States would inevitably dominate India's strategic agenda. American pressure on India to downgrade its relationship with Iran—to which New Delhi acquiesced—was prominent evidence of how this pressure was being applied (Mistry 2014, 88–89). However, only the left-wing parties were in outright opposition to closer India-US relations (Ollapally and Rajagopalan 2012, 33–38). A number of works have illustrated the splintered character of Indian elite preferences on foreign policy (Bajpai 2014; Ollapally and Rajagopalan 2012; Sagar 2009). But, as Ollapally and Rajagopalan note, elite opinion generally has a limited and indirect effect on policymakers, though it can sometimes act as a veto (Ollapally and Rajagopalan 2012, 4–5).

Why did the general transformation of India-US strategic relations not provoke a veto response? Four reasons may be adduced. First, the structure of foreign policy making in India is such that the executive generally has strong control over the process. The parliamentary system of government gives the power to make policy to an executive that enjoys the majority in the legislature (specifically, in India, the directly elected lower house, the Lok Sabha). Moreover, the Indian legislature does not enjoy specific powers over critical foreign policy decisions such as the declaration of war, the signing of treaties, and the adoption of free trade agreements. In effect, the power of Parliament is largely restricted to controlling expenditures and to defeating the government in a vote on a legislative matter. Though the Manmohan Singh government was a weak coalition without a clear majority, this was not easy to do because the sources of political opposition were also weak, as I show just below.

Second, as is also commonly the case elsewhere, foreign policy issues frequently do not have a domestic constituency to answer to, which means that policymakers have a fairly free hand in making decisions. This is particularly true of strategic issues, to which the voting public tends to pay relatively little attention, except on questions of war and peace. India's move to expand strategic cooperation with a specific country other than China or Pakistan (where the possession of territory is involved) is not likely to be the subject of debate in the street or to affect election outcomes.

Third, as noted above, such opposition as there was did not take on a solid character because it came from diverse sources. The main opposition party, the BJP, was not in a position to take strong exception to the shift. The BJP had itself initiated the strengthening of India-US strategic relations by means of the Singh-Talbott talks. Moreover, after the September 11, 2001, terrorist attacks on the United States, Vajpayee had made a startling offer to assist the United States in its military campaign against the perpetrators (Lavoy 2002, 27–28). The left-wing parties were certainly uncomfortable with the policy change but were reluctant to make common cause with the BJP, which they disliked, and were not by themselves sufficiently powerful to dig in their heels against a process that was general rather than focused on specific action.

And fourth, internal resistance from the bureaucracy was significant but not forceful. For instance, officials in the Ministry of External Affairs and the Ministry of Defense balked at the 2002 proposal for Indian ships to escort US supply vessels as a departure from established practice with uncertain ramifications; and foreign policy officials were unhappy about the 2005 Singh-Bush initiative on jointly promoting democracy, which had never been on India's agenda (Raja Mohan 2006, 94–96, 104–5). But Indian officialdom has generally tended to follow the direction given to it by the political leadership, so bureaucratic opposition was not exactly unyielding.

It would take a specific policy decision to galvanize the disparate sources of resistance to come together. This happened after the announcement in July 2005 that India and the United States would work toward establishing civilian nuclear trade.

THE NUCLEAR AGREEMENT AND THE APPEARANCE OF DRIFT

The George W. Bush administration's recognition of the practical and symbolic importance of the nuclear issue led it to agree that the restrictions imposed on India must be loosened. This was easier said than done (Bhatia 2012). There were legal and political obstacles that would be difficult to overcome. On the legal side, domestic legislation prohibited nuclear commerce with states that had not signed the NPT. There was also an elaborate set of international agreements and rules that revolved around the NPT and had the same effect worldwide. In the latter case, an exception made for nuclear trade with India could raise a question mark over the NPT itself because there were bound to be objections from non–nuclear weapons states that had agreed to bind themselves permanently not to seek the bomb. Politically, too, the nonproliferation lobby was well entrenched in the US legislature, the bureaucracy, and nongovernment organizations and would resist a change in the regime's rules. On the Indian side, opposition was bound to come from those unwilling to see a closer India-US relationship, particularly if it cut into India's long and dearly held preference for strategic autonomy. Nonetheless, policymakers on both sides were agreed on making progress.

The strategy adopted was to strengthen defense and strategic cooperation in tandem with the move to alter the rules on nuclear trade. A symbolically significant moment, though without immediate practical results, came with India's offer immediately after the 9/11 attacks to assist the United States with intelligence, military bases, and the use of its air space (*Congressional Record* 2001, 21992). However, India's utility was very limited for this purpose because it does not have direct geographic access to Afghanistan. Vajpayee visited Washington a few weeks later, in November 2001, and the two leaders announced their solidarity in responding to the terrorist threat. The limits to this aspect of cooperation became evident shortly when US support for India after the terrorist attack on its Parliament was less than wholehearted. Though the attack was perpetrated by Pakistan-based terrorists, the United States was loath to put intense pressure on Islamabad, whose cooperation was required in the effort to defeat the Taliban regime in Afghanistan. India, perhaps partly influenced by this, balked at the American invitation to send a peacekeeping force to Iraq in 2003.

Still, strategic cooperation accelerated rapidly in other ways over the next few years. The US-India Defense Policy Group, which had not met since 1998, was revived in December 2001; and the prospect of US arms sales to India was back on the table (van de Wetering 2016, 127). In January 2004, Vajpayee and Bush announced the Next Steps in Strategic Partnership, which envisaged accelerated cooperation on civilian nuclear technology, civilian space programs, high-technology trade, and missile defense. In March 2005 came a remarkable statement from an unnamed White House official that President Bush and Secretary Rice had presented an outline for strategic cooperation to Prime Minister Singh, and that "its goal is to help India become a major world power in the 21st century" (White House 2005a). In June 2005, India's defense minister, Pranab Mukherjee, and US defense secretary Donald Rumsfeld signed a ten-year Defense Framework Agreement, which charted a broad course for working together on security, counterterrorism, nonproliferation, and ensuring freedom of movement with respect to global trade. More specifically, the two sides set themselves on a course of increasing operational cooperation on military exercises and on arms transfers, including technology transfers. For these to become more free-flowing, however, the nuclear trade hurdle had to be surmounted. As long as the web of nonproliferation restrictions imposed by domestic US law and by international agreement among the members of the NSG remained, India would still be a pariah, which was humiliating for it, and would be deprived of access to critical dual-use technologies and materials. The nuclear deal was the logical—though not inevitable—opening for a way out.

When Prime Minister Manmohan Singh visited Washington in July 2005, he and President Bush announced their intent to work toward a formal agreement that would enable India to bypass the restrictions imposed on it by the nonproliferation regime. The details of the nuclear agreement need not detain us here—they have been elaborated on in a number of publications (Bajoria and Pan 2010; Chari 2009; Chaudhury 2014, 213–52; Mistry 2014; Pant 2011; Schaffer and Schaffer 2016; *Times of India* 2008b). A brief outline follows, before I examine the Indian domestic politics of the deal at length.

It was agreed that the United States would engage in "full civil nuclear energy cooperation" with India and that "India would reciprocally agree that it would be ready to assume the same responsibilities and practices and acquire the same benefits and advantages as other leading countries with advanced nuclear technology, such as the United States" (White House 2005b). India would separate its civilian and military nuclear facilities and place the former under permanent International Atomic Energy Agency (IAEA) safeguards; strengthen its nonproliferation controls; work with the United States toward concluding the Fissile Material Cutoff Treaty; and continue its unilateral moratorium on testing. The provision for civil–military separation was a key gain for India: this was the first time that the United States tacitly acknowledged the legitimacy of India's nuclear weapons, despite the latter being formally viewed as a "nuclear non–weapons state" under the NPT.

A number of difficulties stemmed from the agreement. First, there was disagreement on the question of who would decide on the separation of civilian and military facilities. Second, there was resistance in India to IAEA safeguards being established in perpetuity. Third, the United States wanted India's breeder reactors to be brought under safeguards, whereas the Indian nuclear establishment was adamant that they should stay out. And fourth, though this was left in abeyance at the time, the question of future testing was thorny because the United States wanted to include a provision that nuclear cooperation would cease if India were to test. The Indians were particularly sensitive about this because they retained a bitter memory of the United States reneging on a thirty-year agreement signed in 1963 to supply enriched uranium after India's 1974 test (Subramanian 2015, 613–14).

The July 2005 announcement of the planned nuclear agreement evoked considerable debate in both countries. In the United States, Ashton Carter (assistant secretary of defense under Bill Clinton; and later under secretary and then secretary of defense under Barack Obama) gave a detailed opinion to the US Senate on the expected benefits of a deal: support on curtailing Iran's nuclear program; a hedge against China; cooperation on a possible nuclear terrorist threat in Pakistan; joint military action on disaster relief and "stability operations"; potential military basing; preferential treatment for US producers of nuclear energy; preferential treatment for US industry for arms sales; and strengthening nuclear nonproliferation (Carter 2005). Similar, though less optimistic, arguments were made by others (Levi and Ferguson 2006; Ganguly and Mistry 2006). There were criticisms aplenty: the failings of the Indian civil nuclear program; the high cost of nuclear energy in India; India's potential to produce more bombs if a deal freed up its existing fissile material stocks; and the weakening of the nonproliferation regime (Mian and Ramana 2006; Milhollin 2006; Perkovich 2005; Weiss 2006).

On the Indian side, supporters of the nuclear rapprochement emphasized a number of potential gains for India: hedging against China's rise; countering the proliferation of weapons of mass destruction; responding actively against the threat from terrorism and failed states; obtaining access to strategic technologies; accelerating economic growth; and expanding nuclear energy (Bajpai 2006; Ravi 2005; Singh 2005; Subrahmanyam 2005; Virmani 2006). One influential commentator stressed the enormous significance of the proposal for a deal: "For the leading opponent of India's 'nuclearization' to accept us even partially as a nuclear weapons power establishes a benchmark for itself and a new fact of international life for others as well" (Bajpai 2006). Another made the critical point that the July 2005 announcement represented a "tectonic shift in geopolitics," with the United States "now offering to recognize Delhi's strategic parity with Beijing and treat India differently from Pakistan" (Raja Mohan 2005). But critics noted the possible (some thought inevitable) adverse effects: the difficulties involved in civil-military separation of India's nuclear infrastructure; the restriction likely to be placed on future testing; past American failures to keep promises; the likelihood of India becoming a dependent state; and the unlikely prospect of successful joint defense production between technologically unequal nations (Bidwai 2005; Chari 2006; *Indian Express* 2005; Koithara 2005; Subramanian 2005). Some of the criticism was instrumentalist: the BJP admitted as much privately to US Embassy officials (Wikileaks n.d.). But the government was on the defensive right from the start.

These debates continued through the long process preceding the finalization of the agreement through a series of steps. In March 2006, President Bush and Prime Minister Singh issued a joint statement emphasizing the strategic partnership between their countries and their intent to sign a pact on civil nuclear cooperation. The two sides agreed on a separation plan for India's reactors—of the twenty-two then existing, fourteen would be placed under permanent IAEA safeguards. The next step was for the United States to enact enabling legislation that would override the restrictions on nuclear commerce with India. This was done through the Henry J. Hyde United States–India Peaceful Atomic Energy Cooperation Act of 2006, which was signed into law by Bush in December 2006.

This set in motion the next major stage, which was to work toward a "123 agreement," a generic nomenclature for US civil nuclear cooperation agreements with other states under Section 123 of its Atomic Energy Act of 1954. The process was an exacting one for both sides, given that there were major differences between them on important issues: whether the United States would guarantee the supply of reprocessed fuel; whether India would be allowed to reprocess fuel; and whether India retained the right to test. Eventually, the United States agreed to the first two, while the third—the subject of heated debate in India—was left deliberately vague: the term "nuclear test" was not mentioned and, as Under Secretary Burns put it, "India retains the right to test, and the United States retains the right to respond" (quoted by Schaffer 2009, 98). In July 2007, after several rounds of tough negotiations, India and the United States agreed on the text of the 123 agreement, which then had to be approved by the US Congress in order to come into force. A key prerequisite for the 123 Agreement to become law was prior approval by the NSG. This approval—to exempt India from full-scope safeguards—was obtained on September 6, 2008, through vigorous diplomacy by both India and the United States. Eventually, the United States–India Peaceful Atomic Energy Cooperation and US Additional Protocol Implementation Act were passed with comfortable majorities in Congress. The House voted 298–117 for the legislation, while the Senate approved it 86–13. On October 8, 2008, Bush signed it into law.

The time between the initial announcement of the deal and its finalization had been more than thirty-eight months. This prolonged time frame was partly due to the difficult negotiation process. The overall strategic convergence was certainly there, but the devil in the details was of substantial proportions. It was, moreover, complicated by domestic politics, which itself grew out of the distribution of political power. For the purpose of this analysis, which is to identify the domestic political constraints that hampered the Indian side, the negotiating process can be usefully divided into two components. The first stage, between the announcement of the deal in July 2005 and the conclusion of negotiations on the 123 agreement in July 2007, involved a "two-level game," where the two executive leaderships bargained simultaneously with each other and with their respective domestic constituencies (Putnam 1988; Mistry 2014; Pant 2011). Thereafter, the bargaining became a simple, one-level game largely internal to India. The nuclear deal became the centerpiece around which opponents and supporters engaged in intense electorally driven maneuvering. The next subsection investigates these political games in some detail.

Phase 1: Power Distribution and Triangular Domestic Politics

By the time the nuclear deal was announced, the distribution of power in Indian politics was very different from that of the early postindependence years. As noted in chapter 1, the political system had been fragmenting since the late 1980s, and coalition governments were the order of the day until 2014. In the general election of 2004, national-level parties (as opposed to regional parties) secured just two-thirds of the seats in the Lok Sabha, with the two main contestants, the Congress and the BJP, winning 145 and 138 seats, respectively, of the total of 543 (Election Commission of India 2004, 99). Coalition politics was a complicated affair. The Congress-led electoral alliance of 19 parties together won 222 seats and, after some postelection changes involving the departure of two parties and the addition of eight others, the new alliance, now known as the United Progressive Alliance (UPA), with 25 parties and 268 seats—still short of a majority—was established (Sridharan 2004, 5419, tables 1 and 2). Prime Minister Manmohan Singh of the Congress Party headed a weak UPA coalition, which depended on outside support from a Left Front coalition led by the Communist Party of India (Marxist) (CPM), which held 59 seats. Singh's position was uneasy because coalitions had a history of instability, owing to periodic entries and defections in a "revolving-door" system (Kailash and Arora 2016; see also Ruparelia 2005; Tummala 2009). Though his predecessor Vajpayee's coalition had survived in office for a full five-year term, there had been seven governments between 1989 and 2004.

In light of this unstable equilibrium, Singh's prospects for pushing through the nuclear agreement appeared uncertain at best. In the first phase of negotiations, from July 2005 to July 2007, he began with the knowledge that internal resistance was likely to be considerable. The Congress itself had a history of leaning leftward under Nehru and Indira Gandhi, and embracing the United States was not going to be easy. Besides, though nonalignment was no longer the central principle of Indian foreign policy, the long-standing emphasis on strategic autonomy remained its keystone. Foreign Minister Natwar Singh and other senior members of the Congress Party—such as Mani Shankar Aiyar, Makhan Lal Fotedar, Pranab Mukherjee, Arjun Singh, and Ambika Soni—were unhappy with the turn of events; and Sonia Gandhi, who headed the party, worried about the political fallout (Hasan 2012, 11, 14). Singh was determined to push forward. Knowing the delicate position he was in, the prime minister was categorical in directing his team not to accept any curbs on India's nuclear weapons program (Saran 2015, 12).

As late as on the eve of the announcement of the deal in July 2005, there was considerable doubt among some members of the delegation accompanying Singh to Washington, for memories of US sanctions after 1974 were still fresh, and the possibility that the United States would use the deal to impose restrictions on India's nuclear weapons program was worrisome to several of them (Menon 2016, 36; Saran 2015, 6–7; 2017, 207). At one point, Singh decided to scrap the portion of the joint statement pertaining to the nuclear issue and was unwilling even to meet Rice to discuss the issue. However, a meeting did take place. According to Rice, who does not give details on the back-and-forth that transpired at the meeting, she persuaded Singh that this was "the deal of a lifetime" (Rice 2011, 439). However, Shyam Saran, who was a key member of the delegation as foreign secretary, tells us that Singh agreed to proceed only after Rice had acquiesced to changes in the draft statement reflecting the Indian team's insistence that its language should not undermine India's nuclear weapons status (Saran 2015, 6–7). This was the first instance of the bargaining paradox that, in some situations, weakness can be a source of strength (Putnam 1988, 440–41). Because any constraints on India's nuclear weapons program would have killed the deal at its birth domestically, the Indian team on several occasions stuck to its guns under pressure and in effect compelled its American interlocutors to make concessions.

From time to time, Singh also had to contend with more internal complications. Internal politics was one. Before the July 2005 breakthrough, Saran had been playing a leading role in negotiations, and the national security adviser, M. K. Narayanan, had been left out of the interactions (Chaudhuri 2014, 25). This appears to have been resented by Narayanan, who established a separate apex committee to discuss negotiating positions, a group from which Saran was excluded (Saran 2017, 203, 210–11). (Although the national security adviser appears to have been motivated to keep Saran out, the Ministry of External Affairs always has a key senior official, who reports to the foreign secretary, posted in the Prime Minister's Office.)

Later, Natwar Singh, who had become embroiled in a financial scandal and was compelled to resign in 2006, tried (with little success) to mobilize opposition to the nuclear deal among parties that were already against it (*The Hindu* 2006d). But these distortions in the policy setup did not ultimately prevent the negotiations from going ahead.

Two sources of domestic pressure that affected the course of the negotiations were particularly strong in this first phase: the nuclear bureaucracy and the major political parties opposing the deal. The scientists of the Department of Atomic Energy (DAE) played a pivotal role in the internal negotiating process. Nuclear scientists had long enjoyed a privileged position vis-à-vis political decision-making in their field because they ran an organization that had direct access to the prime minister and, because of the secrecy surrounding their covert work on nuclear weapons for many years, were largely protected from public scrutiny (Abraham 1998; Sharma 1983). They were not only custodians of the bomb but also enjoyed the advantage of being specialists in a technology to which few could have access, let alone master. In this sense, the nuclear scientists had always been political, so it was no surprise that they played a critical role in shaping the terms of the nuclear deal. In the discussions leading up to the July 2005 announcement, the Indian delegation included B. R. Grover, a senior DAE scientist, whose role was to vet technical matters and to keep an eye on the negotiations as a whole from the standpoint of his organization (Chaudhuri 2014, 18). Anil Kakodkar, chairman of the Atomic Energy Commission (AEC), the apex body of India's nuclear bureaucracy, was a member of the delegation that accompanied Prime Minister Singh to Washington in July 2005 and played a prominent role throughout.

As mentioned above, the negotiations reached an early breaking point, owing to internal differences in the Indian team. It is a reasonable inference that the AEC chairman had objected to some of the language of the draft announcement because, according to Saran, Singh at this juncture asked Kakodkar to suggest specific changes in writing to meet his reservations. These pertained, among other things, to ensuring that India would have control over the separation of civilian and military nuclear facilities (i.e., on the designation and number of facilities classified as one or the other) and that safeguards over the former would be India-specific and the same as those applied to nuclear weapon states under the NPT (Saran 2017, 208–9). This, according to Saran, was a critical point in the negotiations: "It was only when Kakodkar said he was satisfied with the changes that the prime minister gave the go-ahead" (Saran 2017, 209). Kakodkar and nuclear scientists from the DAE, the functional apparatus under the AEC, played a key role throughout this first phase of the negotiations. Apart from their direct access to the prime minister, they also influenced internal discussions through the national security adviser's apex committee mentioned above, which involved the PMO and the AEC/DAE. Notably, the national security adviser himself was skeptical of the value of the proposed deal (Chaudhuri 2014, 20).

The reluctance of DAE officials to support the deal appears to have been driven by a number of considerations, none of them exceptionable. First, as guardians of the nuclear arsenal, they were in the frontline of those with the responsibility to stave off American efforts to constrain the Indian weapons program. Second, they had been collectively subject to sanctions for more than two decades since the 1974 tests and bore a degree of distrust toward US officialdom (Chari 2007, 3). And third, the prospect of losing control over a substantial portion of what had been a largely untouched bureaucratic empire would have naturally dampened their enthusiasm for the deal—and, indeed, they fought hard to protect their turf from external controls.

Having successfully bargained for the technical bureaucracies' concerns and won substantial gains in the negotiations preceding the July 2005 joint statement, Kakodkar publicly defended the agreement in a long media interview in August (Subramanian 2005a). Here, he stressed that neither the civilian nor the military nuclear programs would be hampered in any way. A senior colleague, K. Santhanam (2005), who had been associated with the 1998 tests, gave an equally positive opinion, focusing mainly on the energy-related benefits of a deal. But India-US differences over the specifics of the proposed nuclear agreement came to the fore over a number of issues. The United States wanted to bring India's fast breeder reactor program under the civilian list, and hence make it subject to IAEA safeguards. Kakodkar asserted that the United States was shifting the goalposts and controls over India's energy security, and nuclear deterrent would result in its being "shackled." He also reiterated that the decision to determine the division of civilian and military facilities "will have to be decided by India and not by others" (Bagla 2006). In August 2006, other leading scientists—former AEC chairman P. K. Iyengar and former director of the Bhabha Atomic Research Centre, A. N. Prasad—backed Kakodkar's stand (*Times of India* 2006b). Two months later, a larger group of eight scientists, including three former AEC chairmen, gave a signed statement to Parliament protesting against what they viewed as a US effort to curb indigenous research and impose constraints on India's nuclear option (*The Hindu* 2006g).

The nuclear scientists received support from other quarters. In the forefront was the leading English-language newspaper, *The Hindu*, which brought out a series of articles reflecting the perspective of the DAE (Bhatt 2006; *The Hindu* 2006b, 2006c, 2006d, 2006g; Iyengar 2007; Ramachandran 2006; Srinivasan 2006a, 2006b, 2007; Subramanian 2005; Varadarajan 2005, 2006a, 2006b, 2007). Criticisms were expressed in other news outlets as well (e.g., Bidwai 2005; Suchitra 2005; Yechury 2006), but no other newspaper brought out such a steady stream of critical commentaries on the nuclear negotiations. The left-leaning *Hindu*, with its series of opinion editorials purveying the nuclear scientists' case against the nuclear agreement, was the link between the atomic energy establishment and the political left, with which it had long been connected. *The Hindu*'s editor-in chief at the time, Narasimhan Ram, was close to CPM general secretary Prakash Karat—both had cut their political teeth as university students in the CPM-affiliated Students' Federation of India. While the CPM led the political charge against the nuclear deal, it brought to bear the scientists' specialist knowledge on the technical aspects of nuclear energy on the arguments against the deal, while *The Hindu* provided a public platform for their criticisms. The three made common cause in building a powerful opposition to the deal's terms as they were initially laid out. The fragile coalition led by Manmohan Singh was placed under enormous pressure, as it was dependent on the CPM and its allies in the Left Front to secure a majority in Parliament.

The CPM was ideologically driven from the start to oppose any kind of accommodation with the United States. On its insistence, the UPA's Common Minimum Programme, drafted in 2004 to pull the UPA and the

Left Front together, had excluded mention of India's relationship with the United States (Chakravarthi 2009, 68). After the 2005 Indo-US joint statement, the CPM's initial response was critical of both the Congress and its predecessor in government, the BJP. In its reaction to the statement, the CPM said, "The BJP-led government had begun the journey of accepting junior partnership of the United States" and the Congress had now marked "an end to India's nuclear disarmament policy" (*The Hindu* 2005c). The smaller Communist Party of India was also critical of the "reversal of India's earlier nuclear policy" and India's pro-US shift (*The Hindu* 2005c). Sitaram Yechury, a member of the Rajya Sabha (the upper house of the Indian Parliament) and of the CPM's top decision-making body, the Politburo, was highly critical of India's vote in favor of a US resolution against Iran at the IAEA in February 2006. In his view, the vote—obviously a quid pro quo for the nuclear deal—represented the recognition that India had "no option but to toe the US line" (Yechury 2006). The CPM's sharply focused response to the ongoing efforts in the United States to amend national legislation reflected the concerns of India's nuclear bureaucracy. It decried the constraints the proposed US bill would impose on India's right to test and claimed that the United States would compel India to sign the Fissile Material Cutoff Treaty (which it had earlier rejected) and coercively bind India to accepting IAEA safeguards in perpetuity (*Times of India* 2006a). It reiterated the party's position on the IAEA vote against Iran that the United States was attempting to "arm-twist" India and compel it to "kowtow to US global strategic designs" (*Times of India* 2006a).

The political scrummage over the first stage of negotiations leading to the nuclear agreement reveals that there was something interesting happening with regard to the dynamics of India's domestic political system. Analysts commonly distinguish the politics of a cabinet system of government (as in India) from a US-type system with a separation of powers (Elman 2000). In the cabinet system, the executive normally enjoys a majority in the legislature, so policymaking tends to be relatively smooth. In a US type of system, both branches must agree on legislation or treaty making, which often involves intense bargaining and "side payments." Moreover, dissatisfied members of the bureaucracy are in a position to exert influence through their connections with legislators, whether directly or through the media (or both). In the present case, the politics of a fragmented Indian polity ruled by a weak coalition government came to resemble a separation-of-powers system. India's atomic energy establishment, a component of a normally compliant bureaucracy, was able to exercise inordinate power not only because of its specialist command of the nuclear sector but also because it was able to enter into an informal alliance with the Left Front and an influential section of the media to put enormous pressure on the government to ensure that its concerns were given due attention.

Notably, the key demands of the atomic bureaucracy were met. The United States ultimately agreed to (1) let India determine the separation of civilian and military facilities (eight out of twenty-two reactors were designated as military); (2) provide assurance of fuel supply; (3) exempt fast breeder reactors from safeguards; (4) accept reprocessing of fuel by India; and (5) leave a modicum of space for India to conduct nuclear tests if necessary. India did make concessions on some issues: perpetual safeguards on civilian reactors (which are not required of formally designated nuclear weapons states under the NPT); an open-ended agreement to work toward the Fissile Material Cutoff Treaty; an oblique restriction on its freedom to test (with built-in qualifiers); and an understanding that it would be on the US side on the issue of circumscribing Iranian nuclear capability. But these were relatively limited concessions that had to be part of a quid pro quo in which India clearly gained far more than it lost.

The outcome of the negotiations effectively met the interests of the DAE. On July 26, 2006 (the same day on which the US House of Representatives passed the Hyde Act), Manmohan Singh met Kakodkar and former senior scientists at his residence for ninety minutes and secured their formal support (Baruah 2006). Though the scientific community continued to watch closely as the negotiations unfolded, this effectively closed the first phase of the triangular politicking surrounding the deal.

Phase 2: Electoral Politics, Coalitions, and the Chicken Game

The so-called 123 agreement—officially, the Agreement for Cooperation between the Government of the United States of America and the Government of India Concerning Peaceful Uses of Energy—was signed in August 2007. This meant that the party–bureaucracy coalition opposing the nuclear deal had fallen apart, leaving the opposition political parties to consider their next step. From this point on, the spotlight was no longer on the specifics of the terms of the agreement, though it remained the formal focus of opposition. The real game was electoral politics. Here, too, the nuclear deal was not an issue that the opposition parties could use to gain public support. As one study shows, nuclear issues were of no consequence in the public mind: the BJP lost three state elections shortly after the 1998 tests; a major 1999 survey showed that the majority of voters were unaware of the tests; and as many as two-thirds of the electorate had not even heard of the nuclear agreement, with the great majority of those who had heard of it regarding it as a secondary issue (Sasikumar and Verniers 2013, 686). The politics of the nuclear deal henceforth revolved around the distribution of power in the Lok Sabha and all political maneuvering aimed at altering or preserving this distribution.

The CPM, which had held fast to its ideological opposition to the nuclear agreement, appears to have given up on persuading the government to bring it to a halt and became increasingly hostile to the UPA, despite the risk of facilitating the BJP's coming to power. Shortly after the signing of the 123 Agreement, its position hardened. General Secretary Prakash Karat said the left-wing parties (i.e., the CPM and its allies) were "unable to accept" the agreement, and asked the Singh government not to operationalize it (*The Hindu* 2007b). A few days later, the CPM Politburo released a formal statement opposing the agreement and announcing that it had "decided to take the issue of the nuclear agreement and the dangers of the strategic alliance with the United States to the people through a nationwide mass campaign" (*The Hindu* 2007a). The following day, Karat publicly rejected the notion that his party might make common cause with the BJP, which had called for a joint parliamentary effort to stall the deal. On the contrary, he argued, the CPM would not join hands with the "pro-imperialist" BJP, which was "infamous for kowtowing to the US" (*The Hindu* 2007c). But a warning followed the very next day in an opinion editorial by Karat (2007): "The Left parties continue to accord priority to having a secular government and keeping the communal forces at bay. However, this cannot be taken as licence by the UPA government to go ahead with a long-term agreement that has such serious implications for India's independent foreign policy and sovereignty."

At this point, the CPM was willing to negotiate rather than withdraw its support for the UPA. Apparently, it wanted to avoid a crisis culminating in another round of national elections at a juncture when it faced significant public criticism in its own political bailiwick: at the time, there was rising opposition to the CPM-led government's acquisition of land for industrial use in the state of West Bengal (Sikri 2009, 179). The UPA, too, was willing to negotiate—more accurately, procrastinate—as elections were due in the state of Gujarat in December 2007. Hence, in the period October–November 2007, with worries about the government's survival rising within the Congress leadership among some UPA allies, it was decided to put the process on hold (Mistry 2014, 154–56). The left-wing parties agreed not to pursue a parliamentary resolution against the deal, while the government assured them the matter would be brought up for a parliamentary debate.

A series of meetings between the left-wing parties and the UPA leadership ensured that the process of decision-making dragged on for several months. But both sides stuck to their guns, and a confrontation became inevitable after they failed to find common ground in June–July 2008. By this time, the UPA's position had hardened considerably, as it had come to other arrangements in order to lessen the impact of the Left's possible withdrawal of support for it. More on this follows.

In the meantime, the UPA tried to persuade the BJP to drop its opposition to an agreement that, after all, was the culmination of a process of India-US rapprochement initiated by the latter. Manmohan Singh said as much to Vajpayee in a meeting that ended cordially on July 26, 2007 (Mistry 2014, 156). The BJP itself went through internal debate, with its top leaders divided on whether to compromise with the government (Mistry 2014, 163–64), and eventually came to a decision not to support the government. Its motives, it appears, were pragmatic from the standpoint of political expediency. According to a leaked confidential document of the US State Department, BJP National Executive member Seshadri Chari had earlier assured the US Embassy in New Delhi that his party's vociferous public opposition to the nuclear deal need not be taken too seriously, as it was "'standard practice' aimed at scoring easy political points against the UPA" (Wikileaks n.d.).

The BJP's opposition to the agreement reflected its internal contradictions. Its own government had previously been willing to offer what it now opposed: placing some reactors under IAEA safeguards (Gupta and Raja Mohan 2005). Nevertheless, the party's leaders insisted that the nuclear deal made India a "junior partner" of the United States, detracted from India's decision-making autonomy, and negatively affected its security (*Indian Express* 2005; *The Hindu* 2005a, 2005b, 2006a, 2006f; Joshi 2005; Vyas

2007). However, there were internal differences. On August 27, 2007, senior leader Lal Krishna Advani set off a debate in the party when he said, "As far as the BJP is concerned—and it is in national interest—we have no objection to a strategic partnership with the US," to which another added "after all, we are in support of India becoming a strong nuclear power and have nothing against strategic ties with the US" (Jha 2007). Backing this position, Mohan Bhagwat, chief of the Rashtriya Swayamsevak Sangh (= National Self-Service Organization), a Hindu cultural organization closely affiliated with the BJP (many of their leaders are shared) "appreciated" Advani's position (George 2007). But three days later, Advani took a U-turn and said the nuclear pact would push India into "strategic subservience to Washington" (*Economic Times* 2007). Clearly, internal party deliberations had forged a common position that, despite reservations about collaborating with the CPM, was now focused on dislodging the UPA from power.

The trajectories of the two major opposition players, the BJP and the CPM-led Left Front, were coming together. The aim was to introduce a motion of no confidence in the Lok Sabha and force the UPA out of office. But the picture was more complicated. Though the UPA was dependent on the CPM to sustain its government, the parliamentary position of the Left Front (which had 59 seats in the Lok Sabha) and the BJP (which had 138 seats) together in the 543-seat Lok Sabha did not give them the capacity to vote the government out. In this situation, the allegiance of a large number of small parties was of critical importance. The Samajwadi (= Socialist) Party (SP), with 36 seats in the Lok Sabha, played a crucial role in the final days of the nuclear deal saga. The SP was the largest party in a "third front" coalition, the United National Progressive Alliance, that was initially trying to warm up to the Left Front. The SP's calculus had nothing to do with the India-US agreement, but plenty to do with the politics of the state of Uttar Pradesh, India's largest state.

The politics of Uttar Pradesh had for some years witnessed an all-out confrontation between the SP and the Bahujan Samaj Party (BSP), a relatively new actor in the state. In 2002, the SP established a coalition government and in 2003 strengthened its seat position by enticing thirty-three BSP legislators over to its side. Nonetheless, the BSP romped home on its own in the 2007 elections. The crisis over the nuclear deal gave the SP and the Congress, which had no love lost between them, an opportunity to strike a deal (Chawla 2008a). As Amar Singh, a senior SP leader put it, referring to the BSP's chief, "We have to deal with a common enemy—Mayawati," and she, along with the BJP, was an enemy "more lethal than Bush" (Chawla 2008b). Speaking at a meeting convened to consider disbanding the United National Progressive Alliance, Amar Singh justified his party's decision to switch sides on the grounds that the BSP was cozying up to the BJP and argued that the SP had effectively no choice but to link up with the Congress (*Business Standard* 2008).

As the SP made its position clear, the Left Front quickly forged an alliance with the BSP, but their numbers were not enough. Amar Singh played a crucial role in the defeat of the no confidence motion initiated by the opposition parties in the Lok Sabha. In the end, the parliamentary vote was won by the UPA government on July 22, 2008, with 275 votes in its favor and 256 against. It was a close shave. The UPA's victory was engineered by means of five defections from the BJP and five from other parties, plus some abstentions (Ansari 2008). These, according to a leaked document of the US Embassy in New Delhi, were facilitated by substantial payments of money to the concerned members of Parliament (*The Guardian* 2011). One Congress member, who had been suspended on disciplinary grounds, voted against his party (Ansari 2008). The deal was done.

EXPLAINING THE DRIFT

The politics of the India-US nuclear deal is a classic case for the early neoclassical realist approach. It underscores distortions in foreign policy making arising from the difficulty governments sometimes have in extracting the political resources required to implement policies crafted in line with systemic incentives. In this case, the policy in question was indubitably the product of structural change in the international system. At the general level, the end of the Cold War and India's vulnerability to the pressures of the global economy—exposed by a major balance-of-payments crisis—gave it strong incentives to revamp its overall strategy toward the external world. It responded by seeking a closer strategic relationship with the United States, opening up its largely closed economy, and shoring up its hitherto covert nuclear weapons capability by going public and building a better-organized arsenal. The relationship with the United States was critical to this new policy framework. It offered the possibility of simultaneously providing ballast for India's national security though a strategic partnership with the United States and attendant economic benefits through trade and investment relations with it. Although the economic benefits were quick to begin appearing, the strategic gains were not, for India could not attain advanced technology or recognition as a "rising power" without breaking out of its isolation as a virtual nuclear pariah. The nuclear deal was a way out of this difficulty.

The dramatic shift in India-US relations evoked domestic political resistance, which was not surprising given the uneven relationship between the once–"estranged democracies." But this did not amount to a powerful force compelling Indian leaders to think twice about their objective. Left-leaning political forces among political parties (including sections of the ruling Congress Party) and academia and bureaucrats schooled in nonalignment had neither the heft to block the change nor the imagination to provide alternatives. Yet, when the nuclear deal itself came up as a logical high point in the rebuilding of the India-US relationship, a serious challenge emerged, even though the deal raised the prospect of major strategic and economic gains. The result was prolonged policy drift over a period of three years as the Indian leadership bargained simultaneously with internal opponents and American policymakers over the terms of the deal. As noted, the playing out of the "two-level game" has been discussed elsewhere. Here, I have examined a notable shift in the character of this game, which underwent two distinct phases.

In the first phase, between the announcement of the deal in July 2005 and the signing of the 123 Agreement in July 2007, the nuclear bureaucracy and opposition parties, particularly the Left Front, came together—with support from the left-leaning press—to attack the deal. In the second phase, after the terms of the 123 Agreement had largely satisfied the atomic establishment, the game changed to a political contest between the UPA and its leading competitors, the CPM and the BJP, with smaller parties—chiefly the SP—playing a critical role in the final outcome, which culminated in victory for the UPA.

A number of analytically interesting points may be made. First, the fragmented distribution of power in Parliament gave disproportionate power to players who would otherwise have been relatively insignificant or at best weak—if loud—protesters. In the first phase, the nuclear bureaucracy—always influential because of its technical control over a strategically important area—was able to impose substantial constraints on political decision-makers because of its linkages with politically motivated opposition parties. In structural terms, the distribution of parliamentary power gave a branch of the executive unprecedented influence in opposing a policy initiated by its political masters, a phenomenon usually seen in a system with a separation of powers, as in the United States. Once satisfied, this prominent source of opposition to the nuclear deal switched sides (though some retired officials remained critical), and its former ally, the Left Front, was left to fend for itself.

Second, the distribution of power gave relatively small political parties unprecedented power to influence the outcome. None of the opposition parties possessed sufficient strength to threaten the UPA government on its own. As a result, an ideologically driven, CPM-dominated Left Front, with only 59 seats in a lower house of 543, was able to lead the charge against the deal. But the weakness of the Left Front meant that, even with the eventual support of the BJP, the largest opposition party, still smaller parties were in a position to make or break the deal. Thus, the SP, with only thirty-six seats, became in effect a king maker or, more accurately, a king saver. The final tally on the parliamentary no-confidence motion shows that parties that were virtually marginal in size mattered as well, though they were far too small to enjoy bargaining power on their own in the normal course.

Third, the fragmentation of domestic political power meant that opposition coalitions were also unstable and constrained by intergroup differences (Kailash and Arora 2016). Though the potential binding agent was a single issue, potential and actual coalitions were subject to the vagaries of changing circumstances and interests in a highly fragmented political system. As noted, the nuclear bureaucracy was active in opposition until its interests were satisfied. Once its main demands had been met, this group bowed out. Initially, the prospect of a party coalition against the deal was limited by the fact that the Left Front could leverage bureaucratic opposition for its cause and hence did not feel the need to forge an alliance with the BJP. The left and the right, which had never really come together on a common platform and were deeply divided on a number of issues, remained apart even after the nuclear bureaucracy opted out. But political expediency required at least a tacit alliance, which was manifest as both the Left

Front and the BJP attacked the government separately, even as the former declared it would have no truck with the latter. But expediency eventually helped forge a joint effort to try and dislodge the government.

Fourth, the final outcome was clearly the result of a degree of political opportunism on the part of players that clearly exceeded most norms of proper political behavior. For those hardline realists who are of the view that international politics is fundamentally amoral, it is still a problematic choice: is national interest compatible with domestic corruption? The point is not marginal. As we will see in chapter 5, disregard for norms can produce high security costs.

Finally, the material distribution of power is not in itself the only arbiter of outcomes. Associated with it is the vital importance of commitment. In a seminal work on why big nations lose small wars, Andrew Mack (1975) draws attention to the critical importance of the balance of commitment. In the present case, one crucial factor was commitment. The UPA coalition was feeble, and its leader, Manmohan Singh, appeared to be the same because he was not a man grounded in electoral politics but a former bureaucrat chosen to lead the party by a Congress leadership wanting to avoid the difficulties that might arise under a party leader of Italian extraction (Sonia Gandhi). We know that Singh had all but given up on the eve of his 2005 meeting with Bush. But once he was personally committed to the pact, the "accidental prime minister" (Baru 2014) was ready to stake his all in the face of periodic opposition from political adversaries and from within his own party.

After the CPM's harsh reaction to the signing of the 123 Agreement in August 2007, the prime minister, in a newspaper interview, threw down the gauntlet: "I told them that it is not possible to renegotiate the deal. It is an honourable deal, the Cabinet has approved it. We cannot go back on it. I told them to do whatever they want to do, if they want to withdraw support, so be it" (quoted by Rediff India Abroad 2007). In June 2008, when party boss Sonia Gandhi seemed to be backing away from the deal, Singh threatened to resign, which forced her to give him the green light (Baru 2014, 244–47). He later affirmed this in a newspaper interview: "I was very clear that if the deal had not gone through, I would have resigned as prime minister" (*Times of India* 2009). The widespread impression that Singh was a weak personality is erroneous. As Sanjaya Baru, who worked closely with him as media adviser, has pointed out, Singh has been tough on a number of serious domestic as well as foreign policy issues (Baru 2013). When push came to shove, the prime minister turned it into a high-stakes chicken game regardless of the personal cost to himself. If he had not, the deal would probably have collapsed.

CONCLUSION

The dynamics of coalition politics relating to the India-US nuclear agreement present a classic case of the kind that Type I neoclassical realism highlights. A shaky coalition entangled in coalition politics had to fight for survival in order to pursue a policy that offered a radically new and positive change for India's security and standing in global politics. Though the deal eventually went through despite a tortuous process, it was a near thing. In theoretical terms, systemic incentives may have been strong, but the structure and process of domestic politics came close to upending the applecart.

Two closing points may be made. The analysis presented here does not assume that policy drift is wholly negative in its effects, as many critics of the UPA's travails have tended to assume. Conceivably, delay might be better than precipitate action that is poorly thought out. In the present case, it is likely that, at least in the first two years, policy drift resulted in an agreement that was more favorable to India than it might have been. But this does not undermine the main point in this chapter: that the structure of domestic politics can play an important role in producing outcomes that a leadership does not want (in this case, prolonged delay) when responding to systemic incentives.

The second aspect worth recalling is that weak coalitions do not necessarily lack levers to boost their prospects. In a fragmented system, small parties seeking power do have strong incentives to stay in or join a multiparty coalition. Interesting parallels can be seen in the ways in which weak coalition governments in Japan and Turkey were able to carry out significant foreign policy changes despite strong domestic resistance, including from their own coalition partners (Kaarbo 2017). In both cases, critical factors were the Turkish and Japanese leaderships' willingness to raise the stakes and risk the fall of their government and the unwillingness of dissident coalition parties to accept the cost of government collapse. In the present case, Manmohan Singh similarly raised the stakes, primarily within his own party, to press ahead. Besides, coalition leaders in a fragmented system have another option: to reach out to small, noncoalition parties to offset the threat from internal dissidents. This is precisely what Singh was able to do by obtaining the collaboration of the SP at the moment of truth (Blarel and Van Willigen 2021). This was not the case when governments in New Delhi struggled to devise policies that would bolster India's position in Sri Lanka, as we will see in the next chapter.

3

INDIA AND SRI LANKA'S CIVIL WAR

The preceding chapter explored the difficulties Indian policymakers faced in responding to systemic incentives vis-à-vis a major power. In this chapter, I examine India's relationship with a small power to show similar—but not the same—dynamics at work. The Indian government, responding to systemic incentives, sought to build a warmer relationship with Sri Lanka and, consequently, keep adversary states from gaining a foothold there. However, though the broad shift toward a more cooperative approach than had been adopted in the past did not prove difficult, Indian policymakers found themselves in difficulty when it came to specifics. Policy was bogged down in the quicksand of domestic politics, where the domestic distribution of power imposed severe constraints.

The backdrop was a prolonged ethnic conflict between the Sinhala-speaking majority and the Tamil minority in Sri Lanka that had been built up since independence from British rule in 1948. The tension intensified over time, periodically breaking out into violence, and ultimately pitched the rebel Liberation Tigers of Tamil Eelam (LTTE), which were seeking independence for Tamils, against the Sinhala-dominated government in a violent civil war. The conflict stretched from 1983 to 2009 and covered four particularly intense phases, which are usually referred to as Eelam War I, June 1983–July 1987; Eelam War II, June 1990–January 1995; Eelam War III, April 1995–February 2002; and Eelam War IV, July 2006–May 2009 (Destradi 2010; Ganguly 2018a; Haelig 2017; Rotberg 1999; Wickramasinghe 2014). The brutality of the war led, according to United Nations estimates, to 80,000 to 100,000 deaths (Nebehay and Pal 2021). The conflict was not just a local one on a small South Asian island but saw involvement by several states—including India, China, Pakistan, and Israel—whereas the participation of the Tamil diaspora was global (Orjuela 2008).

There were strong systemic incentives for India to be closely involved in helping the Sri Lankan government achieve its objectives. First, helping the Sri Lankan government defeat the LTTE was an objective congruent with Indian interests at the time, because a splintered Sri Lanka would have shaken the regional order. Second, assisting in strengthening Sri Lanka's internal security would have consolidated a relationship that had been on a positive trajectory since the mid-1990s. Third, an Indian role in crushing the LTTE would have enabled India to keep its major rivals, China and Pakistan, which had demonstrated an interest in assisting Sri Lanka in the civil war, at bay. Fourth, India would have demonstrated its benign hegemony as a regional stabilizer and set an example of regional leadership that would have been an inducement to other neighbors to follow suit. And fifth, the overall outcome of these gains would have enhanced its status as a regional leader as well as a rising power in global politics.

In the event, what actually happened was quite different. Despite its desire to help Sri Lanka destroy the LTTE, India's role in the conflict was seriously constrained by the distribution of domestic political power. Policymakers in New Delhi faced stiff resistance from the Indian state of Tamil Nadu, which adjoins Sri Lanka, and which played a critical role in shoring up the central government in India at the time. In short, the structure of political power in the Indian political system seriously hampered Prime Minister Manmohan Singh's ability to pursue Indian interests optimally. What Singh's government did do was to try and assist Sri Lanka in a relatively covert way in order to balance his government's domestic political interests with the state's foreign policy interests. The outcome for India was less than desirable because it left open substantial strategic space for its adversaries, especially China, to establish a foothold in Sri Lanka, which was viewed with not a little alarm in New Delhi.

In the next section, I outline the systemic sources of India's strategic approach to Sri Lanka. We have seen in the preceding chapter that a state's relationship with its interlocutors is to a significant degree shaped by the power differential between them. Strong states behave in ways that allow them to maximize their power advantage, and weak states act in ways that might minimize their vulnerability to the strong. During the first four decades after independence, India's relationship with Sri Lanka was the opposite of its relationship with the United States—that is, its behavior toward the former was precisely what it feared about the latter: interventionist and domineering, reflecting an offensive realist perspective on the world around it. The next section shows how, after the watershed years of 1990–91, the Indian approach shifted dramatically—to a defensive realist and less insecure view of the world—which led it to be both more comfortable with major powers and less overbearing vis-à-vis its smaller neighbors. This broad reorientation was not only welcome in Colombo but also did not generate any significant domestic resistance within India.

In the subsequent section, I show how political resistance grew rapidly in Tamil Nadu with respect to India's supportive role in Sri Lanka's prosecution of Eelam War IV. As Indian policymakers struggled to pursue their objective, the ground seemed to slip from beneath them and, eventually, left them well short of their goal of a strong India–Sri Lanka relationship buttressing India's security as well as its profile as a rising power. Finally, I summarize the findings of the chapter and show how it dovetails with the broad pattern of material factors shaping policy drift identified in chapter 1 while simultaneously highlighting the finer differences between the India-US and India–Sri Lanka cases.

INDIA AND SRI LANKA: THE OFFENSIVE REALIST PHASE, 1947–91

I take as my starting point the useful distinction between offensive and defensive realist worldviews. The focus here is not so much on the analytical distinction made by scholars of international relations as on the outlook of states, or—to be more precise—the outlook of policymakers in their making of foreign policy strategy (Christensen 1996; Fiammenghi 2011; Glaser 1996; Lieber 2007; Montgomery 2006; Rendall 2006; Snyder 2002; Snyder and Lieber 2008; Taliaferro 2001–2; Tang 2010; Zakaria 2008). In the worldview of offensive realist states, they must perpetually seek to maximize power in an anarchic world in the search for security—a quest always out of reach, which is the fundamental "tragedy of great power politics" (Mearsheimer 2001). This perspective regards the world as one in which other states are without exception existing or potential security threats to which one should respond accordingly by maximizing power to the extent possible, if necessary by employing armed force. In contrast, defensive realist states understand that to seek power relentlessly is only to invite greater insecurity, high costs, and the risk of ruinous war stemming from ever-higher tensions. Most analysts tend to focus on one or the other of the two forms of realist outlooks. In my view, states can and do sometimes change their worldviews, as Tang (2008) has tried to show with respect to China.

India's strategic outlook before 1990–91 was essentially in accord with an offensive realist perspective—that is, a tendency to base policy on deep-rooted fear of others' power and on the need to act unilaterally whenever possible against the sources of fear. Though it did not, in a standard offensive-realist sense, seek continual expansion, it tended to view the world around it as uncertain and as a constant source of actual or potential aggression against it; and hence to respond to its security fears by assertive and sometimes military means. As a strong power in its neighborhood, it did use military force to expand its power and defend its interests from time to time. Shortly after independence in 1947, it used force to absorb the state of Hyderabad, the ruler of which had acquiesced to British dominance but now showed a desire to attain sovereign status. In 1960, India again deployed force to expel the Portuguese from their colony in Goa. In 1971, the Indian Army engineered the birth of Bangladesh through a military campaign against Pakistan. In 1981, India deployed a frigate in the Bay of Bengal to shut Bangladesh out of the disputed New Moore / South Talpatty Island (Roy-Chaudhury 1999). And in 1987, Indian Air Force transport aircraft escorted by Mirage fighters dropped relief packages over Sri Lanka against opposition from Colombo, which presaged the arrival of the Indian Army in that country. The last instance—to which I return below—was one that seemed to confirm Sri Lanka's perception of India as a constant source of insecurity (Kabir 1996; de Silva 1999; Sivarajah 1999).

India's proclivity for intervention among its neighbors produced insecurity-driven resistance from Sri Lanka and other small neighbors. And by the late 1980s the neighbors' fears were growing along with India's expanding military capabilities—including a nuclear-powered attack submarine and long-range maritime patrol aircraft leased from the Soviet Union—which brought a widespread perception that it had now assumed the role of regional policeman (Copley 1988; Munro 1989). To be fair, Sri Lanka had earlier asked for and benefited from Indian intervention. In 1971, when its government was threatened by a major left-wing insurgency launched by the Janatha Vimukthi Peramuna (= People's Liberation Front), India—itself in the throes of leftist rebellion in several of its states—provided Sri

Lanka with military assistance in the form of Indian Air Force helicopters (Moorthy 2011, 210–11).

India's intrusive role in Sri Lanka was driven by its early perception of threats emanating from other players that had the capacity to intervene in the region. During the Cold War era, as S. D. Muni (1993, 19) has pointed out, "the extension of extra-regional great power rivalry gave India a sense of weakness and vulnerability in the regional context." Even before independence, Nehru had considered an "Eastern Federation"—comprising China and India, along with Afghanistan, Burma, Ceylon (later renamed Sri Lanka), Iran, Malaya, Nepal, and Siam, designed to keep the big powers at bay—though he subsequently (in 1945) proposed a smaller South Asian Federation of India with Afghanistan, Burma, Iran, and Iraq (Muni 1993, 14). The notion that Ceylon was critical to Indian security was embedded in Indian thinking. Congress Party president Pattabhi Sitaramaya averred as much in 1949: "It cannot be that Ceylon is in friendship with a group with which India is not in friendship" (quoted by Muni 1993, 32–33).

Indian intervention in Sri Lanka became more substantial as deteriorating ethnic tensions between the majority Sinhala and minority Tamil groups of the population came to a boil in the 1980s (Bandarage 2009; Senadhira 2000; de Silva 2012). India's policymakers saw the worsening situation as detrimental to their national interests in a number of ways (Dixit 1998, 14–15). First, they feared a deep societal fissure in Sri Lanka would facilitate a closer linkage between Tamils in Sri Lanka and their counterparts in India, which had negative security implications because the latter had harbored secessionist sentiment in the postindependence years. This perspective has been challenged. Sankaran Krishna has argued that India was largely indifferent to developments in Sri Lanka and that Prime Minister Indira Gandhi securitized the issue for her own reasons—to boost her party's fading prospects in Tamil Nadu and to enhance her leverage over Colombo (Krishna 2001, 4–8). He notes that there was no serious outcry in Tamil Nadu when the Indian Army launched a military campaign in 1987 against the LTTE (Krishna 2001, 11). But this interpretation is not entirely convincing, for the big picture does reflect Indian insecurity on a range of issues pertaining to its strategic environment, as is made clearer just below.

Second, India viewed the active presence of other states in Sri Lanka's security affairs with apprehension. Starting in the early 1970s, Indian anxiety had grown as the United States and China leaned toward Pakistan during the 1971 crisis and Washington imposed sanctions against New Delhi for its 1974 nuclear test (Sridharan 2016, 53). Under President Junius Jayawardene (1978–89), Sri Lanka displayed a marked preference for drawing closer to the United States (Bullion 1995, 77–80). While India sought to keep the United States out of the Indian Ocean by calling for its designation as a "Zone of Peace," Jayawardene suggested at the 1983 summit of the Nonaligned Movement that the island of Diego Garcia, where the United States has a major military base, be delinked from the proposal (Bullion 1995, 76). Reversing a 1972 decision, Jayawardene in 1980 allowed foreign warships to visit the northeastern Sri Lankan port of Trincomalee—close to the Indian coast—if they were not at war or carrying nuclear weapons (Fernando 2002, 78). J. N. Dixit, India's high commissioner in Colombo during the critical phase from 1985 to 1989, explicitly refers to Indian worries at the time with respect to the United States and other countries (Dixit 1998, 14–15). The Indian government believed that Sri Lanka was receiving assistance from Israel and Pakistan to counter the Tamil agitation and that the United States intended to establish an intelligence base in the guise of a Voice of America radio station in western Sri Lanka and a possible intelligence base in Trincomalee. There were reports that the US Central Intelligence Agency, Israel's Mossad, and British mercenaries were active on the island and that China and Pakistan were training Sri Lankan forces and providing them with military equipment (Effendi 2007, 41; DeVotta 2010, 43; Suryanarayana 1988, 39–40).

Sri Lanka's quest for military assistance from countries other than India was seen as contravening Indian security under a policy framework that developed under the premierships of Indira Gandhi and Rajiv Gandhi during the 1980s (Hagerty 1991; Sen Gupta 1983). This policy, which came to be known variously as "India's Monroe Doctrine," the "Indira Doctrine," or the "Rajiv Doctrine," held that "India will not tolerate external intervention in a conflict situation in any South Asian country if the intervention has any implicit or explicit anti-Indian implication" (Sen Gupta 1983). India's willingness to intervene was implicit in this unofficial doctrine, which was conveyed to the United States, to the United Kingdom, and to India's neighbors, including Sri Lanka (Sen Gupta 1983). In 1983, when the killing of Sri Lankan soldiers by Tamil militants and the consequent slaughter of Tamil civilians triggered a major crisis, India made preparations for possible military intervention. Though this did not happen, an Indian Army brigade was placed on alert for dispatch as a peacekeeping force (Bobb 1983). The Sri Lankan leadership was acutely conscious of the threat, and Jayawardene is said to have told his cabinet that "if India, by some chance, decided to invade us, we will fight and may be lose, but with dignity" (quoted by Kabir 1996, 37).

Though Dixit is unsurprisingly coy about India's intrusive role in Sri Lanka, he does mention that India's external intelligence agency, the Research and Analysis Wing, was involved in attempting to broker a compromise between the Sri Lankan government and Tamil militant groups (Dixit 1998, 3–4). In fact, Indian backing of Tamil extremist groups was substantial. Large numbers of Tamil militants established themselves in Tamil Nadu, where the state government let them set up camps for ideological and military training (Gupta 1984). Retired Indian military and paramilitary officers were employed to impart instruction to the guerillas. According to a report in *India Today* magazine, the state government was supportive of the numerous Tamil groups, while the central government provided some of their leaders with Indian passports and generally turned a blind eye to their activities (Gupta 1984). The LTTE built up a support network in the state, incorporating "smugglers, fishermen, political activists, transport operators, businessmen and corrupt officials" (Suryanarayan 2009).

Subsequently, India's Jain Commission, set up in 1991 to inquire into the assassination of former prime minister Rajiv Gandhi, revealed, among other things, that Tamil Nadu chief minister M. G. Ramachandran (widely known as "MGR") had given financial assistance to the LTTE, that the Government of India had provided the militants with large sums of money, and that the central government was fully aware of the military training camps set up by them. All this emerges from a Tamil Nadu state police report cited by the commission (Joshi 1997a, 1997b). The commission's report also refers to the seizure of surface-to-air missiles, AK-47 rifles, mortar shells, hand grenades, and other military equipment from the LTTE in November 1986—materials that were then "returned to them under pressure from Shri P. Chidambaram, the then internal security minister" (cited by Joshi 1997a).

Under Rajiv Gandhi's prime ministership (1984–89), India's intercession in its southern neighbor's affairs became more intense. The larger strategy behind India's intervention in Sri Lanka was to ensure that neither the militants nor Colombo should win the internal conflict. If the former became ascendant, the potential risk of a transnational Tamil movement would rise; if the latter gained the upper hand, there would be domestic repercussions in India. In January 1987, the balance in the Sri Lankan civil war tilted toward Colombo, which launched a major thrust, Operation Liberation, against the LTTE. The Indian government, critical but not willing to intervene directly, sought to assuage the political pressure building in Tamil Nadu by providing humanitarian aid to the beleaguered Tamil population in Jaffna in northern Sri Lanka. Besides, New Delhi may have wanted to preempt China and Pakistan, both of which had offered humanitarian aid (Bandarage 2009, 131). But the Sri Lankan government refused Indian assistance. This led to a brief military confrontation. In June 1987, a flotilla of nineteen fishing boats rented by the Indian government to carry food, medicines, and fuel and led by the Indian Coast Guard vessel *Vikram* was stopped by the Sri Lankan Navy and forced to turn back (Sirohi 1987).

India immediately launched Operation Poomalai (= Garland), which involved the dropping of aid packages by Indian Air Force transport aircraft accompanied by Mirage fighters (Weisman 1987). India's minister of state for external affairs, Natwar Singh, told Sri Lanka's high commissioner in New Delhi that "any resistance would be met by force" (cited by Kadian 1990, 10). Indian high commissioner Dixit's warning to Sri Lanka's minister for national security, Lalith Athulathmudali, as recounted in a later interview, was more graphic: "Even if a single plane is shot at, these Mirages will fan out and destroy all your air fields" (cited by Krishna 1999, 152).

This episode compelled Jayewardene's government to suspend its military campaign and to consent to the Agreement to Establish Peace and Normalcy in Sri Lanka (July 29, 1987), more widely known as the India–Sri Lanka Accord (Gooneratne 1996, 275–78). The agreement was designed to produce a political settlement brokered by India that would end the civil war. But the effort went awry as the LTTE, after initially agreeing to the deal, resumed fighting. The Indian Peace Keeping Force (IPKF), sent to supervise the surrender of arms and ensure stability, ended up fighting the LTTE in a fruitless insurgent war (Kadian 1990). The signal failure of the campaign is attributable to inadequate intelligence, the absence of local support, and the need to limit the use of force lest India's Tamils take umbrage (Ganguly 1998, 215–16). Eventually, the IPKF was withdrawn in March 1990.

This conflict, sometimes called "India's Vietnam," has since had a significant influence on Indian strategic behavior, making governments reluctant to contemplate military deployments overseas, with the exception of peacekeeping under the United Nations flag. More broadly, this was the last phase of India's proactive efforts to police the region in the offensive realist phase of India's strategic outlook. As seen in chapter 2, the twin shocks of the Cold War's end and a balance-of-payments crisis brought a dramatic change in India's worldview and external policies.

INDIA'S DEFENSIVE REALIST TURN AND COOPERATION WITH SRI LANKA: UNPROBLEMATIC SHIFT

The about-face in India's strategic worldview in 1991 meant that the world was no longer deeply threatening to post–Cold War Indian policymakers, who were far more confident than their predecessors in dealing with the sources of power. One reason was the decision to become a nuclear weapons power with the 1998 tests. The tests did, as we shall see in chapter 5, create unanticipated problems vis-à-vis Pakistan; but on the whole, they brought a sense of security in dealing with big players, primarily China, which had (and still has) a much larger economy and military capability. Moreover, as we have seen in chapter 2, the tests brought an unexpected dividend, in that the United States now began to consider India a serious player on the strategic landscape and to seek a strategic partnership with it. This in turn brought major gains: investment and technology, extensive military collaboration, and India's inclusion in several (though not all) components of the nuclear nonproliferation regime.

Another reason for the new sense of confidence in New Delhi was the positive gain from India's radical shift in economic policy. India's gross domestic product growth rate rose quickly, and with it the expectation that it would soon be a major economic player despite its enduring problems of poverty and underemployment. This became evident when India's gross domestic product, in terms of purchasing power parity, overtook that of Japan in 2011 (Banerji and Shah 2012). In addition, rapid growth meant India was in a position to build its conventional military capability quickly without having to devote a sizable proportion of its gross domestic product to this end. A major effect of all these developments was the achievement of a rapid rise in India's international status (Basrur and Sullivan de

Estrada 2017). It was now able to find a seat at many tables, ranging from the Group of Twenty major economies to the family of institutions centered on the Association of Southeast Asian Nations, the Shanghai Cooperation Organization, and new multistate configurations such as the BRICS (Brazil, Russia, India, China, and South Africa) and IBSA (India, Brazil, and South Africa). In this changed environment, India's self-image increasingly became that of a state on the cusp of becoming a major power.

How did this new outlook affect India's strategic perspective and behavior? First, it meant that India was no longer prone to a deep sense of insecurity. In the past, it had been fearful of big powers; now, it sought to play the power game with them through multiple strategic partnerships and to benefit from it. With respect to its smaller neighbors, India no longer had the tendency to view their other strategic and economic relationships with anxiety, though it remained watchful about the degree to which such relationships might have a negative impact on Indian interests. Second, India was no longer fearful of the global economy, which it began to view as a realm of opportunity rather than risk. The new interest in integrating with the capitalist system opened up avenues for cooperative relationships with other states big and small. As an increasingly open economy, India was now comfortable with building mutually profitable trade and investment relationships with its neighbors as a pathway to stability. Likewise, neighbors that once viewed it with a degree of suspicion could now be induced to see it as an opportunity rather than a threat.

Third, in this increasingly interdependent world, an optimal strategy was one that minimized costs, particularly with respect to overseas military action, the price of which had been brought home by the IPKF's painful experience. India's aggressive defense of its interests had not yielded regional stability or an acquiescent set of neighbors, most of which remained wary of it and sought both to keep their distance and to draw closer to other major powers. As a result, post–Cold War India eschewed military intervention both among its immediate neighbors and in more distant theaters. This in turn made it less of a threat to its neighbors than in the past. It would hardly have escaped their notice that, since the IPKF episode, India's armed forces showed no serious interest in overseas involvement—a marked contrast to the first four decades of its independent history.

In consequence, India undertook a major shift from emphasizing its hard power to underscoring its soft power (Wagner 2005). The change in India's attitude toward its neighbors was exemplified by the so-called Gujral Doctrine, named after Inder Kumar Gujral, who was minister for external affairs during the years 1989–90 and 1996–97, and then prime minister from April 1997 to March 1998. The doctrine laid down five principles of Indian foreign policy: India would not insist on reciprocity in relations with its small neighbors; no South Asian state should allow its territory to be used against another; all should eschew interference in one another's internal affairs; all must respect one another's sovereignty and territorial integrity; and all disputes should be settled peacefully and bilaterally (Gujral 1997; Murthy 1999, 639–40). The framework was a unilateral and nonofficial one, but it gave India's neighbors the important commitment that it would not intrude in their political life on the understanding that they would not engage with third countries in ways inimical to Indian interests.

Not all India's neighbors responded with alacrity to its new strategic persona. Nor were they consistent in their responses. Nevertheless, significant changes are apparent. The earliest occurred in the India–Sri Lanka relationship. A joint commission was set up in 1992 to work on areas of cooperation, including trade, investment, science and technology, culture, and education. Given the sharp tensions between the two countries during the IPKF episode, the turnaround from the early 1990s was remarkable. For Sri Lanka, there was room for optimism. From India's standpoint, the IPKF experience had made it clear that its capacity to use force to meet its regional security concerns was limited. Besides, such sympathy as Indians had for the LTTE was shattered by the assassination of former prime minister Rajiv Gandhi in May 1991, which precipitated a government crackdown on it (Sridharan 2016, 60).

Domestic political change in Sri Lanka facilitated an improved relationship. Chandrika Kumaratunga, who was elected president in 1994, was prepared to craft a more cooperative future; and Sri Lanka's strategy shifted from balancing to bandwagoning (Gamage 2017, 7–11). India, with its large market, was seen as an opportunity, particularly in light of the slow progress in regional negotiations toward the South Asian Free Trade Area (Gamage 2017, 8). Accordingly, negotiations on a free trade agreement (FTA) commenced soon after Kumaratunga took office. The India–Sri Lanka Free Trade Agreement (ISFTA) was signed in December 1998 and the pact took effect in March 2000. Sri Lanka benefited significantly as its trade deficit with India declined during the first decade after the FTA had been signed, from 82.36 percent of total bilateral trade in 2000 to 68.62 percent in 2010 (calculated from International Monetary Fund n.d.). From the Indian standpoint, the breakthrough was an exemplar, as Sri Lanka was the first among India's immediate neighbors to seek a close economic relationship with it. On the investment front, Indian foreign direct investment (FDI) in Sri Lanka grew steadily, and India became one of the largest investors in the country both in terms of annual inflows and aggregate FDI stock (UNCTAD n.d.).

India also sought to cement its strategic links with Sri Lanka. Discussions on a possible defense cooperation agreement (DCA) were mooted. A joint statement in October 2003 announced that both sides had agreed on commencing talks "with a view to concluding a defense cooperation agreement at the earliest" (Joint Statement 2003). The systemic incentive was obvious. As *The Hindu* remarked, "It is no secret that this convergence arises mainly from the threat posed by the Liberation Tigers of Tamil Eelam and its goal of a separate Tamil state in the North-East" (*The Hindu* 2004a). In addition, a DCA would have preempted other states from stepping in to undercut India's strategic position through enhanced military support for Colombo in the civil war.

In the meantime, even as the civil war continued, there was no significant resistance within India to the departure in foreign policy. Why was there so little opposition to the change in Indian policy? There is some indication that India's foreign policy bureaucracy was less than enthusiastic about the Indian political leadership's push to build bridges with Sri Lanka, possibly owing to inertia. In a personal interview, a former minister in the Kumaratunga cabinet recalled that there was resistance to the FTA from officials in the Indian Ministry of External Affairs. However, bureaucratic opposition was overruled by the Bharatiya Janata Party (BJP) leadership's personal intervention (Interview 2004).

A more likely source of opposition was Tamil Nadu. But though there has always been an undercurrent of sympathy in the state for the Sri Lankan Tamils, and notwithstanding links between Tamil Nadu's political leaders and militant groups in Sri Lanka, the civil war and the fate of the LTTE were not major political issues. One reason was a cultural distance between the two groups. In Tamil Nadu, postindependence politics were characterized by the rise of an anti-Brahmin movement that sought the social uplift of the lower castes. In Sri Lanka, the major Tamil social group is the dominant Vellalar caste, which sees itself as the standard bearer of Tamil tradition and has close links with the Brahmins (Pfaffenberger 1981). Furthermore, as Bryan Pfaffenberger notes, the "Ceylon Tamils [as they were known earlier] deem the mainland to have undergone such drastic social change that only they continue to adhere to the ancient patterns of social relations that constitute Tamil civilization" (Pfaffenberger 1981, 1148). Consequently, the political connections between the Indian Tamils and their Sri Lankan counterparts have never been deep. Seeing themselves as unique, the latter have never felt the urge to unify with the Tamils of the mainland (Pfaffenberger 1981, 1148).

As Krishna (1999, 59–100) has observed, the politics of the two Tamil groups have been very different. Secessionism among the Indian Tamils, which emerged from resistance to what was seen as northern Brahminical dominance, was in decline when the crisis began brewing in Sri Lanka. In contrast, secessionism among the Sri Lankan Tamils emerged as resistance to Sinhala domination after independence and intensified after the killings of 1983. Hence, efforts by Sri Lankan Tamil leaders to garner support from fellow Tamils across the Palk Strait drew expressions of support from Indian Tamils, both leaders and public, but little more (Krishna 1999, 93–94). In January 1981, Tamil Nadu chief minister MGR, known to be sympathetic to the Sri Lankan militants and to have provided them with financial assistance, was critical of Tamil United Liberation Front leader Appapillai Amirthalingam's appeal for support and affirmed his government's preference for maintaining good relations with the governments of neighboring countries (Krishna 1999, 94–95).

On the other hand, the involvement of militant Sri Lankan Tamil groups in violence within India was the source of considerable public anger in Tamil Nadu. In August 1984, a major explosion in Madras's (the pre-1996 name for Chennai) airport left thirty dead; Sri Lankan Tamil militants were known to be involved in bank robberies and extortion from the rich; and Douglas Devanandan, chief of the Eelam People's Revolutionary Liberation Front (EPRLF), was involved in the killing of an Indian civilian in November 1986 (Suryanarayana 1988, 79). In June 1990, the LTTE massacred thirteen top leaders of a rival militant group, the EPRLF, as well as two Indians, in Madras (Subramanian 1999).

Importantly, as Krishna notes, there was no major outcry when the IPKF went to war with the LTTE: "Here was an Indian army killing hundreds, if not thousands, of Sri Lankan Tamils in a war that lasted nearly three years—and yet the political fallout in Tamil Nadu seemed hardly to bear out such claims [of the significance of the Tamil Nadu factor]" (Krishna 2001, 11). Rajiv Gandhi's emissary to ailing All India Anna Dravida Munnetra Kazhagam (AIADMK) chief MGR later wrote that the latter promised his support (Parthasarthy 2000). Moreover, the issue of the civil war in Sri Lanka played only a peripheral role in the elections to the state legislature in 1988 (Krishna 2001, 11; Parthasarthy 2000). Though the pro-LTTE Dravida Munnetra Kazhagam (DMK) gained a majority in the 1989 state assembly elections, the DMK lost out to the Congress-AIADMK alliance in the parliamentary elections in Tamil Nadu (Parthasarthy 2000).

The limits of the transnational ethnic linkage are underscored by the relative lack of interest in Tamil Nadu in the fate of the so-called Upcountry Tamils (also called Indian Tamils or Estate Tamils). These people are concentrated in the central hills of Sri Lanka and have close historical linkages with Tamil Nadu, from where many of them were brought as indentured labor during the nineteenth and twentieth centuries. In contrast, the Jaffna Tamils of northern and eastern Sri Lanka have had an independent existence over a much longer period. Indeed, the AIADMK's MGR was born in Kandy among the Upcountry Tamils but showed little interest in their fate even as the Indian and Sri Lankan governments wrestled over their citizenship (Sooriyanarayan 2002, 94).

As noted above, the killing of Rajiv Gandhi led to widespread public anger in India (Gopalan 2002, 48–49). The LTTE was outlawed by the Government of India in 1992, while in Tamil Nadu, the AIADMK, which had won power the previous year, cracked down on the LTTE (Sridharan 2016, 60). Indeed, all the Tamil Nadu political parties that had flirted with Sri Lankan Tamil militants turned away from the LTTE. Periodic attempts by the LTTE to rebuild its relationship with the Indian government failed. At a press conference in 2002, LTTE chief Velupillai Prabhakaran indicated that his group was keen to revive good relations with India. In a press interview, S. P. Thamilchelvan, the head of the LTTE's political wing, tried again: "We hope New Delhi will revisit the entire gamut of engagement with the Tamil Tigers. . . . We expect and hope that there is an attitudinal change in New Delhi" (*Sunday Island* n.d.). But the Government of India's response was cold.

India's major disaster relief efforts in Sri Lanka also turned the tide of public opinion there. After a severe cyclonic storm resulting in serious flooding in May 2003, the Indian Army and the Indian Navy activated Operation Denim and sent in supplies and personnel to help the victims. A report on the deployment noted that, in contrast to the departure of the IPKF in 1990, Indian forces were given a warm sendoff by the Sri Lankan defense minister at a ceremony where they were awarded certificates of appreciation and tribute was paid to the IPKF personnel who had died earlier (Sambandan 2003a). India's standing in Sri Lanka was also vastly improved by its swift response to the tsunami disaster in 2004, which took a toll of over 30,000 fatalities (CNN 2005). On the same day as the tragedy, the Indian Navy launched Operation Rainbow, which dispatched nineteen ships, four aircraft, and eleven helicopters to Sri Lanka, the Maldives, and India's own territories (Sakhuja 2005). Indian assistance to Sri Lanka included $22 million for immediate and long-term relief; the deployment of two Indian Navy ships for clearance operations at Trincomalee (one of them was later converted into a hospital ship); and arrangements for transport aircraft and helicopters to convey relief supplies (Price 2005, 15). India also granted Sri Lanka a three-year moratorium on debt in light of the severe consequences of the tsunami disaster (Sambandan 2005c).

A significant outcome of the new warmth was that, in December 2003, Sri Lanka decided to grant citizenship to 168,141 Upcountry Tamils, who had been in a limbo of statelessness for decades (Sambandan 2003b). The general picture, then, was that India's position vis-à-vis Sri Lanka was on a positive trajectory.

The Indian government's policy of engaging Sri Lanka and attempting to keep other states—in particular China and Pakistan—at bay appears to have worked quite well starting in the 1990s. A key factor in the central government's ability to carry out its policy without having to worry too much about its domestic fallout was the distribution of domestic political power at the time. During the period when India began to play an active interventionist role in Sri Lanka—that is, after 1983—the central government was under the firm control of a Congress Party majority. In the 1980 general election, the Congress under Indira Gandhi had won a comfortable majority, securing 353 of 542 seats in the Lok Sabha. In the 1984 election, the Congress—this time with Rajiv Gandhi at the helm after his mother's assassination—had performed even better, winning 415 seats (*Indiavotes* n.d.; hereafter, all election statistics are drawn from this source).

Consequently, the central government's policy vis-à-vis Sri Lanka was not subject to serious challenge.

Nor was it confronted. As we have seen, ethnic links between Indian and Sri Lankan Tamils did not constitute a tricky obstacle for the two leaders. When violence against Tamils in Sri Lanka broke out in 1983, there were certainly protests: political parties in Tamil Nadu vied with one another to portray themselves as defenders of the Sri Lankan Tamils' cause, not least because of the approaching 1984 elections for both the central and state legislatures. The AIADMK's MGR sent a multiparty delegation to New Delhi to press for government intervention in Sri Lanka; DMK chief M. Karunanidhi collected 10 million signatures to petition the United Nations, resigned from the state legislature in protest, and formed the Tamil Eelam Supporters Organization, which called for military intervention; and MGR led a statewide general strike (Thomas 1995, 63–65). But these were largely symbolic activities, and there was no serious mass agitation in Tamil Nadu, even when Indian forces fought the LTTE. Indeed, the ruling Congress at the center also found it expedient to support the general strike, even as it maintained that the crisis in Sri Lanka was an internal issue, while Prime Minister Indira Gandhi told Parliament that her government was opposed to a Tamil state in Sri Lanka (Thomas 1995, 64–66).

It was only starting with the 1989 general election that the political picture underwent a drastic change—with profound consequences for the formation of governments in New Delhi—and a tug-of-war between the center and Tamil Nadu began to shape Indian policy toward Sri Lanka. The weakening of the center occurred at precisely the time when its policy toward Sri Lanka underwent a major change from one of balancing the Tamil rebels and the Sri Lankan government to one displaying a distinct pro-Colombo tilt.

SPECIFIC ISSUES, DOMESTIC POLITICS, AND THE APPEARANCE OF DRIFT

Once its war with the LTTE had broken out, India's position was no longer that of an outsider intent on ensuring some sort of equilibrium between the Sinhala and Tamil populations of Sri Lanka. From this time onward, Indian policy began to make a distinction between the LTTE and the general Tamil populace in Sri Lanka. India would work to defeat the former and simultaneously try and protect the interests of the latter. Hence, Indian policymakers now pursued a narrower objective that envisioned success in terms of an India-assisted victory for the Sri Lankan state, which would enhance India's position with the latter. However, this new approach quickly became entangled with the political complexities of an increasingly decentralized Indian polity. Simultaneously, electoral politics in Tamil Nadu became increasingly competitive for reasons that had nothing to do with politics at the central level but were driven in good part by the Sri Lanka issue. This engendered center–state tensions, and the national government became increasingly vulnerable to state politics.

In the 1989 national election, the Congress won a paltry 197 seats and had to yield power to a United Front coalition led by Vishwanath Pratap Singh, who headed a minority government surviving with support from opposition parties. Thereafter, all elections up to (and excluding) the 2014 general election brought to office governments led by parties that did not enjoy a majority in the Lok Sabha. As a result, national governments tended to be wary of pursuing policies that might generate major problems for them in Parliament. Throughout the 1990s, India played a cautious role in Sri Lanka (Krishna 2001, 13). Even as the relationship between the two countries underwent a profound change, as described above, India's involvement in the civil war was limited, despite the emergence of strong anti-LTTE sentiment after Rajiv Gandhi's assassination.

The domestic politics of Indian policy toward Sri Lanka and its refusal to play an active role in the political resolution of the crisis are reflected in three episodes: India's disinclination to assist Colombo when its troops appeared to be on the verge of a major defeat in 2000; the Indian government's inordinate caution about signing the DCA with Sri Lanka, the prospects for which eventually faded away; and India's reluctance to provide extensive military assistance to Sri Lanka during the final phase of the civil war.

The 2000 Crisis

The first major test for Indian policy in Sri Lanka came when the Sri Lankan Army began to lose ground to the LTTE in the north in 1999–2000 (Bandarage 2009, 162–75; Hashim 2013, 88–131; Moorcraft 2012, 34–37). At the time, the BJP's Vajpayee, as leader of the National Democratic Alliance coalition, was prime minister. In December 1999 government forces incurred heavy casualties and lost control of about 1,000 square kilometers of territory in Vanni. In April 2000, the LTTE gained control of the army's base at Elephant Pass, leaving 30,000 troops trapped on the Jaffna Peninsula. President Kumaratunga appealed to India for assistance, but she acknowledged in an interview that this was something "which India had said they cannot give" (quoted by Subramanian 2000). Kumaratunga also wanted the Indian government to help bring the LTTE to the table, but this too did not happen. The Indian response was instead to avoid grasping the opportunity to intervene on behalf of Colombo (Murthy 2000).

Jaswant Singh, Vajpayee's minister for external affairs, visited Colombo in May 2000 but officially offered only a credit facility of $100 million (Cherian 2000). Meanwhile, pressure was growing for military intervention. A respected columnist, reflecting the prevailing elite view in New Delhi that a victory for the LTTE would raise the specter of a unified Tamil homeland, argued for the employment of the Indian Air Force to strafe and bomb the LTTE's forces (Jha 2000). But the Vajpayee government was circumspect, and Jaswant Singh made it clear that "the question of military involvement in Sri Lanka is not an option we consider as open" (Cherian 2000).

At the same time, there was a strong incentive to help Colombo because the latter had begun acquiring military assistance from several countries: Pakistan, Israel, South Africa, and North Korea, among others (Aneja 2000; Hargreaves et al. n.d., 10, 12, 44). China was as yet not involved. But Pakistan, according to one report, airlifted multibarrel rocket launchers and other equipment on an emergency basis (Mir 2009). Hence, India quietly offered a modicum of military aid. It was reported that the Indian chief of air staff, Air Marshal A. Y. Tipnis, flew to Sri Lanka and visited several air bases along with a senior technical officer. But Indian military assistance was limited to the tightening of coastal vigilance through Operation Pasha, a joint surveillance mission by the Indian Navy and Coast Guard aimed at cutting off supplies to the LTTE, and a day-long naval-cum-coast guard exercise that included a destroyer as a show of force (Aneja 2000).

Why was India ambivalent in its response? The BJP's position was precarious: after the 1999 elections, it had emerged as the largest party in Parliament, but it held only 182 of 543 seats and relied on the support of twenty small parties and half a dozen independent members. In the background was harsh experience. In 1996, the BJP's minority government had stepped down less than two weeks after assuming office because it had failed to cobble together a majority. In 1998, the BJP had formed a second coalition government but constantly struggled to remain in office as its numerous allies threatened its stability in their efforts to bargain for their interests (Ramakrishnan 1998). Eventually, the government was brought down in 1999 by the AIADMK, which walked out of the coalition. The AIADMK's exit was occasioned not by any policy issue but by New Delhi's refusal to dismiss the government of its rival in Chennai, the DMK, which held power in the state. The BJP's policies in its third coalition government (from 1999) were thus conditioned by bitter experience, and Prime Minister Vajpayee was careful not to anger regional parties. After the AIADMK's exit, the DMK joined the National Democratic Alliance (it switched to the United Progressive Alliance, or UPA, in 2004) in a classic act of political opportunism. But the DMK's tally of seats was relatively small: it held 12 of the 39 Lok Sabha seats from Tamil Nadu.

The Tamil Nadu legislature itself had a history of seesaw power shifts between the two regional parties (Racine 2009, 454). The distribution of seats between the DMK and the AIADMK in the state assembly swung sharply with each state election. The ratio was 24:133 in 1984, 151:27 in 1989, 2:164 in 1991, and 173:4 in 1996. In the meantime, small parties such as the Pattali Makkal Katchi (PMK) and the Marumalarchi Dravida Munnetra Kazhagam (MDMK) were trying to carve out political space for themselves by, among other things, making vociferous appeals to Tamil nationalist sentiment. The DMK, trying to retain its position in Chennai, was caught between the BJP's pro-Colombo leanings and the shrill pro-LTTE rhetoric of the small regional parties (Viswanathan 2000). DMK chief M. Karunanidhi expressed conflicting sentiments in quick succession, at times pro-LTTE and at times "sympathetic" to the Government of India's position (Panneerselvan 2000).

In effect, the PMK and the MDMK, which held five and four seats respectively in Parliament, and which were even weaker at the state level with four and zero seats respectively, were able to severely circumscribe the scope of action for Vajpayee's government. The symbolic power of Tamil nationalism, combined with the unpredictability of coalition politics in Chennai and New Delhi, prevented the Indian government from taking more decisive action, which would have turned the military tide and strengthened Indian influence with Colombo. Eventually, the war on the Jaffna Peninsula swung in favor of the Sri Lankan Army, but the fact remains that India lost a major opportunity to establish a solid strategic position in Sri Lanka owing to the exigencies of domestic politics.

Defense Cooperation Agreement

Notwithstanding India's diffidence on the Jaffna crisis, the relationship between the two countries remained sound. The defense dimension remained low-key but made some progress. Indian policy aimed at providing Sri Lanka with military assistance—without, however, risking a political backlash at home. India helped Sri Lanka with military training, intelligence, and "nonlethal" military equipment, a somewhat loose definition because this did include an armed offshore patrol vessel (*The Hindu* 2004). A joint statement on the occasion of Prime Minister Ranil Wickremesinghe's visit to India in October 2003 referred to the "ongoing cooperation in training and the supply of equipment to the Sri Lankan defense forces." It also noted that "the two sides will commence discussions with a view to concluding a defense cooperation agreement at the earliest" (Joint Statement 2003). In December 2004, the Indian Coast Guard and the Sri Lankan Navy took part in their first joint exercise—Operation Eksath (= together)—in which two Indian and five Sri Lankan vessels focused on search and rescue, antipiracy, and pollution control (Sambandan 2004). There appear to have been some differences between the two countries. An agreement under which India was to repair a key air strip at Palaly on the Jaffna Peninsula apparently did not pan out because Colombo rejected India's condition that no other country be allowed to utilize the facility (Berlin 2011, 14; Gokhale 2009, 122).

But domestic politics was the main obstacle. Sri Lanka pressed for a DCA, but Indian leaders were cautious. At a press conference in New Delhi in May 2004, India's external affairs minister, Natwar Singh, was noncommittal, admitting that the DMK "naturally" had an interest in the talks, but said they would continue. He was quick to emphasize the standard public position of the government, saying that "we very much hope that a peaceful, negotiated solution will be found which will maintain the unity, territorial integrity and sovereignty of Sri Lanka" (Baruah 2004). According to one source, the DCA was close to being finalized but was derailed by the DMK, which was strongly opposed to it (Muni 2004, 94). But even if it had been formalized, the DCA had apparently not been designed to establish a firm Indian military commitment to Sri Lanka (*The Hindu* 2004). Again, a critical opportunity to gain a strong position in Sri Lanka was lost as the demand for the DCA had come from the Sri Lankan government. Once Colombo had defeated the LTTE, it lost interest in the DCA (DeVotta 2010, 49). Less institutionalized cooperation did continue (Gokhale 2009). But the tipping point for a close defense relationship had passed. Though India did subsequently upgrade the level of its military assistance, China had by then gained an advantage by providing Sri Lanka with substantial quantities of defense equipment.

India and Eelam War IV

The Government of India was similarly constrained when Colombo sought to augment its military sinews and make a concerted effort to win what was the final stage of Eelam War IV, which it did in 2009 (Hashim 2013, 132–96; Moorcraft 2012, 126–48; de Silva 2012, 180–204). For Indian policymakers, the systemic incentives to intervene were strong. China's role in Sri Lanka was growing. In October 2007, Colombo signed a deal with Export Import Bank of China to obtain $306 million toward the cost of constructing Hambantota Harbor (AidData n.d.). A March 2008 press report noted that Chinese aid to Sri Lanka—encompassing port, highway, and electric power development—had jumped to $1 billion (*Times of India* 2008a). Chinese military aid was also substantial, encompassing Jian-7 jet fighters, which were given as a gift; armored personnel careers; and a host of other weapons (Pandit 2008b). Pakistan, too, was providing considerable military aid, and in August 2008 proposed a defense pact with Sri Lanka (Samanta 2008). India did provide military assistance—rather more than was widely known at the time—in the form of at least two patrol vessels for the Sri Lankan Navy, M-17 helicopters, and radar systems (Gokhale 2009; Unnithan 2007). But domestic political constraints meant that it was cautious in doing so, which permitted its strategic rivals to enhance their profiles in Sri Lanka.

In 2004, Prime Minister Manmohan Singh of the Congress headed a multiparty UPA coalition with the DMK as a partner. Once again, the main party was weak: the Congress had only 145 seats in a house of 543. The DMK had 16, while two other allies were pro-LTTE parties: the PMK, with 6 seats; and the MDMK, with 4. In the Tamil Nadu assembly, the DMK was in power, with 173 seats; the PMK had 20 seats; and the MDMK none from the 2001 state elections. But another small party, the Viduthalai Chiruthaigal Katchi (VCK), which was allied with the DMK, favored an independent Tamil Eelam (= Nation) in Sri Lanka. The DMK, therefore, was not inclined to take a strong position against the LTTE. Once again, New Delhi's options were circumscribed by its precarious alliance and the presence in it of parties that were themselves caught up in the uncertainties of state politics in Tamil Nadu.

The government's indecision, caused by its desire not to upset the coalition applecart in New Delhi, also affected other policies, notably on economic liberalization (Tummala 2009). In this particular instance—of policy toward Sri Lanka—the tune was clearly called by political swings in Tamil Nadu. In the state, the DMK was in power in 2006, but with a coalition, and its own seats numbered just 96, well below the level required for a majority on its own in the 234-seat house. In March 2007, the MDMK abandoned the DMK; and in March 2009, the PMK followed suit. Both joined hands with the AIADMK, which, in the run-up to the next round of general elections in 2009, also became aggressively Tamil-nationalist. The DMK could do no less. When LTTE leader S. P. Tamilselvan was killed in November 2007, the DMK publicly mourned his death, and party chief Karunanidhi himself penned a eulogy for him (Mohan 2008). In October 2008, Karunanidhi orchestrated a threat of mass resignation by his party's members of Parliament if the government did not, among other things, compel Sri Lanka to order a cease-fire (*Indian Express* 2008). Defense Minister Pranab Mukherjee dashed to Chennai to persuade Karunanidhi to change his mind, which he duly did (*Indian Express* 2008b). The DMK chief felt obliged to wave the ethnic flag, but he was surely aware that his party's relationship with the Congress was an interdependent one. The DMK was a partner in the Congress-led UPA coalition at the center, while the Congress was a partner in the DMK-led coalition in Tamil Nadu. If anything, the Congress was in a better bargaining position because its government in New Delhi could have survived with external support from parties not in its coalition, whereas the DMK was not so well positioned in Tamil Nadu (Sridharan 2016, 163).

In May 2009, on the eve of elections, with the LTTE on the verge of defeat, both Karunanidhi and AIADMK leader J. Jayalalitha called for the establishment of Tamil Eelam (*India Today* 2009). Both also went on a fast during the campaign for the 2009 elections, giving the Sri Lanka issue a prominent place in their poll planks (Raman 2009). All this reflected the "hyperpragmatism" of the extremely competitive electoral dynamic of the time (Sahadevan 2007, 35). With the national government constantly worrying about its survival, the domestic distribution of power trumped systemic incentives in shaping foreign policy.

The volatility of Tamil Nadu politics needs to be explored a little further in order to understand how it affected India's Sri Lanka policy. As with the politics that shaped many of the pulls and pushes related to the India-US nuclear agreement, here too the driving force was the constant jockeying for electoral advantage among the regional parties. There is no evidence that the voting public was persuaded by the ethnic rhetoric of the competing Tamil parties. Nonetheless, it came to occupy a central place in the competition. As we know, the central government was weak and dependent for its survival on coalition partners, which made the allegiance of the main parties from Tamil Nadu, the DMK and the AIADMK, critical. Just as the National Democratic Alliance under Vajpayee was susceptible to Tamil Nadu politics, so after 2004 the UPA under Manmohan Singh was vulnerable to pressures from the state. As we have also seen, the major state parties themselves were plagued by uncertainty about their prospects for every election. The pattern of large swings from 1984 to 2006 identified by Racine (2009), which affected the state throughout the period and later, made for a high degree of uncertainty for parties that were essentially populist in their appeal and style (Wyatt 2013).

Though the DMK and the AIADMK originally had a somewhat different social base—with the latter tending to appeal more to lower social strata—the exigencies of electoral politics had diffused their differences: both had to appeal to the support base of the other in order to widen their catchment area. Given the uncertainties of electoral outcomes, competition for popular support intensified, which opened up space for smaller parties to try and expand their base. The major Tamil parties now began to compete intensely for allies among small parties like the MDMK, the PMK, and the VCK. Wyatt observes that support for all the parties was in decline starting in the late 1990s (Wyatt 2013, 377), but the data show otherwise. None of the small parties had a substantial following, whereas the DMK and the AIADMK between them commanded between 62.1 and

66.9 percent of the vote between 1991 and 2006 (calculated from *Indiavotes* n.d.). However, it was the unpredictable nature of election outcomes in Tamil Nadu—the wide swings referred to above—that caused the big two to engage in what Wyatt correctly identifies as competitive outbidding for the support of the small parties (Wyatt 2013, 377).

The small parties were in the unusual position of not commanding large followings but nevertheless being given attractive incentives (e.g., ministerial positions in government) to switch sides between the two major parties. And because they were not really cut from significantly different political cloth in terms of their ideas or social bases, the small parties tended to pick up on symbolic issues and try and mobilize support through street agitation. For instance, S. Ramadoss launched the PMK in 1987 on a platform demanding reservations for the Vanniyar caste, of which he was a leader. But because the other parties also co-opted members of the Vanniyar caste, he resorted to the tactic of street agitation on a number of issues to stir up support. One of the causes he took up was that of the Sri Lanka Tamils (Racine 2009, 469–71).

Other parties like the MDMK adopted the same tactic and espoused a vociferous ethnic nationalism. Given the uncertainties surrounding elections, the larger Tamil parties also found it expedient to declare their commitment to the Sri Lankan Tamil cause. The symbolic appeal of this ethnonationalism may not in itself have gained them significant support, but they could not risk *losing* votes on this count and, besides, it was a low-cost flag to wave. In effect, the small parties drove national politics owing to the fragmentation of the political structure at the central level and the simultaneous volatility of the political structure at the state level in Tamil Nadu.

The Indian government's position was tricky. Policymakers were aware that if they failed to offer significant support to the government in Sri Lanka, they would leave the way open for China and Pakistan to entrench themselves. On the other hand, the demands of Tamil Nadu's ethnic nationalists were not acceptable. Shivshankar Menon, India's foreign secretary at the time, acknowledges that, if his government had pressured President Mahinda Rajapaksa, "we would have effectively written ourselves out of Sri Lanka for the next decade or more, sacrificing our maritime and other interests in Sri Lanka and abdicating a geopolitically strategic neighbor to other powers" (Menon 2016, 96). Hence, they tried to avoid intervening formally in Sri Lanka and yet to provide Colombo with considerable military aid, though in ways that did not unleash strong political reactions in Tamil Nadu.

The Indian fear of being "written out" of Sri Lanka was reflected in National Security Adviser M. K. Narayanan's blunt warning: "It is high time that Sri Lanka understood that India is the big power in the region and ought to refrain from going to Pakistan or China for weapons as we are prepared to accommodate them within the framework of our foreign policy" (quoted by Behuria and Sultana 2013, 91). The Sri Lankans could hardly have been unaware of India's anxieties as well as its potential to intervene and were careful to assuage Indian concerns through regular consultations. Years later, a senior member of the Mahinda Rajapaksa cabinet told this author in a matter-of-fact way that "India was the most important country to keep with us; the only country that can intervene" (Interview 2017). Indeed, as with his predecessors, President Rajapaksa's first overseas visit was to New Delhi (Subramanian 2005). But he returned with no assurances of support for his campaign against the LTTE. Nevertheless, the two governments arranged an informal series of regular meetings of their senior ministers and bureaucrats—the so-called troika—to maintain continuous engagement between them. On the Indian side were National Security Adviser Narayanan, Foreign Secretary Menon, and Defense Secretary Vijay Singh, while Sri Lanka was represented by the president's senior adviser, Basil Rajapaksa, Defense Secretary Gotabaya Rajapaksa, and Secretary to the President Lalith Weeratunga. Apart from communicating on the telephone, the troika met at least five times during the period 2007–9 (Behuria and Sultana 2013, 90).

From the Sri Lankan standpoint, the best thing about India's role was that it permitted the conduct of the war to go ahead unimpeded (Hashim 2013, 184). From the perspective of India's policymakers, they made the best of an awkward political position. The Tamil Tigers were clearly a serious threat. They had fought the Indian Army, had assassinated a former prime minister, and were now moving toward developing an air strike capability that might someday be able to target sensitive nuclear and space installations along India's southern coast (*The Hindu* 2008; Moorthy 2011, 242). They also posed a more insidious threat through their dual network of drug and arms trafficking, which linked Afghanistan, Pakistan, Tamil Nadu, and Sri Lanka (Moorthy 2011, 246–47).

Caught between systemic pressures and domestic constraints, India's policy was indecisive, effectively allowing its strategic rivals to enhance their role through the provision of military aid to the Sri Lankan government. Beginning in 2005, China annually provided $1 billion in aid, which helped Sri Lanka stabilize its finances (Hein 2017, 88, citing Glenn 2015, 33). In March 2007, China began investing heavily in Sri Lanka, providing 80 percent of the funding for the construction of Hambantota Port (Destradi 2010, 613). Chinese military assistance also grew rapidly starting in 2007, when, after the withdrawal of US aid on human rights grounds, China stepped in to fill the vacuum and became the largest supplier of military aid to Sri Lanka (Hargreaves et al. n.d., 12; Marshall 2009). This included antiaircraft guns, JY-11 surveillance radars, ammunition, and, in 2008, a generous gift of six F-7 (also termed Jian-7) jets (Hargreaves et al. n.d., 12). With China (and also Russia) providing political protection at the United Nations and bilateral trade rising rapidly, Sri Lanka's relationship with it strengthened immensely. In striking evidence of this, President Rajapaksa visited Beijing as many as six times during his tenure in office (Hein 2017, 87–88; Gardner 2009).

Pakistan also became a significant provider of military assistance to Sri Lanka. It had for some time been giving Colombo advice on logistics and counterinsurgency (Hargreaves et al. n.d., 10; Suryanarayana 1988, 39). Colombo's purchases of Pakistani military supplies, which began in 1999, totaled $50 million by 2007 and thereafter increased rapidly (*Sri Lanka Guardian* 2008). In May 2008, Sri Lanka's Army commander, Lieutenant General Sarath Fonseka, visited Pakistan to finalize a major arms deal that included twenty-two Al-Khalid tanks worth $100 million and other weapons worth $65 million, of which $40 million was for the air force and the balance for the army. According to reports, one shipload of military supplies was sent to Sri Lanka every twelve days to help it in its final drive for victory over the LTTE (Jabbar 2010; Rediff India Abroad 2009b). In January 2009, the defense secretaries of the two countries met and agreed to increase cooperation on military training, exercises, and intelligence sharing (Mir 2009). Later that year, Pakistani foreign minister Shah Mahmood Qureshi offered his Sri Lankan counterpart, Rohitha Bogollegama, a draft agreement on defense cooperation (*Dawn* 2008). Meanwhile, India was procrastinating over its own DCA with Sri Lanka.

The warming relationship between Sri Lanka and India's strategic adversaries brought increasing pressure on policymakers in New Delhi. National Security Adviser Narayanan voiced his concern at a lecture in the capital, saying: "We have to ensure that India's pre-eminent position in the region is not compromised by Sri Lanka seeking arms from elsewhere" (*Times of India* 2008c). Indian officials were worried by what appeared to be a larger pattern. As an unnamed senior official said, "The story of Myanmar is being repeated in Sri Lanka. China is already all over the island nation with a flurry of arms deals, oil explorations, and construction projects like the Hambantota Port" (quoted by Pandit 2008b). Lieutenant General Fonseka was forthright: "It is only after India told us that it cannot supply offensive weapons that we looked at other options" (quoted by Gokhale 2009, 128). But India found itself unable to do much. Hamstrung by domestic constraints, the Indian government sought to offer alternative carrots. One was a soft loan of $100 million for Sri Lanka to make defense purchases, but with the proviso that these would be restricted to "defensive" equipment (Samanta 2008). Under pressure from the rising crescendo of election-oriented protests against Tamil casualties in the Sri Lankan civil war, Congress president Sonia Gandhi sought to assure the public that India would not provide Colombo with arms that could be used against civilians, "whose welfare remains a matter of utmost concern" (*The Hindu* 2006e).

The hesitancy displayed by the Government of India in providing military assistance to the Sri Lankan government did not mean that its contribution was marginal. On the contrary, though always cautious in trying to avoid domestic repercussions, India supported Sri Lanka in numerous ways and from well before the onset of Eelam War IV in 2006. From time to time, India unobtrusively transferred weapons systems to Sri Lanka. In 2000, the latter purchased an armed offshore patrol vessel, the *Sayura* (Hashim 2013, 175). The ship was fitted with new armaments before being transferred (*Naval Technology* n.d.). This was in addition to other vessels that the Sri Lanka Navy acquired from Israel and the United States (Hashim 2013, 175). In June 2003, it was reported that India had deployed reconnaissance aircraft to help track and destroy LTTE vessels and that the Sri Lankan government had also sought the advice of a retired Indian naval officer of admiral rank to advise it (*Indian Express* 2003). The Indian Coast Guard and the Sri Lankan Navy carried out a joint exercise in December 2004. In June 2005, the foreign ministers of the two countries let it be known that they were discussing the transfer of radars to bolster Sri

Lanka's air defense system (India, Ministry of External Affairs 2005). Once the transfer of equipment had taken place, it came to be known that Indian technicians were deployed in Sri Lanka on training and maintenance duties (*Daily News and Analysis* 2008). In December 2005, the two countries conducted their first joint naval exercise (Sambandan 2005b). In light of the air threat from the LTTE, antiaircraft guns were also supplied to Sri Lanka.

Meanwhile, the long-standing practice of training Sri Lankan officers and soldiers had been continuing. In 2008, in a bid to bolster its position in response to China's growing presence in Sri Lanka, India expanded its training programs. It was announced that in 2008–9, roughly five hundred Sri Lankan officers and other ranks would receive training at various institutions specializing in, among other subject areas, counterinsurgency, gunnery, antisubmarine warfare, and a number of technical subjects. Two special courses were also arranged for officer cadets from Sri Lanka (Pandit 2008c).

While India tried to play a low-key role during Eelam War IV, it was kept abreast of Sri Lanka's military operations by top military officials (Gokhale 2009, 124). The Indian government also tried to assist Colombo's military efforts to the extent it could without stimulating opposition in Tamil Nadu. With the help of vessels obtained from India and of Indian and American intelligence inputs, the Sri Lankan Navy was able to deal the LTTE a body blow by systematically destroying a large portion of its "floating arms warehouses"—some of them on faraway seas in the vicinity of Australia and Indonesia—in 2006–7. The material destroyed in these operations included aircraft parts, bullet-proof vehicles, and diving equipment (Gokhale 2009, 125–27; Hashim 2013, 174–76). The Indian Navy also deployed attack vessels against the LTTE in the Palk Strait between northern Sri Lanka and Tamil Nadu (Gokhale 2009, 127).

To counter the air capabilities being developed by the LTTE, India quietly gave Sri Lanka Indra-II Doppler radar systems in 2005, though these had little utility against the relatively low-technology LTTE capability of the time, which consisted of microlight aircraft (Dikshit 2005). In 2006, India also gave Sri Lanka a gift of five Mi-17 helicopters, with the condition that they be painted with the colors of the Sri Lankan Air Force. These enabled the Sri Lankan Army to operate deep inside LTTE-held areas (Gokhale 2009, 121). The one occasion when Indian military presence was highly visible in Sri Lanka was in August 2008, when the 15th summit meeting of the South Asian Association for Regional Cooperation was held in Colombo. At the time, at India's insistence, Sri Lanka permitted the deployment of Indian naval ships, antiaircraft guns, and helicopters in the vicinity of its capital (Gokhale 2009, 123–24). Interestingly, on this occasion, India asked President Rajapaksa to try and conclude the civil war before the Lok Sabha elections, scheduled for 2009 (Gokhale 2009, 124). Clearly, Indian military assistance was important in helping Sri Lanka win Eelam War IV. But it was not comparable to the role played by China, which provided it with major weapons systems as well as infrastructure investment and political backing in international institutions.

As the civil war tilted against the LTTE and reached its final and most violent stage, India had to battle growing internal protests. The general election of 2009 was nearing and political parties in Tamil Nadu stepped up their campaign to intervene on behalf of their fellow Tamils. By this time, the focus had shifted from saving the LTTE to saving the Tamil population of Sri Lanka. This was certainly an issue that acquired more political traction. Unlike the LTTE, which had earned a bad reputation because of its association with ruthless violence, the Tamils of northern Sri Lanka were hapless victims of the war. Caught between the brutality of the LTTE and a military prepared to overlook large-scale civilian casualties in the drive for final victory, they were subject to excessive violence from both sides. According to the International Crisis Group (2010, 5, 6n23), the number of civilian fatalities in the last five months of the war was somewhere in "the tens of thousands," with the great majority being killed by government forces. A United Nations–mandated panel report tentatively put the number of civilian deaths as up to 40,000 (United Nations 2011, 41).

But the view from New Delhi had less to do with human rights concerns and more with Indian strategic priorities. External Affairs Minister Pranab Mukherjee told the Rajya Sabha (the upper house of Parliament), "In our anxiety to protect the civilians, we should not forget the strategic importance of this island to India's interests" (quoted by *Indian Express* 2008e). Referring to the growing influence of China and Pakistan in Sri Lanka, he further said, "We cannot have a playground of international players in our backyard," and added that it had been conveyed to Colombo that India would "look after your security requirements, provided you do not look around" (quoted by *Indian Express* 2008e). India's inclination was to lean toward the Government of Sri Lanka while publicly pressing for restraint on its part and averring that its primary concerns were for the civilian populace (Subramanian 2011). Accordingly, as evidenced by leaked US government cables recounting his visit to Colombo, Mukherjee made it clear that India would not try to moderate the Sri Lankan military campaign but that "military victories offer a political opportunity to restore life to normalcy in the Northern Provinces and throughout Sri Lanka after twenty-three years of conflict" (quoted by Subramanian 2011).

But Indian policymakers were caught in a difficult situation as the tumult of Tamil Nadu politics in the run-up to the 2009 elections became ever more raucous with all the state's parties taking up the Tamil cause, resulting in clamorous rhetoric, demonstrations, strikes, fasts, and even suicides (e.g., *Indian Express* 2009; Kolappan 2009; Murari 2009a, 2009b). The uproar subsided once President Rajapaksa had declared the end of major military operations in late April 2009. But the outcome was hardly one calculated to please Indian policymakers. Less than a year later, China consolidated its gains with the announcement that it would extend loans of $200 million for the construction of an airport in southern Sri Lanka; and another $100 million for the construction of a railway line (BBC News 2010).

India's ambivalence was also very visible in its conflicting votes on UN pressures against Sri Lanka's conduct of the war. In May 2009, with international criticism against it rising, Sri Lanka introduced a resolution in the United Nations Human Rights Council emphasizing its sovereign right to conduct the war without external interference. India voted in favor (MacInnis 2009). Subsequently, under pressure from coalition partners, the UPA government voted against Sri Lanka in 2012 and 2013 (Mitra 2017), then abstained in 2014 (Balakrishnan 2014). The hard-to-establish foothold in Sri Lanka as a strategic partner was slipping as India was again proving to be inconsistent and, from the standpoint of its southern neighbor, unreliable.

EXPLAINING DRIFT

India's policy toward Sri Lanka and its Eelam War IV once again corresponds closely to the early phase of neoclassical realist analysis. Systemic incentives were pursued by policymakers, but domestic politics seriously constrained them. The desired objective was to back the Government of

Sri Lanka and promote Indian security interests in two ways. First, India wanted to help destroy the LTTE, which was viewed with increasing alarm as it began to transition from a guerilla band to a military power with the emerging (if limited) capabilities of a proto-state, including a naval and an air arm. Second, a major Indian role in defeating the LTTE would have entrenched India's strategic position in Sri Lanka by ensuring that its rivals—mainly China, but also Pakistan—were prevented from establishing their influence in the country. A third potential gain—a reasonable inference, though not backed by the available evidence—was that a close relationship with its southern neighbor would have encouraged other South Asian states to have similar relationships with India, with positive results for India's security as well as its international status as a rising power.

But India was consistently hampered from pursuing its goals by domestic politics. As in the case of India-US relations, the overall transformation in the tenor of India–Sri Lanka relations, best exemplified by their signing of an FTA barely a decade after the Indian Army's unwelcome arrival on Sri Lankan soil, did not meet with significant resistance within India. But on the specific issue of the civil war and India's role in it, the policy faced strong resistance. The fragmentation of India's domestic political structure left the national government increasingly susceptible to the demands of those political parties in the state of Tamil Nadu that were its coalition partners. These parties in turn were driven not so much by a profound concern for their fellow Tamils in Sri Lanka—commitment to whom was more symbolic than genuinely deep—than by intense electoral contestation accompanied by ethnically colored competitive outbidding at the state level.

India repeatedly held back from a role that would have given it an advantageous position by shaping the end game in Sri Lanka. President Rajapaksa wanted India to be a player—along with the United States, the European Union, Japan, and Norway—in the peace process: "India is the main country, we have to get them involved in the peace process" (Sambandan 2005a). But India stayed out of it. Again, Colombo's first port of call for weapons to combat the LTTE was New Delhi, but India was unwilling to offer the kind of assistance that could have made it the primary contributor to Sri Lanka's needs, thereby ceding first place to China. Even in the case of investment in Hambantota Port, where India viewed China's entry with alarm, Sri Lanka approached Beijing only after India had turned it down (Rediff News 2010). As a result of its indecisive policy, India was left well short of its objective of strengthening its strategic position in Sri Lanka. China established a firm standing in the country as a major arms supplier, while Pakistan also acquired a stake in it. China's gain was in addition to its enormous advantage as a wealthy source of FDI. If India had been the primary provider of military aid for Sri Lanka, this would have offset China's financial advantage. As it turned out, China became the main source for both.

The India–Sri Lanka case is similar to the India-US one, in that the tentativeness of Indian policy was due to the fragmented structure of domestic politics and the resultant weakness of coalition governments in New Delhi. In both cases, small parties that in themselves did not carry much weight—the DMK and the AIADMK in the present instance, and the Communist Party of India (Marxist) in the India-US nuclear deal—were able to exercise inordinate influence in hindering policymakers' pursuit of security objectives. But there is also a key difference. Unlike in the India-US case, the source of the problem faced by New Delhi in executing policy toward Sri Lanka was the competitive ethnic politics set in motion by relatively marginal parties (e.g., the MDMK, the PMK, and the VCK), which enjoyed very little direct appeal with the electorate but were able to set the agenda by playing upon the vulnerabilities of the larger Tamil Nadu parties. This tells us something about the unexpected ways in which what Susan Strange (1988, 25) called "structural power"—the ability to set the agenda or "shape frameworks"—can sometimes work. In certain circumstances, a political agenda might be set by fringe actors rather than by hegemonic players.

For Indian policymakers, the choice was a rational one. As with the India-US nuclear deal, the cost of a decisive policy that disregarded the opposition would have been high, very likely bringing about an early collapse of the government. In the India-US case, however, the cost of *not* pursuing the policy all the way would have also been very high. India would almost certainly have missed the strategic bus that helped it establish a strong security relationship with the United States, without which it would have been left isolated and vulnerable to both China and the nonproliferation regime. Hence, Manmohan Singh eventually (and successfully) risked all in a final throw of the political dice over the nuclear deal. Singh's policy—and, indeed, Vajpayee's earlier policy—toward Sri Lanka was less loaded with serious implications. For one, India was able to retain significant influence with Sri Lanka because it did manage to play a substantial, though not primary, role in that country's prosecution of Eelam War IV. More importantly, though China may have gained substantially by establishing a strong position in Sri Lanka, the loss to Indian security was not as severe as might have been the case if the India-US nuclear deal had failed. Ultimately, as a senior minister in the Mahinda Rajapaksa government has privately acknowledged, Sri Lanka's leaders recognize that its giant neighbor is a fact of strategic life with which it must live, so they are aware they cannot afford to trample on its sensitivities (Interview 2017).

CONCLUSION

The thrust of this chapter has been to demonstrate how system-driven policy preferences have been faced with serious obstacles by the distribution of domestic political power in India. As shown in chapter 2, a broad policy reversal has been carried through because it has not produced sufficient direct effects to spur opposition groups into action. Indian governments seeking closer relations with the United States and Sri Lanka have done so despite stirring criticism on the part of those who might have preferred otherwise. But once more narrow and focused policies falling under the already established general policy have been introduced, opposition groups have been stimulated by varying interests (not necessarily related to the issue at hand, as we have seen in both cases) to mobilize resistance, thereby building oppositional coalitions or commandeering the agenda of big parties to threaten the survival of weak ruling coalitions and consequently to dilute and delay policy.

In the India-US case, the BJP saw an opportunity to try and overthrow the Congress-led ruling coalition, even though the policy pursued by the latter was no different from its own and hence joined forces with the ideologically antagonistic Communist Party of India (Marxist). With respect to India's Sri Lanka policy, the dynamic was similar, in the sense that it was driven by coalition politics, but was different in another way: very small regional parties engaged in ethnic outbidding in order to attain a modicum of power at the state level took control of the political agenda at the state level and, through this, shaped policy at the central level. The big difference between the two cases is that the stakes were much higher for central policymakers trying to reorient India toward the United States. Failure to conclude the nuclear deal would have left India deeply uncomfortable and still in a relatively weak position in global politics. Hence, Prime Minister

Manmohan Singh grasped the nettle and forced his own party to risk its political survival. Indian policy toward Sri Lanka was not subject to such powerful pressures, which made policy drift relatively tolerable. In short, though the material dynamic was similar, the cost/benefit calculus was very different.

In these two chapters, the key to understanding policy drift has been the material distribution of power and the central government's lack of sufficient control over the levers of policy. In the next two chapters, I turn to a very different phenomenon: policy is suboptimal not because policymakers lack control but because they fail to exercise the control they do have in a responsible and accountable way.

Part II

RESPONSIBILITY DEFICITS

4

NUCLEAR STRATEGY

In chapters 2 and 3, we have seen how Indian policymakers adopted policies that responded to systemic incentives. But domestic politics acted as a serious drag on the implementation of specific aspects of those policies. Key policy decisions pertaining to relations with the United States and with Sri Lanka were severely constrained by a material factor: the domestic distribution of power. In this chapter, I focus on a different set of kinetics. Indian governments responded to systemic incentives by crossing the nuclear threshold—in the military capability sense—but have failed to produce optimal policies, not because of domestic structural obstacles but owing to their failure to exercise moral responsibility. The resultant policy drift is what I have called "voluntary," as opposed to the "involuntary" drift observed in chapters 2 and 3. The conceptual difference between the two, it bears recalling, relates to whether policymakers have control over the environment in which they function. In involuntary drift, which occurs under pressure from the distribution of domestic political power, they do not; in voluntary drift, where that structure is not a significantly inhibiting factor, they largely do. In this chapter, I treat policy drift as voluntary because policymakers have substantial control over the policy process but fail to exercise their responsibility in fashioning cost-effective policies. This shortcoming represents what I called a "responsibility deficit" in chapter 1—that is, a substantial gap between what policymakers themselves broadly (and responsibly) desired and what was actually done, owing to their failure—and not inability—to act in morally appropriate ways.

In this chapter, I show that Indian policymakers have yet to develop a clear sense of what is required to exercise nuclear deterrence and, specifically, what is meant by "minimum" deterrence. As a result, nuclear strategy has developed a deep internal contradiction and exhibits two sets of incompatible features. On one hand, it retains the minimalist character of deterrence posture initially espoused under the rubric of "minimum deterrence" by, among other things, refraining from actively deploying their weapons. On the other hand, it leans toward a maximalist posture by investing in weapons systems that are well beyond the requirements of a minimum deterrence strategy. Contrary to the impression held by some analysts, the roots of the problem lie not in the pathologies of bureaucratic politics or civil–military relations but in the failure of the political leadership to make the effort to grasp the essence of nuclear deterrence.

With respect to nuclear strategy, the gap between intent and outcome is the result of confusion in coming to grips with fundamentals. The foundation of nuclear strategy is a set of principles that are applied to national security objectives. These have to do, fundamentally, with the purposes accorded to nuclear weapons, the kinds and numbers of weapons required to achieve these objectives, and the posture best suited to meet the objectives. Having decided that a minimalist form of nuclear deterrence was a core requirement for national defense, Indian policymakers still remain unclear about how deterrence works and about the instruments required for it. This is a persistent problem because strategic thinking and posture draw from ideas about the nature of deterrence that are inherently maximalist.

The broad framework utilized in chapters 2 and 3 is retained in this one. I begin with a brief survey of the historical background for India's acquisition of the bomb, in what was a process of reluctant nuclearization. The shift from the nuclear circumspection of the first four decades after independence to the development of a usable nuclear arsenal, which took place in stages culminating in the nuclear tests of 1998, was a response to the growing perception of external threat. The concept of minimum deterrence was declared an optimal option, providing for security without incurring extensive costs and risks. Once the shift had taken place, however, the inherent contradictions within Indian strategy began to appear. These have intensified in the two decades and more since the 1998 tests and show little sign of being understood, let alone reconciled.

My analysis reviews India's slow and cautious responses to systemic pressures, which ultimately led to the 1998 tests. I then look closely at the concept of "minimum deterrence" through the lens of foundational arguments about the requirements of effective deterrence—many of them stated by Indian military and political leaders at the outset—from which I draw some elementary principles. The actual working of deterrence is shown to be in accord with minimalist principles. Thereafter, I demonstrate the divided character of Indian nuclear strategy by showing how one part of it remains unchanged and minimalist, while another has moved definitively away and adopted a maximalist trajectory. I show how this schizophrenic strategy stems from the conceptual confusion in thinking about nuclear deterrence. In the concluding section of the chapter, I bring in the cost/benefit framework utilized in earlier chapters to explain why this messy situation has continued unchanged and identify shortcomings in responsibility and accountability as its chief source.

HESITANT NUCLEARIZATION

Neoclassical realism in its Type II form holds that systemic conditions generate significant incentives for national policy, though actual policies may vary, depending on a variety of factors operating at the domestic level. The United States and the Soviet Union crossed the nuclear threshold with alacrity, spurred by the perceived threat from adversaries. India's long and slow process of undertaking the shift from a nonnuclear to a nuclear power was shaped by systemic factors—the threat from China and Pakistan, and later the pressure applied by the nonproliferation regime—but simultaneously restrained by deep misgivings about the catastrophic potential of nuclear weapons. Security concerns about China stemmed from defeat in the 1962 Sino-Indian War and the Chinese atomic test of October 1964, followed by four more between then and December 1966. In April 1967, Prime Minister Indira Gandhi wrote to French president Charles de Gaulle that the Chinese threat had made it increasingly difficult to confine India to the peaceful use of atomic energy (Sarkar 2015, 944). Yet Indian leaders had long avoided a definite decision to cross the nuclear threshold on essentially moral grounds. The national leaders Mohandas ("Mahatma") Gandhi and Jawaharlal Nehru had repeatedly expressed their abhorrence of nuclear weapons, with the result that antinuclear sentiment had embedded itself in their thinking (Anand 1998; Bandyopadhyaya 2003, 286–321). Their successors took the same line.

The long-term consequence of this tension was a strategic culture characterized by the constant interplay between systemic pressure and normative restraint (Basrur 2001). The pathway to the bomb was a long and slow one (Basrur 2001; Cohen 2001, 157–84; Jaipal 1977; Kapur 1998, 352–53; Malik 2010; Mukherjee and Sagar 2018; Perkovich 1999; Subrahmanyam

2018). The crossing of the nuclear threshold was an incremental process that took decades and was accompanied by intense debates. Indian leaders never allowed their deep moral reservations about the bomb to eclipse an underlying element of realism. Nehru, who had deep misgivings about nuclear weapons, acknowledged in a file noting that nuclear technology carried the "built-in advantage" of being available for defense if necessary (Kapur 1976, 193–94). As the weight of security concerns grew, the Indian response was to inch forward cautiously. Nehru's successor as prime minister, Lal Bahadur Shastri, responded to China's first test by authorizing the secret Subterranean Nuclear Explosion Project to develop Indian nuclear-weapons capability but ordered that the program stop well short of testing (Subrahmanyam 2018, 27). Indira Gandhi—though in many ways a hard-boiled realist—rejected nuclear deterrence as "untenable" (Pande 1989, 363).

This normatively shaped circumspection on the bomb was also influenced by uneasiness about the negative political impact of the bomb, as exemplified in a secret letter written by Laxmi Kant Jha, secretary to Mrs. Gandhi, to a colleague, wherein he brooded on the tension between going nuclear in response to the Chinese threat and the prospect of "losing the ideological battle against China in the process" (quoted by Sarkar 2015, 945). Mrs. Gandhi eventually chose to test (1974), but to eschew the stockpiling of warheads, though she did later authorize a missile development program during the 1980s. The approach adopted was an uneasy compromise: Indian leaders stopped short of developing a nuclear arsenal but nevertheless kept the door open for the possibility of crossing the threshold by slowly developing the technical capabilities required for producing atomic weapons and the means of delivering them. Even the doughty opponent of nuclear weapons, Morarji Desai, who succeeded Mrs. Gandhi as prime minister in 1977, accepted the majority opinion of his inner cabinet and authorized resumption of nuclear weapons development in 1979 (*The Hindu* 2004b).

Over time, security concerns grew, as the China threat was matched by a Pakistani threat from the early 1970s onward. The latter development prompted Prime Minister Rajiv Gandhi, an advocate of a universal nuclear ban, to cross the nuclear threshold and order the building of a small covert arsenal (Chengappa 2000, 331–32; Subrahmanyam 2018, 44). But Indian capabilities remained very limited, and there was little effort to build an organizational structure around the weapons.

INDIA'S NUCLEAR COMING OUT: NO DOMESTIC FALLOUT

After the end of the Cold War, a major source of threat was the pressure applied on India by the United States–led nonproliferation regime to roll back its covert nuclear weapons program (Saksena 2006). It was this that proved to be the last straw for what had become by then an increasingly untenable policy position. The decision to test was first made by Prime Minister P. V. Narasimha Rao in December 1995; but he held back, partly under pressure from the United States, which learned about Indian preparations in advance, though also because the policy community was divided over the political and economic costs that would follow (Subrahmanyam 2004a, 593). Eventually, Vajpayee took the plunge and carried out the tests of 1998.

Why did India cross the threshold? A number of explanations have focused on the domestic factors at work: the Bharatiya Janata Party's ideological proclivities (the symbolic value of asserting national power), the party's desire to consolidate its hitherto precarious electoral gains, and the lobbying of interest groups, especially the nuclear bureaucracy (Abraham 1998; Bajpai 2009; Ganguly 1999; Perkovich 1999; Sharma 1998). But these explanations are inadequate. First, as Ganguly (1999) notes, explanations at the domestic level of analysis fail to acknowledge that the Bharatiya Janata Party had long incorporated the need to go nuclear in its platform. Second, we know that Vajpayee himself had a history of doubts about the morality and the strategic value of the bomb (BBC News 2002; Subrahmanyam 2004b). And third, India had serious security concerns, owing to perceived threats from China and Pakistan as well as the US-led nonproliferation regime (Malik 1998; Paul 1998). The last was particularly irksome because India and the United States had long been on opposing sides of the regime, which India regarded as a threat to its status as well as security (Paul 1998). A realist explanation, therefore, stands on strong ground.

The 1998 tests did not meet with much domestic opposition. Antinuclear intellectuals and left-wing parties did object, arguing that India could ill afford the expense of a nuclear arsenal; that China would now target it (which they oddly assumed it had not done before); that Pakistan, which had followed suit with its own tests, would now have the opportunity to intensify its support for insurgency within India; that costly international sanctions would be imposed on India; and that India's global image would be diminished (Malik 2010, 237–45). But on the whole, there was little public opposition to the dramatic change in India's position on nuclear weapons (Bhaumik and Gupta 1998). As some pre-1998 studies have shown, there had never been much public concern about nuclear weapons (Cortright and Mattoo 1996, 117–18; Nandy 1972, 1535). After the 1998 tests, public opinion was positive and the Vajpayee government drew popular support, not least because it had cocked a snook at what was widely seen as the shallow nonproliferation moralizing of the United States (Malik 2010, 241, 245). The costs, to the extent that there were some, were not the result of domestic opposition but came from external reaction. The United States imposed sanctions and was followed by Australia, Japan, and other countries. But the spate of sanctions receded after President Bill Clinton withdrew them just six months later (Morrow and Carriere 1999). At this point, then, Indian policymakers faced no serious pressures with regard to unfolding a nuclear strategy and an organization to match it.

The fitful nuclearization process outlined above was certainly a kind of "drift" (Sarkar 2015). But though this is not entirely an inaccurate description, the drift thus far had been a conscious one characterized by much debate. Moreover, it had been about a single decision: whether to cross the nuclear threshold; though, once the bomb had been covertly acquired, it was more a question of declaratory policy. The policy drift described next relates to the *content* of strategy over time and has been largely unconscious: it does not seem that policymakers are even aware of their confusion.

THE DRIFT IN STRATEGY

Nuclear strategy began to stray from the straight and narrow immediately after the tests. Having crossed the nuclear Rubicon, Indian policymakers were clear that their understanding of deterrence was minimalistic. The immediate official announcement after the tests proclaimed adherence to "minimum" deterrence, as announced by Prime Minister Vajpayee in Parliament (Sagar 2009, 244). But what exactly *is* minimum deterrence? Certainly, there has been no shortage of contemporary discussion and debate over minimum deterrence on a global scale (Chalmers, Somerville, and Berger 2011; Doty 2009; Forsyth 2016; Hoeber 1978–79; Payne and Schlesinger 2014; Schneider 2014; Sokov 2007). Doctrinal questions have been widely discussed in India, as I show in some detail below. Although the question "what does it take to deter?" is inherently resistant to precision, the concept must at least rest on recognized assumptions and principles and, equally, on evidence drawn from strategic experience. Granted, deterrence is hard to prove. It can be said to work when an adversary does not do something, but it is hard to prove what has not happened. This difficulty has caused debates over the workability of deterrence, which may be said to be lacking in empirical grounding. Much of the literature cited above and later in this chapter lacks a systematic exposition about the fundamentals of minimum deterrence. The same applies to India's declared doctrine of "credible minimum deterrence."

The rest of the story in this chapter is about India's deviation from its own declared nuclear doctrine of minimum deterrence, a meandering passage that is imperfectly understood by policymakers and strategic experts. My critique is explicitly about deviation from what policymakers themselves see as their objectives. To fully comprehend the concept of minimum deterrence, it is necessary to define it—a task that few have attempted in a systematic way, and certainly not the Indian government. In chapters 2 and 3, policy objectives, though not always explicitly spelled out, were quite clear from the thrust of policy efforts. The deviation here follows much the same pattern: an objective is stated, policymakers begin by acting in accordance with it, and deviation occurs. The difference is that, in the present case, the discordance that appears is not the consequence of the structure of domestic power but lies within policymakers' own sphere of capability and responsibility—in the conceptualization (or, really, the lack of it) of the policy itself.

To assess the initial correspondence of Indian doctrinal thinking with minimalism, I begin with a discussion of the assumptions and principles of minimum deterrence as an ideal type and show that, at the outset, Indian doctrinal thinking was close to it but not consistent with it. To arrive at this ideal type, which has not been done at length in the literature cited above, I review a debate on the basic principles of deterrence that took place in the heyday of the Cold War between two foundational exponents of nuclear strategy. Albert Wohlstetter, a reputed American thinker from the RAND Corporation, represents what might be called nuclear orthodoxy, with his systematic enunciation of deterrence doctrine—one that still exercises a powerful influence around the world, including in India. Ranged against him is Patrick Blackett, a largely forgotten British physicist who challenged Wohlstetter's thinking, starting with first principles. The debate is particularly interesting because both were men of scientific temperament and yet differed enormously on the working of nuclear deterrence. Wohlstetter was a mathematician and systems analyst; Blackett a physicist (he won a Nobel Prize in 1948) and defense adviser to the wartime British government (on Wohlstetter, see Rosecrance 1991 and Zarate and Sokolski 2009; on Blackett, see Howard 1991 and Nye 2004).

The chief differences between Wohlstetter and Blackett were as follows. First, the edifice of Wohlstetter's views on deterrence was built on the risk of surprise attack, a concern that grew out of the American experience of Pearl Harbor, on which his wife, Roberta Wohlstetter, had written a major study (Wohlstetter 1962). In his view, deterrence was not "automatic," and a nuclear Pearl Harbor was in the cards because an adversary might judge that it would stand to gain an advantage from a major surprise attack (Wohlstetter 1958; see also Wohlstetter 1959). He also believed the Soviet Union had the advantage of secrecy in launching a first strike because of its authoritarian system, in contrast to the democratic American system (Wohlstetter 1958, 8). Blackett, conversely, downplayed the risk of a surprise first strike, arguing that any strike must be preceded by preparations that will be visible to the target state (Blackett 1961, 11–12).

Second, Wohlstetter (1958, 16) believed that deterrence can only be effective if the possible damage to an attacker is vast. The Soviet Union, in his view, having survived 20 million deaths in World War II, would be willing to absorb high levels of damage in a nuclear war. Rejecting this, Blackett (1961, 12) argued that Russia had a history of defending against attack rather than aggression and that "any country which has experienced the horror of losing 20 million people in one war is very unlikely to take any avoidable risk of it happening again." Third, the combination of the two points made above—the risk of a surprise attack, and the need to pose the threat of massive damage to deter—led Wohlstetter (1958, 7) to lean heavily on the concept of "second-strike capability"—that is, the ability to survive a first strike, to "make and communicate the decision to retaliate," and to reach and destroy a large number of enemy targets after penetrating enemy defenses. Blackett (1961, 10–11) retorted that a state contemplating aggression could not afford to assume that it could knock out all enemy forces in a first strike and that, given the massive destructive power of atomic weapons, there would always be the risk of millions of fatalities arising from even a relatively small counterstrike.

Fourth, for Wohlstetter it followed that, to ensure that large-scale damage would be caused after surviving a first strike, a state would need to possess large and diverse forces. A small force would not be able to deter a larger one effectively (Wohlstetter 1961, 363–64). A favorable balance of forces was therefore desirable. Blackett, because he believed the damage requirement for deterrence is not very large, demurred and argued that an attacker five times stronger than a defender would still be deterred since the cost imposed on the former by the latter's retaliation would remain unacceptably high. It followed that no country could enjoy nuclear superiority in any practical sense (Blackett 1961, 11–12).

The debate has an important bearing on how states determine their nuclear doctrines and postures. The practical implications of the two arguments, which are summarized in table 4.1, diverge considerably for decision-makers seeking to determine the allocation of resources. The table shows how very different doctrines, weapons requirements, and postures follow from the two perspectives.

The Wohlstetter "model" is essentially maximalist, and the Blackett "model" is essentially minimalist. These are, of course, ideal types, but they help us place the nuclear powers somewhere along a spectrum. The United States and the Soviet Union / Russia, with their giant arsenals of cutting-edge weapons systems, are closer to the maximalist end, while China, India, and Pakistan, all of which have much smaller and less sophisticated arsenals, are closer to the minimalist end, although all three have been drifting in significant ways toward the maximalist side (Basrur 2013). As I show below, the Indian position has in important respects shifted away from the minimalist end of the spectrum and toward the maximalist side.

The ideal-type Wohlstetter and Blackett models are deductive, relying on inferences rather than on evidence of the actual working of nuclear deterrence. It does have more empirically grounded echoes in contemporary debates over the bargaining advantages of a favorable balance of nuclear capabilities (Kroenig 2018; Sechser and Fuhrmann 2017). But these confrontations are in many cases not really of the kind that threaten nuclear war—for example, those cited by Kroenig over Congo in 1964 and Nicaragua in 1984 (Kroenig 2018, 154, table 1). I take a closer—though necessarily brief—look

Table 4.1 Practical Implications of the Wohlstetter-Blackett Debate

Aspect of Debate	*Maximalist Approach (Wohlstetter)*	*Minimalist Approach (Blackett)*
Basis of deterrence	Certainty of damage	Risk of damage
Required damage levels	Very high	Not very high ("unacceptable")
Quality and quantity of weapons systems	Large and varied; favorable balance desirable	Sufficiency easily achieved with small numbers; balance unimportant
Survivability of forces (and desirability of a triad)	Imperative	Not a major concern
Deployment	Hair-trigger alert	Relaxed (active deployment not necessary)
Targeting	Countervalue as well as counterforce (military targets)	Countervalue (especially cities)

at empirical evidence from tensions between six pairs of nuclear rivals and their hostile interaction to consider what their strategic behavior implies for the Wohlstetter and Blackett models. I focus on confrontations where the possibility of war was either partially realized through actual combat or came close to being realized. The six pairs are: during the Cold War era, the United States and the Soviet Union, the United States and China, and the Soviet Union and China; and, during the post–Cold War period, the United States and North Korea, India and Pakistan, and India and China. In all these confrontations, the presence of nuclear weapons at varying levels of capability prevented the outbreak of a full-scale war. Equally significant from the standpoint of the present analysis, variations in the balance of capabilities between the two contestants had no significant bearing on the outcome. (At the time of finalizing this book—the spring of 2022—there have been substantial tensions between the United States and Russia and between the United States and China, but no military confrontations.)

The Cuban Missile Crisis (1962) between the United States and the

Soviet Union concluded with a compromise in which the former agreed to withdraw its missiles from Turkey, while the latter did the same with its plan for missiles in Cuba (Hershberg 1995; Lebow and Stein 1994; Munton and Welch 2007). At the time, Soviet warheads, numbering 3,346, were a small proportion (13.10 percent) of the 25,540 possessed by the United States (Norris and Kristensen 2013, 78, figure 2). There is no evidence that the balance of forces had any bearing on the outcome, nor that any advantage (from the Wohlstetter perspective) accrued to the United States, which alone possessed "second-strike capability."

During the Vietnam War, Chinese and American aircraft clashed occasionally in the air and, on a larger scale, with Chinese antiaircraft batteries firing at US planes (Chen 2001, 227; Levering 2005, 104; Goldstein 2003, 748; Stoessinger 1994, 83–84; Zhai 1998, 107). Though no crisis occurred, there was a significant risk of escalation of combat, and both countries exercised caution in not allowing that to happen. Once again, the nuclear balance was distinctly in favor of the United States. As late as 1969, China's 50 warheads were a minuscule proportion (0.18 percent) of the 27,552 possessed by the United States (Norris and Kristensen 2013, 78, figure 2). Yet the latter refrained from a preemptive war against China's fledgling arsenal and tolerated significant combat losses. In short, neither the favorable balance enjoyed by the United States nor China's lack of second-strike capability affected the outcome.

In yet another instance of serious confrontation involving limited combat, Soviet and Chinese forces clashed repeatedly over their disputed border starting in the mid-1960s, which led to considerable fighting in 1969, when there seemed to be a very real threat of nuclear war (Gelman 1982, 26; Chang 1990, 44–45, 285–86; Lewis and Xue 1988, 51–72, 213). At the time, the nuclear balance heavily favored the Soviet Union: in 1969, China's 50 warheads constituted a tiny 0.47 percent of the Soviet total of 10,671 warheads (Norris and Kristensen 2013, 78, figure 2). However, as in the preceding cases, there is no evidence that the distribution of capabilities influenced the outcome of the confrontation, which was an agreement to withdraw and negotiate.

Similarly, the nuclearization of North Korea sharpened the ongoing tension between it and the United States (Mazarr 2007; Manning 2002; Roehrig 2006). Why did the United States, with its enormous conventional and nuclear strength, hold back from a nuclear strike? It is not clear how many warheads North Korea had in its possession in 2006; as late as 2013, one reasonable calculation—on the basis of its estimated plutonium stockpile—was that the number could at best have been around 8 to 12 (Norris and Kristensen 2013, 78, figure 2). If we reckon the number to be 8 in 2006—likely an overestimation—this would have amounted to a tiny 0.10 percent of the 7,853 in the US arsenal at the time. Pyongyang should have been very vulnerable to American pressure, but its minimal capacity was sufficient to cause Washington to be cautious, particularly because it was known that many of North Korea's nuclear facilities were well concealed (Cumings 2003; Shanker and Sanger 2003).

The confrontations between India and China along their disputed borderlands in 2017 and 2020–21 reflect the same pattern seen above (Basrur 2019; Bloomfield 2021; Menon and Kanisetti 2021; Westcott 2021). The imbalance in capabilities was considerable. A report dated January 2018 put India's warhead numbers, 130 to 140, at about half of China's 280; and the proportion was similar in 2020, with India's warheads at 150 and China's at 320 (SIPRI 2018, 2021). Nevertheless, both sides demonstrated equal nuclear prudence, and China's greater weight in numbers had no bearing on the outcome (in the latter case, until the time of writing in the spring of 2022).

The case of India and Pakistan is interesting because it is different in one respect (Chari, Cheema, and Cohen 2007; Cohen 2013; Ganguly 2002; Ganguly and Hagerty 2005; Paul 2005). The two are relatively small nuclear powers, but, though both have lacked second-strike capability in the Wohlstetterian sense, mutual deterrence has clearly been in place through a series of crises from the late 1980s onward. During the Kargil crisis in 1999, both were estimated to possess just 8 warheads, while in the crisis of 2001–2, India was believed to have 23 and Pakistan 26 (Norris and Kristensen 2013, 78, figure 2). The two crises revealed that small nuclear arsenals do deter and that assured second-strike capability based on large and varied forces (as required by Wohlstetter) is not the sine qua non of effective deterrence.

The conclusion is inescapable that Wohlstetter's view of the requirements of deterrence is off the mark and that Blackett's assessment is more accurate. Regardless of the balance of nuclear forces, states faced with the prospect of nuclear conflict have been deterred from going to war, including a full-scale, conventional war. In essence, Blackett's conception of how nuclear deterrence works is correct: the potential to inflict limited damage, a relaxed posture, and relatively small forces constitute the requirements of deterrence. In short, deterrence by definition occurs at a minimal level. The rest is window dressing. Some support for Wohlstetter's view has appeared recently. Keir Lieber and Daryl Press (2006) have argued that advances in counterforce technology have undermined deterrence. But in light of how actual crises have played out, one wonders whether decision-makers contemplating a first strike will be content to depend on the kind of computer modeling they use.

Conceptualizing Minimum Deterrence: Strategy Adrift

The discussion above shows that, to arrive at a clear and sensible nuclear doctrine and attendant posture, it is necessary to begin with fundamentals. Although, in several respects, early Indian thinking was close to the minimum ideal type outlined above, it was never consistent and systematic to begin with, and there is no evidence that India's civilian and military leaderships have given methodical consideration to nuclear doctrine based on available evidence rather than preference derived from the opinions of others. Instead of starting with first principles based on empirical evidence, it has been erratic, drawing from both the minimalist and maximalist strains identified above. While claiming ownership of minimum deterrence, it has picked up a vocabulary replete with concepts ("vulnerability," "survivability," "second-strike capability") that are anything but minimalist, for they are drawn from writings that clearly reflect—whether or not they have read him—the writings of Albert Wohlstetter, writings that facilitated the accumulation of tens of thousands of warheads and an open-ended spiral of arms racing that persists today.

In contrast, almost nothing of Blackett's views is known in India today despite the fact that he played an important part in establishing the foundations of India's defense establishment. Blackett was a friend of Nehru and regularly stayed at the Indian premier's residence on his visits to the country. He was appointed as a defense adviser by Nehru and wrote a seminal report on the organization of India's defense (Blackett 1948). This report, which led to the establishment of the Defense Science Organization, later called the Defense Research and Development Organization—which produces India's nuclear missiles today—was welcomed by Nehru (1948). Nehru was also familiar with Blackett's ideas on nuclear weapons and had read his *Atomic Weapons and East-West Relations* "with considerable profit" (Nehru 1957). Blackett was also a close friend of Homi Bhabha, who headed India's civilian nuclear program at the time and was a strong advocate of the bomb.

There is also evidence that Blackett's thinking about nuclear weapons issues was known to a wider Indian audience at the time. In April 1949, an Indian journal, *The Thought*, carried a review of his *Military and Political Consequences of Atomic Energy* (Review 1949). Interestingly, *Atomic Weapons and East-West Relations* was reviewed in the official military journal, *Sainik Samachar* (= *Military News*), with the reviewer noting his "plea for the reduction of nuclear weapons to the absolute minimum" (Karunakaran 1960). Perhaps Blackett's views on deterrence have faded because there was little interest in deterrence doctrine and practice when he was writing, and perhaps too because strategic history has not received the kind of attention it needs in India.

In the early years of Indian deterrence thinking, there was nevertheless considerable overlap between Blackett's ideas and that of some Indian thinkers. As one study has shown, most experts favored small numbers of weapons (even some hawks thought less than a hundred would suffice), a nondeployed posture, the capability to inflict unacceptable (rather than massive) damage, and a no-first-use (NFU) retaliation-only posture (Basrur 2001). However, none was consistent. For instance, even as he expounded a minimalist vision in which a triad of land-, air- and sea-based weapons would not be necessary and nuclear balancing with adversaries would not be required, External Affairs Minister Jaswant Singh, in a wide-ranging interview on the requirements of deterrence, stressed the importance of "credibility" and "survivability," terms that reflect Wohlstetter's maximalist thinking (*The Hindu* 1999). This was clearly not based on historical evidence, of which there was plenty at the time from the history of the Cold War. As I have shown, in none of the crises mentioned above is there evidence that these concepts were at all relevant. It is a glaring reflection of the weakness of Indian deterrence thinking that the term "credible" is almost always attached to "minimum deterrence" without clarity on what precisely is meant by this. In all the crises touched on above, there was never any question of "credibility" in assessing even the most minimally capable of adversaries.

But to avoid ambiguity, it is useful to define what is meant by minimum deterrence in concrete terms. Drawing from table 4.1 and adjusting for certain specific aspects of doctrinal choice in the Indian doctrinal context, I define several characteristics that differentiate a minimalist from a maximalist model of deterrence. The characteristics are as follows.

Basis of Deterrence

The minimalist model rests on posing a risk to the adversary (who cannot know in advance the extent of damage that will be inflicted), while the maximalist one insists on certainty of successfully targeting the adversary. It follows that "credibility" is not central to the first position but is vital to the second.

Required Damage Levels

Minimum deterrence is based on "unacceptable damage" of an unspecified level. This is inherently difficult to quantify, but is generally understood in contradistinction to the maximalist approach, which tends to base its requirement on a very large quantum of damage or on a substantial proportion of the adversary's population (say, in the millions).

Quality and Quantity of Weapons Systems

From the perspective emanating from Blackett's thinking, sophisticated and large arsenals are not required because the risk of unacceptable damage can be posed with small numbers of relatively simple weapons. In contrast, because they need to be certain of inflicting large-scale damage, those espousing the Wohlstetter perspective tend to favor high-quality weapons in substantial numbers. Minimalists are confident that balances do not matter very much: larger arsenals can be deterred by smaller arsenals capable of causing unacceptable damage. But for maximalists, balances are important because they affect the ability to cause massive damage after absorbing a first strike.

Warhead Testing

Warhead testing is a subcategory of the quality of weapons systems, but it needs to be singled out in the Indian case given that the limited number of tests carried out thus far by India—one in 1974 and five in 1998—has raised questions about Indian capabilities, particularly about the claim that India tested a thermonuclear weapon in 1998. From Blackett's standpoint, testing is not a critical issue: weapons are generally reliable, and thermonuclear bombs are not essential for the levels of damage capability sought. From the Wohlstetter perspective, because certainty is critical, warheads need to be tested, and the testing of thermonuclear weapons is particularly necessary since they can more easily inflict the large-scale damage necessary for effective deterrence.

Survivability

Adherents of minimum deterrence do not worry too much about the survivability of their weapons. In their view, the enemy cannot be certain of preventing a level of retaliation that will cause unacceptable damage. Those who abide by Wohlstetter's thinking worry a great deal about survivability because they fear that the enemy, by striking first, could deprive them of second-strike capability—the capacity to retaliate in a big way—and the knowledge of this would undermine deterrence. Hence, the possession of a triad of weapons systems—and particularly of nuclear submarine–based weapons—is critically important for them.

Deployment

For a minimalist, a relaxed posture of nondeployed and even unmated weapons in peacetime is ideal because they are less threatening and can be assembled when required. Maximalists would ideally like to be fully prepared with deployed weapons that can be quickly launched.

No First Use

In minimalist thinking, no first use, or "retaliation only," is the centerpiece of deterrence, a contestable point because adversaries are scarcely likely to rely on a declared posture. NFU has been a hotly debated issue. Minimalists swear by its defensive nature and assert that the possibility of retaliation is sufficient to deter, whereas maximalists assert that an NFU posture, which they equate with nondeployment, leaves its adherents vulnerable to a debilitating surprise attack.

Targeting

There is much dispute over the relative merits of massive retaliation and flexible response. Minimalists argue that deterrence works best with the threat of an all-out response to the adversary's crossing of the nuclear threshold. Lower-level options in the form of tactical nuclear weapons raise the risk of an early resort to the use of nuclear force. Maximalists retort that massive retaliation is not credible: why risk mutual suicide in response to a limited attack? The use of tactical nuclear weapons restricts the likelihood of an all-out conflagration.

In light of these categories, it is now possible to gauge where India stands with regard to its official claim to adhere to a minimum deterrence strategy.

India's Divided Strategy

India's slow move toward nuclear capability produced a minimalist strategic culture, which envisaged a small nuclear arsenal with few warheads and delivery vehicles, but one that was inconsistent (Basrur 2001, 2006; O'Donnell 2015). In a long interview in the aftermath of the 1998 tests, Jaswant Singh explained that Indian doctrine did not require more tests, a deployed force (let alone an alert one), or warfighting capability; parity in capabilities was not essential, and neither was a triad; NFU was a central principle; and the distribution of capabilities was not important: "we shall not . . . pursue an open-ended program" (*The Hindu* 1999). In all these respects, Singh stood squarely in the minimalist camp as defined above. But, in other ways, when asserting that minimum deterrence was a "dynamic" concept subject to change and in stressing the need for "survivability of assets" to ensure the "credibility" of a nuclear arsenal, Singh was willy-nilly expressing a Wohlstetterian perspective.

It is not difficult to empirically check the observable key aspects of minimalism/maximalism in Indian nuclear strategy. Below, I look at the evidence with respect to eight criteria: the basis of deterrence (certainty vs. risk); the damage levels believed to be required; the quality and quantity of weapons needed; the position on nuclear testing; the issue of survivability as reflected in the building of a sea-based deterrent; the kind of deployment needed; the priority given to NFU; and the preference for targeting (countervalue vs. counterforce).

There has been much debate in the public realm on these questions (Chari 2014; Jaishankar 2017; Joshi and O'Donnell 2019, 149–55; Kampani 2014a; Lalwani and Haegeland 2017; Rajagopalan 2016b). A brief review of where India stands on the criteria noted above is instructive.

Basis of Deterrence

Although the discourse in India is tolerant of imbalances—there is relatively little concern expressed with respect to China's far greater warhead numbers and more advanced delivery capabilities, such as in multiple warhead missiles—the basis of deterrence leans the other way. The officially used nomenclature of Indian nuclear doctrine—"*credible* minimum deterrence" (emphasis mine)—places it within the maximalist category because credibility is about the certainty of retaliation. Vajpayee told Parliament in December 1998 that "ours will be a minimum credible deterrent" (quoted by Sagar 2009, 244). The quasi-official Draft Nuclear Doctrine (DND) brought out by the National Security Advisory Board in August 1999 repeatedly uses the term "credible" in the text and also stresses the importance of communicating will to the adversary. The 2003 statement on doctrine similarly begins by stating the objective of building a "credible" minimum deterrent. One suspects that this term is used reflexively, without much thought given to what it implies. But that is precisely the source of the problem: a lack of clarity on basic concepts, which places "credible" and "minimum" side by side in what is an oxymoronic term.

Required Damage Levels

The notion of "unacceptable damage" is central to minimum deterrence. And this is a concept that has been emphasized in official Indian statements. The requirement of damage levels has never been publicly quantified, but the focus on "unacceptable damage," combined with the preference for a relatively small arsenal, implies that very high levels of damage of the kind seen in American and Soviet/Russian thinking are not envisaged. Still, there is ambivalence in official thinking. The DND speaks of "punitive retaliation with nuclear weapons to inflict damage unacceptable to the aggressor," which obliquely implies a limited damage requirement. But the 2003 press release refers to retaliation that will be "massive and designed to inflict unacceptable damage," which implies that "unacceptable" damage must be largescale. This brings to mind Robert McNamara's definition of unacceptable damage as the capacity to destroy from a fifth to a fourth of the Soviet population and half to two-thirds of its industry (Treverton 1989, 196). Though Indian thinking may not go that far, the scale of retaliation announced officially is close to a maximalist conception of what is appropriate.

Quality and Quantity of Weapons Systems

Indian officials have implied that they do not seek a large and sophisticated arsenal and that they do not wish to enter into arms races. Vajpayee was categorical in his very first statement before Parliament: "We do not intend to engage in an arms race" (Statement to Parliament by Prime Minister Vajpayee, May 27, 1998). However, there is no clear statement of the requirements of minimum deterrence. On the contrary, it has periodically been asserted that minimum deterrence is flexible; as one official put it, the "idea of minimum deterrence cannot be etched in stone" (quoted by Raja Mohan 1998). Similarly, Jaswant Singh's view of deterrence as "a dynamic concept" that is "firmly rooted in the strategic environment, technological imperatives, and national security needs" (*The Hindu* 1999)—on the face of it a commonsense statement—is one that keeps the door open to large arsenals. The Indian position clearly leans toward maximalism. Broadly, India has been developing and acquiring a wide range of weapons. These include a nuclear triad and missiles with substantial ranges, such as the 5,000+ kilometer–Agni V and the intercontinental ballistic missile (ICBM)–range (8,000–10,000 kilometers) Agni-VI (Kristensen and Korda 2020). Periodic reports have appeared about India's development of multiple warhead or multiple independently targetable reentry vehicle (MIRV) missiles, maneuverable warheads, and hypersonic cruise missiles. But while the quest for a wide variety of weapons systems continues, the number of warheads has not, so far as we know, risen significantly in relation to what India could produce. Though fissile material (notably, reactor-grade plutonium) for a much larger number of warheads is available, the actual number remains relatively low (Tellis 2019). In sum, India is ambivalent: maximalist on variety, and minimalist on numbers.

Warhead Testing

From a minimalist point of view, a limited number of tests is sufficient to prove capability. For maximalists, the more the tests, the better, because tests provide for reliability and incorporate diverse designs. The total number of nuclear tests carried out globally thus far (with simultaneous tests counted as 1 test) is 2,056, of which the United States has carried out the maximum of 1,030 (Nuclear Testing Tally 2019). In comparison, India's tally of 6 tests is very small. But immediately after the May 1998 tests, the Indian government announced a unilateral moratorium on testing (Statement to Parliament by Prime Minister Vajpayee, May 27, 1998). This generated considerable controversy within the atomic energy establishment, with leading technical experts like P. K. Iyengar and A. N. Prasad holding that more tests were essential, though others, led by R. Chidambaram (who led the 1998 testing team), held that they were not (Karnad 2008, 66–69; see also Iyengar 2009, 38). The debate went public in 2009, when K. Santhanam, a senior scientist who had been involved in the tests, claimed that the specific test that had sought to validate a thermonuclear design turned out to be a "fizzle" and more testing was needed (Ahmed 2009; Parashar 2009). But the government dismissed the claim and has since then held fast to the moratorium (*Outlook* 2009). In this instance, the official position has been tenaciously minimalist and India has stuck to its self-imposed moratorium since 1998. This is partly due to the fear of sanctions, but the more important point is that no hint of serious interest in testing has come from official sources. In any case, the debate over testing that has taken place relates to thermonuclear weapons, not nuclear warheads generally. India remains committed to a minimalist position.

Survivability and the Need for a Triad

From a minimalist perspective, survivability is not a major concern. An adversary contemplating a first strike cannot be certain that a substantial retaliation will not follow. Yet official (and unofficial) discourse is replete with the term. Vajpayee told Parliament in his May 1998 statement that Indian deployment would be of a kind "that ensures survivability and capability of an adequate response" (Statement to Parliament by Prime Minister Vajpayee, May 27, 1998). Similarly, the DND repeatedly emphasizes survivability as a basic requirement for deterrence. The emphasis on survivability has profound consequences. It lends itself to the widespread belief that a nuclear triad is essential for a true deterrent force because nuclear-powered submarines carrying nuclear-tipped missiles are said to be the least vulnerable to a first strike. Jaswant Singh did explicitly state in his 1999 interview that a triad is not essential (*The Hindu* 1999). But the need for a sea leg has become an unquestioned orthodoxy in Indian thinking and is reflected in the determined bid to build an "invulnerable" subsurface naval capability. Official thinking is assuredly maximalist. The largely unquestioned rationale for the capability is that the sea leg is the most "survivable" leg of the triad. The quest for submarine-launched ballistic missile capability is in fact an old one, going back to as early as 1967, but has never been based on a clear conceptualization of its strategic role (Joshi 2019; O'Donnell and Joshi 2014).

Deployment

With regard to posture, the Indian position has been consistently minimalist. India's nuclear weapons are not deployed in alert mode but, like those of China and Pakistan, kept in an unassembled state (Chakma 2011, 13–14; Ghoshal 2016). From a minimalist standpoint, active deployment is not necessary for effective deterrence. The DND, for instance, calls for capability for shifting from "peacetime deployment to fully employable forces," which implies that the normal posture it prefers is nondeployed. Jaswant Singh, in his 1999 interview, holds that retaliation "does not have to be instantaneous" and that India rejects launch-on-warning and hair-trigger postures (*The Hindu* 1999). Though occasional claims have been made that India has shifted to active deployment, there is no evidence of such a shift. But the sea leg cannot be operationalized meaningfully without mated weapons. The official position, therefore, is ambivalent. Although the practice has generally been to keep warheads and delivery vehicles separate, a shift to mated weapons has at least in principle been partially accepted with the cannisterization of warheads. As Sundaram and Ramana (2018, 162) observe, cannisterization is "a necessary, although not sufficient, step to moving away from the no first use policy," though the abandonment of NFU is not necessarily inevitable. There is no evidence that the Indian arsenal has shifted to an active or alert mode. India's position remains minimalist, though technology has opened up the possibility of a switch to the maximalist position.

No First Use

As mentioned above, NFU is a deeply embedded concept in Indian strategic thinking. Vajpayee's statement in Parliament after the 1998 tests affirmed a "policy of no-first-use with a minimum deterrent" (quoted by Sagar 2009, 244). It is also clearly implicit in Jaswant Singh's statement above that retaliation need not be immediate. The DND, too, affirms that "India will not be the first to initiate a nuclear strike." To the extent that NFU is practical (after all, who knows who will launch first in a severe crisis?), it would seem to be a bedrock principle. But it *has* been questioned from time to time. In November 2016, Defense Minister Manohar Parrikar questioned its viability, though he said this was his personal opinion (Singh 2016a). Similarly, in August 2019, Defense Minister Rajnath Singh indicated that change in the policy was possible and that "what happens in future depends on the circumstances" (Siddiqui and Murud 2019). But thus far these carefully worded statements have not, so far as we know, translated into a move to shift policy. On this point, minimalism rules. Yet it is also a fact that there have been shifts in the precise content of NFU. Originally, the concept was a blanket and unqualified one. But the 2003 statement on doctrine made two notable changes. First, it said that "nuclear weapons will only be used in retaliation against a nuclear attack on Indian territory or *on Indian forces anywhere*" (emphasis added), which appears to have been aimed obliquely at Pakistan and China, with both of which India has territorial disputes. Second, it asserted that "in the event of a major attack against India, or Indian forces anywhere, by biological or chemical weapons, India will retain the option of retaliating with nuclear weapons." That said, official Indian thinking conforms to minimalism.

Targeting

India's officials have opted for countervalue or city targeting as against counterforce targeting or nuclear warfighting, as Jaswant Singh explicitly asserted (*The Hindu* 1999). But there has been considerable debate over the doctrinal principle of "massive retaliation" against a nuclear attack (Clary and Narang 2018–19). Critics have argued that massive retaliation is not a plausible threat against low-level attacks, for instance the use of tactical nuclear weapons. From this perspective, a "flexible response" strategy of countering threats at different levels is favored by some experts (Clary and Narang 2018/19; O'Donnell 2019). But, as of now, there is little sign of a change in India's official position, which remains firmly minimalist. It is sometimes argued that India is shifting toward a counterforce strategy as it has been developing dual-use short-range missiles such as the 150 kilometer-range Prahaar missile and the 300+-kilometer BrahMos cruise missile (Clary and Narang 2018/19, 28–31; Narang 2014, 171). But while the

Table 4.2 A Divided Strategy

Aspect of Strategy	*Minimalist Preferences*	*Maximalist Preferences*
Basis of deterrence		X
Required damage levels		X
Quality and quantity of weapons systems	X (quantity)	X (quality)
Warhead testing	X	
Survivability and need for a triad		X
Deployment	X	X
No first use	X	
Targeting	X	

possibility of nuclear use is inherent in such dual-use systems, there is no evidence that warfighting has been considered seriously within the government. Minimalism remains unchanged in this respect, though dual-use technology leaves space for a shift.

The overall position can be seen in table 4.2, which illustrates the split in Indian strategy. On the basis of deterrence, the quality of weapons, and survivability (and the possession of sea-based weapons), Indian strategy is maximalist; on all other counts, despite some ambiguities, it remains minimalist.

The discussion above shows the ambivalence in Indian strategy, which lacks coherence and consistency owing to an inadequate grasp of the fundamentals of nuclear deterrence. Table 4.2 highlights the divided character of the strategy. Out of eight criteria, Indian strategic thinking is clearly minimalist in only three, clearly maximalist in three, and split between categories in two.

Intellectual Ambivalence and the Drift: Nuclear Experts and Minimum Deterrence

In this subsection, I utilize the eight criteria employed above to assess the tenor of experts' thinking about the requirements of nuclear deterrence. Because none has attempted a methodical and comprehensive discussion on nuclear strategy, not every criterion employed here to define deterrence has been discussed by each author. The purpose here is to gauge where strategic thinkers stand in a holistic sense by systematically placing them within the appropriate boxes of minimalism and maximalism. Elsewhere, I have examined earlier thinking both before and after the 1998 tests to demonstrate the ambiguity pervading Indian nuclear doctrine (Basrur 2006). In this subsection, I look at similar ambivalence prevailing within more recent articulations. I review at length five thinkers closely related to the policy-making process, all of whom were involved with post-1998 nuclear policy to a greater or lesser degree and all of whom have written and spoken about the requirements of nuclear deterrence.

Two of the five are former apex-level civilian officials; two are former military officials who had commanded nuclear forces; and one is a former military officer who, postretirement, was part of the civilian policy structure for national security. These are, respectively, Shivshankar Menon, a retired foreign secretary and subsequently national security adviser; Shyam Saran, a retired foreign secretary, former chairman of the National Security Advisory Board, and former chairman of a think tank; Lieutenant-General (retired) B. S. Nagal, a retired army officer who headed India's Strategic Forces Command while in service and later a major army-related think tank; Admiral (retired) Arun Prakash, who retired as chief of naval staff and chairman of the Chiefs of Staff Committee; and Lieutenant-General Prakash Menon (retired), who postretirement became a military adviser to the national security adviser and later joined a prominent think tank.

Shivshankar Menon

Menon is generally supportive of official doctrine and strategy, which he considers "today the best policy" (Varadarajan 2016). Hence, I treat his views as in accord with the official position when he does not offer an opinion.

Basis of deterrence. Though not expressly stated, his view appears mixed. On Pakistan's capability, he acknowledges that, even if Pakistan exaggerates its capabilities, India cannot call its bluff (Varadarajan 2016), which means that risk is the basis of deterrence. Elsewhere, he emphasizes that deterrence must be "credible" (Varadarajan 2016) and "assured" (Menon 2016, 107, 108), which leans toward certainty of damage.

Required damage levels. He is supportive of massive retaliation and asserts that "retaliation will be big" (Varadarajan 2016).

Quality and quantity of weapons systems. There is no thorough discussion of this, but I attribute this to his tacit acceptance of current acquisition policy, which—as shown above—is maximalist. But he is positively minimalist when he states that "matching" an adversary's capabilities is not important (Menon 2016, 108).

Testing. Menon does not discuss this, which implies that he is comfortable with the official minimalist moratorium.

Survivability and the need for a triad. Survivability is seen as essential and, in his view, should be backed by a sea-based capability as part of a "genuine triad" (Menon 2016, 108, 112; Varadarajan 2016).

Deployment. This, too, is not discussed, which means he is in accord with the ambivalent official position of nondeployment of weapons generally, which does not apply to submarine-launched ballistic missiles.

No first use. Menon is generally supportive of NFU, regarding a first-use doctrine as "destabilizing" (Menon 2016, 110, 116). But he qualifies this by saying that "circumstances are conceivable in which India might find it useful to strike first, for instance, against an NWS [= nuclear weapons state (in a generic sense)] that had declared it would certainly use its weapons, and if India were certain that adversary's launch was imminent" (Menon 2016, 110). Thus, he is both minimalist and maximalist, without explaining the contradiction.

Targeting. He finds nothing wrong with the official position and rejects the notion that there is a difference between tactical and strategic weapons (Menon 2016, 111). This places him on the minimalist side.

It is clear from the above that Menon's position in the minimalist/maximalist divide is ambivalent. Broadly, he is in the minimalist category on six issues and in the maximalist category on six (with an overlap in four).

Shyam Saran

Basis of deterrence. Leaning into maximalist territory, Saran repeatedly stresses the importance of "credibility," which he elucidates in Wohlstetterian terms, implying certainty of damage (Saran 2013a, 12; 2014).

Required damage levels. Like the 2003 official statement, Saran asserts that retaliation will be "massive and designed to inflict unacceptable damage" (Saran 2013b). The term "massive" brings him to the side of the maximalist position.

Quality and quantity of weapons systems. There is not much discussion on this, but he does mention "long range missile capability" in an approving tone (Saran 2013a, 13). He also obliquely recommends the acquisition of enhanced capability with respect to land-based and sea-based missiles (Saran 2013a, 18–19). This places him in the maximalist category.

Testing. Given his unswerving support for India's nuclear doctrine and posture, it may reasonably be inferred that Saran's thinking is in line with the minimalist official stance.

Survivability and the need for a triad. Saran explicitly affirms the "survivability" of India's arsenal and the value of its triad (Saran 2013a, 12–13; 2014).

Deployment. As above, Saran does not discuss this specifically but may be presumed to be inclined to accept the present official stance, which is ambivalent.

No first use. Again, without discussing its merits, Saran seems to approve of this "central tenet" of India's nuclear doctrine (Saran 2013a, 29).

Targeting. Saran supports the official position on massive retaliation and asserts that "the very distinction between strategic and tactical weapons is untenable" (Saran 2014). This makes him a minimalist.

Like other minimalists, Saran straddles both the minimalist and maximalist positions.

B. S. Nagal

Basis of deterrence. Nagal favors the "credibility principle"—that is, the adversary must "know that India can and will retaliate" (Nagal 2014a, 16). To this end, signaling intent is crucial (Nagal 2014b, 8, 9, 12). From one's own perspective, capability must be "assured" and "fool-proof" (Nagal 2019, 218). This puts him unquestionably on the maximalist side.

Required damage levels. These are high. Indian strategy must plan to destroy a large number of targets, both civilian and military, to ensure that "recovery and reconstruction is long and costly" (Nagal 2014b, 12). Further, the adversary's "entire land mass" and "certain sea zones" must be targeted (Nagal 2019, 220), and "the weapons in the arsenal must all be in the thermonuclear range" (Nagal 2019, 221–22).

Quality and quantity of weapons systems. Nagal is clear that minimum deterrence is "not minimum in size" but "is a dynamic concept related to strategic environment, technological imperatives, and the needs of national security" (Nagal 2014a, 13). Balancing is important: "Adversary arsenal size, technological advances, defensive and offensive forces, protection and C4ISR [command, control, communications, and computers; and intelligence, surveillance, and reconnaissance] are factors for consideration whilst arriving at the size, delivery means and yield of the deterrent" (Nagal 2014a, 13; see also 2014b, 9). India does possess second-strike capability, but "China has an advantage in numbers and range" (Nagal 2015, 13–14). This is a classic Wohlstetterian view. He recommends the acquisition of MIRV and MaRV (manoeuvrable reentry vehicle) capability (Nagal 2014a, 17; 2014b, 10; 2015, 11; 2019, 220–21). Hypersonic and Earth-penetrating weapons are also desirable (Nagal 2019, 221). But he is somewhat self-contradictory in arguing that "pressure to increase the size of the arsenal . . . should be resisted" (Nagal 2014b, 14). In his view, strategic stability requires a "robust strategic nuclear balance" (Nagal 2015, 3).

Testing. Nagal does not discuss the case for more tests, but he does say that India need not doubt its own capability (Nagal 2014a, 17). Computer simulation obviates the need for testing (Nagal 2014b, 9; 2019, 221). This is one area where he is decidedly a minimalist.

Survivability and the need for a triad. Nagal supports the idea of a triad: each leg carries advantages, and the sea leg is "practically invulnerable" (Nagal 2014a, 16; see also 2014b, 12). He is positive on the contribution of missile defense to survivability (Nagal 2014, 17; 2019, 222).

Deployment. He is open to more active deployment because he favors inclusion of launch on warning as an option (Nagal 2014a, 14). He argues that, during the Cold War, high alert levels added to credibility (Nagal 2014b, 9).

No first use. Holding that China's commitment to NFU cannot be trusted (Nagal 2019, 216), Nagal opts for a policy of ambiguity that allows for other options, such as launch on warning (Nagal 2014a, 14; 2019, 216–17). This places him among the maximalists.

Targeting. Nagal discusses the pros and cons of tactical nuclear weapons and finds the latter outweigh the former (Nagal 2014a, 12). He plumps for massive retaliation as carrying several advantages, including minimization of damage to one's own population centers and the problem of escalation attached to counterforce strikes (Nagal 2014a, 14–15), but in a later work he opts for a mix of both strategies (Nagal 2019, 217).

Although overwhelmingly maximalist in his views, Nagal nevertheless makes important concessions on testing and targeting.

Arun Prakash

Basis of deterrence. Prakash (2014, 2–3) is critical of "existential deterrence" and argues for a more "credible" deterrence backed by strong capabilities and organization.

Required damage levels. There is no focused discussion of this in his work.

Quality and quantity of weapons systems. Prakash does not like the idea of a minimal arsenal. He leans toward ICBM capability (Prakash 2014, 4) and calls for submarine-launched ballistic missiles with a range of 8,000–10,000 kilometers (ICBM range) on the ground that can be fired from "safe havens" (Prakash 2018; see also Prakash 2014, 5). He is favorably inclined toward technologies such as MIRVed missiles (Prakash 2014, 5).

Testing. The controversy over the yields of India's 1974 and 1998 tests, in Prakash's view, has led to a "credibility deficit," creating a "real chance of deterrence breakdown" (Prakash 2012, 5). Prakash is of the view that, among other things, India's moratorium on testing "calls for reflection at the highest level" (Prakash 2014, 4). The clear implication is that India needs more tests.

Survivability and the need for a triad. Prakash emphasizes survivability by "hardening, mobility or concealment" (Prakash 2014, 5) and believes that nuclear submarines are the "best way to provide invulnerability" to India's deterrent (Prakash 2018; see also 2014, 5–6).

Deployment. It would be fair to assume that Prakash favors active deployment because no one has made the case that nuclear weapons can be kept demated from nuclear submarines.

No first use. Prakash is uncomfortable with India's "hastily made commitments," such as NFU (Prakash 2014, 4).

Targeting. In Prakash's view, counterforce strategy is untenable: he describes Pakistan as having "stepped into the dangerous realm of tactical weaponry" with the short-range Nasr (Prakash 2012, 8).

Clearly, Prakash is a consistent maximalist, standing on that side of the divide in most categories, but he hews to a minimalist line on targeting.

Prakash Menon

Basis of deterrence. Menon is clear that the basis of deterrence is uncertainty about potential damage, which places him firmly on the minimalist side (Menon 2019).

Required damage levels. These are not discussed at length in his writings, but Menon does imply that one does not need to possess the capacity to inflict large-scale damage: a "residual capacity to strike a limited number of significant targets is sufficient to deter" (Menon 2018, 191). This is a minimalist position.

Quality and quantity of weapons systems. Menon (2018, 90) takes a maximalist position with respect to the quality of weapons, arguing in favor of multiple warhead capability and, for the future, hypersonic vehicles. But he leans toward minimalism when he rejects the notion that large arsenals are desirable: "the natural impulse to seek survivability in size must be resisted" (Menon 2018, 191).

Testing. Menon does not offer any comments on this issue. Given that he has been quite outspoken in his criticisms of policies with which he does not agree, I take his position to be in line with national policy, which has been minimalist.

Survivability and the need for a triad. Like many who otherwise espouse a minimalist perspective, Menon regards the concept of "invulnerable" second-strike capability as the bottom line of deterrence capability (Menon 2019, 11). Accordingly, he has a positive view of the sea leg of the triad (Menon 2012; 2019, 84, 89).

Deployment. Again, he does not discuss this subject specifically. For the same reason as given above, I treat his views as being in line with the official position, which makes it ambivalent.

No first use. Menon (2019, 85) firmly rejects first use: a first-use decision is "virtually impossible to justify."

Targeting. Menon (2018, 86–87) emphatically rejects flexible response, dismissing the idea of calibrated nuclear use as a "theoretical mirage."

Taken as a whole, Prakash Menon's strategic preferences reflect a largely minimalist standpoint. But the exceptions—his belief in the centrality of survivability and second-strike capability, his preference for high-technology weaponry, and his likely acquiescence to the ambivalent official position on posture—erode this position significantly.

Summing Up

What does a composite picture of these views tell us? Table 4.3 demonstrates that the proportion of minimalist to maximalist ideas in them is not very high, both individually and in the aggregate. Note that the preferences

Table 4.3 Experts' Views: Proportion of Minimalist to Maximalist Preferences

Expert	*Minimalist*	*Maximalist*	*Minimalist as Proportion of Total*	*Minimalist as Percentage of Total*
Shivshankar Menon	6	6	6/12	50.00
Shyam Saran	4	5	4/9	44.44
B. S. Nagal	3	7	3/10	30.00
Arun Prakash	1	6	1/7	14.28
Prakash Menon	7	3	7/10	70.00
Total	21	27	21/48	43.75

Note: Totals vary owing to either absence of views or overlapping views in one category. Preferences that are partially minimalist and maximalist are counted as 1 on each side.

of the two top civilians, one a former national security adviser, are evenly divided. Also significant is the fact that all five are at least partly on the maximalist side with respect to the two areas where national policy exhibits a maximalist character—that is, the quality of weapons (but not numbers) and the importance of survivability as the basis of a triad.

Table 4.4 looks at the same data from a different angle: how much support is there for a minimalist position on each of the six criteria? The picture is instructive. There is limited support for the minimalist position on the quality and quantity of weapons taken together (none at all on quality alone, as the individual choices show), and none on the triad. Of the remaining four, there is an even division on NFU, strong support for minimalism on testing and targeting, and greater support for the maximalist position on the basis of deterrence, the required level of damage, and posture. The numbers are broadly in line with the record on what has been done and with official thinking.

EXPLAINING THE DRIFT: THE RESPONSIBILITY DEFICIT

As we have seen, in actions as well as in thinking, there is a duality in Indian strategic thinking. The split has been sustained largely unobserved, let alone explained. How do we account for it? A number of explanations might be offered, but these can for the most part be discounted.

Table 4.4 Proportion of Minimalist Preferences to Maximalist Preferences per Component of Deterrence

Component	*Minimalists*	*Maximalists*	*Minimum as Proportion of Total*	*Minimum as Percentage of Total*
Basis of deterrence	2	4	2/6	33.33
Required level of damage	1	3	1/4	25.00
Quality and quantity of weapons	3	4	3/7	42.86
Testing	4	1	4/5	80.00
Survivability and triad	0	5	0/5	0.00
Posture	3	4	3/7	42.86
No first use	3	3	3/6	50.00
Targeting	5	1	5/6	83.33

Note: Totals vary owing to either absence of views or overlapping views in one category. Preferences that are partially minimalist and maximalist are counted as 1 on each side.

The Domestic Distribution of Power

Chapters 2 and 3 demonstrated how the policies of weak central governments have been held hostage by small veto players. But this does not apply to nuclear strategy because of its esoteric nature. Few understand it, and hence most are inclined to go with the official position. More important for present purposes, the minutiae of nuclear strategy do not impinge on partisan political interests in the way that the policies discussed in the preceding chapters show. There has been no politically significant opposition to Indian nuclear strategy and posture.

The Strategic Enclave

Arguments about the technical bureaucracy's enormous power and capacity to push its agenda have been influential (Abraham 1998; Perkovich 1999). But it has been shown that despite sometimes pushing hard, nuclear scientists have never by themselves managed to persuade even weak prime ministers to authorize testing (Basrur 2001, 189–90). The same applies to the missile producers of the Defense Research and Development Organization, who have repeatedly stated that political approval is a prerequisite for introducing new weapons systems such as ICBMs and MIRVed missiles (Aroor 2013; Interview 2019).

Strategic Culture

Shifts in India's once-minimalistic strategic culture have been identified (Basrur 2001; O'Donnell 2015; Shidore 2015). But these analyses, while providing valuable insights, do not explain fully the dynamics of the shift. Basrur explores the political-ideational divergence; O'Donnell focuses on changes in discourses; and Shidore identifies a shift from "moralism" to "realism." The analysis here goes further by examining the ideational tensions visible in Indian thinking and practice and pinning down their source, which is epistemic rather than simply "cultural," though the former impinges on the latter. Narang suggests the possibility of "multiple strategic cultures" emerging (Narang 2014, 51). If one disaggregates strategic culture into multiple subcultures, fair enough. But from a holistic perspective, and to emphasize the dysfunctional nature of Indian strategy, it would be more appropriate to describe Indian strategic culture as having a split or schizophrenic character.

External Pressure

One interesting explanation is that international nonproliferation pressure compelled the Indian bomb program to operate in tight secrecy, causing it to become dysfunctional (Kampani 2014b). Although this analysis does not directly aim to do so, it throws light on a possible reason why Indian strategy is inconsistent. It points to the possibility that secrecy bred poor understanding of doctrine. But this remains a facilitating condition rather than a direct cause of the problem. Once nuclear weapons had been adopted, clear thinking on the requirements of deterrence was an imperative. O'Donnell's argument that "realism" grew in Indian thinking and that this explains the shift toward maximalism is insightful, but his discussion on the discourse shows this to be an enabling factor rather than a direct one in producing doctrinal shift. Realism does not inherently carry a preference for maximalist nuclear strategy.

Civil–Military Relations

The often-uneasy relationship between the civilian and military branches of the state might be the cause of India's doctrinal ambivalence. The civilian authority kept the defense forces at arm's length for much of the early years of nuclear-strategic thinking (Koithara 2012; Prakash 2014). Hence, it could be said, there was not only slow organizational development but also a lack of intellectual cross-fertilization and development of doctrine. To be sure, many problems related to military effectiveness can be traced to an "absent dialogue" between the civilian and military branches of government (Mukherjee 2020). But the critique does not really apply in the present context. As the review of Indian thinking above shows, there is no substantial difference between civilian and military conceptions of nuclear deterrence in Indian thinking. This also means that, contrary to Narang's claim, strategic culture does not operate "through, and only through, civil-military relations" (Narang 2014, 52). Still, both Mukherjee and Narang have identified something problematic about civil–military relations, which I examine below.

The Responsibility Deficit

The only persuasive explanation is that the Indian leadership's ambivalent understanding of nuclear deterrence reflects a lack of effort to come to grips with it, which in turn speaks of a lack of moral-political responsibility. Political leaders from Nehru onward had tight control over nuclear weapons policy. Yet, even as the process of nuclearization went incrementally ahead, and even as there was intense debate over whether to cross the threshold, no effort seems to have been made to evaluate systematically and on the basis of available evidence the basics of nuclear doctrine: the purpose of possessing nuclear weapons, how deterrence works, and—accordingly—the kinds of weapons that ought to be acquired and the kind of posture adopted. Although the accumulation of vast arsenals by the big powers was viewed with distaste, there was no effort to consider at length the question: how does deterrence operate? By the late 1980s there had been a series of Cold War crises between nuclear powers, so there was empirical ground for examination; but no such inquiry took place. Nor is there much evidence of efforts to reflect at length on India's own experience as a nuclear power that has been embroiled in a series of crises with other nuclear powers.

Critically important questions have not been investigated. Take the question of the sea leg of the triad. Is a sea leg desirable? What are its pros and cons? There is no evidence of any investigation of such questions. On the contrary, the initial green signal given was to develop a nuclear reactor without a clear sense of the submarine on which it would be placed (Joshi 2015, 33–36). Until 1998, the pursuit of undersea nuclear technology was confined to nuclear-powered submarines, and interest in submarine-fired nuclear weapons emerged only after the tests (Joshi 2019). Subsequently, no critical assessment of the strategic value of undersea nuclear weapons is known to have been done (O'Donnell and Joshi 2014). To the extent that there is a strategic rationale for it, the case has been made entirely on the basis of a principle—assured second-strike capability—that has no grounding in historical fact but is central to American nuclear theology, which, ironically, has often been dismissed with contempt.

After 1998, there was no change in this muddled approach except that, as the construction of an arsenal and an organizational structure around it proceeded, the leadership seemed to have abdicated control over the formulation of doctrine. The DND, the first document known to try and weave a conceptual picture of nuclear doctrine and posture, was put together by the National Security Advisory Board, a motley group of mainly civilian and military bureaucrats ranging from minimalists to maximalists. Rather than basing the document on a careful study of nuclear strategy and its practical working, the DND was a compromise outcome that completely lacked consistency (Pant 2008, 74).

It is customary to say that political leaders have little technical knowledge and hence cannot be expected to understand the intricacies of military strategy. But if nuclear weapons are instruments that can threaten the survival of society or at least inflict catastrophic damage within a matter of minutes or hours, it is surely the responsibility of the civilians who have their finger on the button, so to speak, to thoroughly understand what their decisions rest on. As Srinath Raghavan notes, "the chain of accountability is clear: the military is responsible to the political leadership, who in turn are answerable to the people" (Raghavan 2012, 131).

The problem stems from the peculiar character of defense policymaking in India. Indian civil–military relations involve a grand postindependence bargain, "an implicit agreement between the military and political leaderships that allowed the Army freedom of action within the institution in return for submitting to the new nationalist leadership on political-strategic matters" (Dasgupta 2008, 209). Under this bargain, the formulation of military strategy is left to the armed forces, while the civilian authority holds the right of approval, especially with respect to spending. Consequently, the civilian leadership has assumed that strategizing on nuclear weapons is not part of its jurisdiction under the bargain. Going to war no doubt is, so policymakers maintain tight control over posture and any action that might lead to war. But the formulation of military strategy—and, by extension, the choice of weaponry—is considered the domain of the military, though subject to civilian approval of costs (Raghavan 2012, 123). More broadly, there is a marked lack of civilian expertise on many defense matters (Mukherjee 2020, 243–44). Lacking adequate knowledge, political leaders tend to rely on bureaucrats, who are the connecting link between political leaders and the military (Mukherjee 2020, 279). But civilian officials are not well informed on the intricacies of nuclear doctrine either, as the analysis here demonstrates.

The problem, then, is not structural but the epistemic weakness of the civilian leadership. If the civilian holders of political power have been unobstructed and yet failed to arrive at a clear understanding of nuclear strategy and its practical requirements, the only explanation for an inconsistent and confused doctrine and posture is a responsibility deficit. This is a malady that has other symptoms, as I will show in the next chapter. For the present, suffice it to say that this includes the larger problem of failure to develop an efficient national security organizational structure in line with the government's own recommendations (Joshi 2014).

CONCLUSION

Growing threat perceptions led India to cross the nuclear threshold after much internal resistance. Although the process had been under way incrementally since the early years after independence, the nuclear tests were a definitive statement that India as a nuclear power had come to stay. The dramatic shift did not bring strong negative consequences in the domestic arena, and the road seemed clear for the development of an arsenal on the basis of an officially articulated doctrine of "credible minimum deterrence."

The doctrine and accompanying posture almost immediately ran into difficulties because it was built on uncertain ground and no one quite knew what was meant by minimum deterrence. The result was not so much a nuclear "counterrevolution," as one critic has observed (O'Donnell 2019), but an unconscious mix of two distinct approaches to nuclear strategy, the minimalist and the maximalist. As a result, I have shown, India's nuclear posture acquired a schizophrenic character. On some counts—such as nondeployment, abstention from testing, and rejection of tactical nuclear weapons—it has held fast to its minimalist moorings. On others—predominantly, the building of excessive capabilities—it has proceeded on a maximalist tangent. This has produced an incoherent strategy, which has become more and more dysfunctional over the past two decades.

The analysis here engages in what I referred to in chapter 1 as a "backward-mapping" approach to locating responsibility—that is, on "how problems faced at the implementation stage might have their origins in the policy process" (Gregory 1998, 520–21). It is clear from the detailed discussion of both official and nonofficial thinking (in the latter case, of former officials) that the fundamentals of deterrence have been inadequately understood, which has resulted in ambiguity about the basis of deterrence and the acquisition of a range of weapons without doctrinal justification. The latter calls into question the cost-effectiveness of strategy and highlights the problem of resource wastage. It also generates a tendency toward arms racing. Pakistan, in particular, has responded to India's growing weapons acquisitions with attempts to match them.

How has this internally inconsistent strategy been sustained? The basic problem is the lack of initiative in engaging with nuclear history and doctrine. The civilian leadership has, to borrow obliquely from Cohen and Dasgupta (2010, 147), defined civilian control as civilian dominance but not taken seriously the task of assuming responsibility for it. This lack of responsibility has not been seriously challenged either from within the Indian state or from domestic political critics, for a number of reasons.

First, there has been no clearly visible cost. Nuclear costing is generally hidden from public view by distributing its components—for example, aircraft used as launchers for nuclear weapons are budgeted under the conventional force, while manpower expenditures are similarly distributed among dual-role personnel in the armed forces. But even so, the financial burden is not likely to be large because the size of the arsenal (thus far) and its surrounding infrastructure are small in comparison with India's defense forces, expenditures on which account for a fairly small proportion of gross domestic product. Such objections as there might be are drowned in strong threat perceptions about China and Pakistan, with both of which India has experienced major crises in recent years.

Second, the secretive character of the nuclear weapons program combines with its esoteric specialist nature to keep it largely opaque and beyond the understanding of the public and even the interested elite. Hence, as observed in chapter 1, there is a substantial degree of "agency loss," which means willingness on the part of the principal (the public) to bear with deviation from the optimum by the agent (the government).

Third, there is some gain from the continuity of minimalist posture. The low profile in testing and deployment reinforces the Indian government's oft-stated claim to be a "responsible" nuclear power and thereby enhances its overall prestige.

And fourth, rising capabilities also yield benefits by generating the image of India as a major power. Arguably, the nuclear tests and subsequent buildup were critical in changing the American view of India from an "emerging" power to a "rising power."

In sum, the policy drift has been sustained by a cost/benefit calculus that is not as yet costly. When it will reach a tipping point and be reversed is an open question.

5

CROSS-BORDER TERRORISM

On November 26, 2008, a team of terrorists launched a commando-style attack on India's commercial capital, Mumbai, exacting a toll of 166 deaths and immediate property damage of about $18 million (Maria 2020, 380; Roy et al. 2011, 273–74). The attack, which lasted 60 hours, aroused not only deep public anxiety about everyday security but also outrage against Pakistan, whence the perpetrators had come, and evoked a sense among many Indians that their government had failed them. A number of studies have recounted in detail the events of those fateful days, bringing out the inadequacies of the Indian state's preparedness and emergency response (Basrur et al. 2009; *Hindustan Times* 2009; Kelly and Rizvi 2015; Maria 2020, 373–512; Rabasa et al. 2009; Rath 2014; Scott-Clark and Levy 2013; Unnithan 2014). But surprisingly few analyses have attempted to engage the subject from a scholarly and theoretical perspective.

The Mumbai attack was a high point in an ongoing chain of major terrorist strikes that began with the series of multiple blasts that took place in the same city in 1993. Other bombings followed. These attacks presented the Indian government with a serious two-faceted problem: how to respond adequately to both the external and internal dimensions of repeated attacks by terrorist groups based in Pakistan. Externally, India needed to deter Pakistan from providing groups like the Lashkar-e-Taiba and the Jaish-e-Mohammed with a territorial base and material assistance for carrying out cross-border strikes. In the domestic realm, India needed to strengthen internal security and adopt appropriate political measures to stave off or at least respond effectively to such attacks. But the Indian response was unequal to the task. Externally, it lacked the capacity to act decisively against Pakistan because of material factors beyond its control. Domestically, it was ineffective not because it lacked control but because it was demonstrably slack in exercising political responsibility in a policy realm where it did have considerable control.

Rather than adopt a balanced and comprehensive approach to the problem, Indian policymakers focused inordinately on its external facet, seeking to hold Pakistan responsible and attempting to find ways to stem the attacks through a combination of coercive military pressure and international diplomacy. The tack failed to deliver the expected results because Pakistan, a nuclear-armed state, could not be pressured to back off. This underscored the need for a well-thought-out internal policy to minimize the domestic costs of the incessant tide of cross-border terrorism. But India's internal security response was unquestionably ineffectual, and policy drifted in a half-hearted tide that facilitated the Mumbai attack. Rather than look at the specific responses to the numerous attacks after 1993, this chapter closely examines the well-documented case of the Mumbai catastrophe in 2008. It highlights the failure of responsibility on the part of the central and state governments and the repeated instances of failure of accountability in its aftermath, which left the door open for the recurrence of similar attacks thereafter.

The central question I ask is about responsibility. If there is a policy shortcoming, scholars tend to find explanations related to problems of decision-making, diverging political interests, the inertia of bureaucratic politics, and so on. Rarely do we raise the question: who is responsible, and in what way? This is important because (1) those making decisions must be held accountable so that future decisions are made in the light of this accountability and the consequences that follow from it; and (2) if responsibility is not assigned, and those found responsible not held accountable, there is every likelihood that the failure will recur. On one level, the problems related to the Mumbai attack were material—it was all about organization and capabilities, as we will see—but these were not beyond the control of policymakers. The sources of the multiple failings that constituted policy drift over a long period lay in a sustained responsibility deficit and the poor working of the accountability mechanism in a society and political system that had all the necessary arrangements for both.

To be sure, all scholarly effort is ultimately about making the world a better place. Yet it is also true, in my view, that "objective" realities need to be complemented by the choices we make. And choices are ultimately what make us responsible to a greater or lesser extent for what befalls us. Social science, uneasily caught in the tension between will and necessity, tends to fall back on probability, usually failing to acknowledge that a focus on probability obfuscates the place of will and therefore of moral responsibility.

My general argument, initially set out in chapter 1, is that responsibility depends on the degree of control one exercises over people, processes, and institutions in a specific context. To the extent that there is such control, decision-makers who make choices can be held responsible. And, especially in a democracy—though, arguably, even with respect to an all-powerful Hobbesian sovereign—the state is responsible to the people it is obliged to protect. In assessing the Indian state's responses to the Mumbai attack, I try to gauge the extent to which such responsibility applies because, in my view, the degree to which (1) the state and its agents exercise responsibility, and (2) they are held accountable, determines not only the quality of governance but also the probability of such tragic events recurring. This, I think, is a more appropriate way of considering the probability of an event occurring in the future than simply focusing on "objective" factors.

The analytical framework of this chapter is as follows. In the next section, I outline the long, slow buildup to the Mumbai attack. There were plenty of signposts, so there is no question of surprise that the incident should have taken place. Thereafter, I focus on the Indian state's response to Pakistan, the external source of the attack. This aspect of policy was—and remains—beyond the control of Indian policymakers. To this extent, they cannot be held responsible for failing to curb cross-border terrorism at its source. But this makes the second aspect—tackling the flow of perpetrators closer to their targets—even more crucial. Accordingly, I turn to the domestic policy context and the Indian state's failure to provide adequate security to its people. The imperatives of prevention and response vis-à-vis catastrophic terrorist acts were in substantial part a responsibility that was not met, owing to the state's failure to make responsible decisions and to act at the domestic level both before and during the attack. The resulting "responsibility deficit" permitted the tragedy to occur.

As in the preceding chapter, the discussion on responsibility here elaborates on its initial elucidation in chapter 1, where I introduced Robert Gregory's distinction between "backward" and "forward" mapping in ascertaining responsibility. The former pertains to the acts (or absence of them) that created vulnerability to terrorism before the attack; the latter to the acts or omissions that represented failures to respond appropriately at the time of the crisis. Finally, I examine the question of accountability, which is a logical and ethically appropriate follow-up to the attribution of responsibility, and I assess what was done to hold those who did not meet their moral obligations accountable. I argue that weak accountability—the failure to hold those responsible for the tragedy fully accountable—perpetuates the problem and creates the permissive conditions for the recurrence of similar catastrophes in the future.

THE BUILDUP TO MUMBAI

Political violence in the form of insurgency, terrorism, and secessionist movements has been a constant feature of India's independent history. In a sense, this was inevitable in a society struggling to establish a nation-state amid unrelenting competition among disparate social groups based on class, religion, language, caste, and tribal identities (see, e.g., Gupta 2001; Singh 2001, 2018). Although much Indian and global attention has focused on groups inspired by extremist Islamic motivations, in fact, a wide range of organizations are involved in acts of political violence in India, many of them driven by other causes. As listed by the South Asia Terrorism Portal, there were in mid-2020 as many as seventy-six active terrorist groups and seventy-nine proscribed groups dedicated to various causes (South Asia Terrorism Portal n.d.–d). Moreover, the majority of these organizations have sprung from within India, though a number of them have (or have had) a presence in neighboring Afghanistan, Bangladesh, Myanmar, Nepal, Pakistan, and Sri Lanka.

In the prelude to Mumbai, Islamic extremism was the main source of terrorist-perpetrated fatality, but not overwhelmingly so. The data on the period just before the Mumbai attack are illustrative. Of the main theaters of terrorist attack (Islamist violence in Kashmir and other areas, ethnic movements in the northeast, and left-wing movements in the heartland of northern and central India), Islamic extremism accounted for 55.96 percent of all fatalities in 2005; 48.59 percent in 2006; and 31.97 percent in 2007 (calculated from South Asia Terrorism Portal n.d.–a). This is significant, because the issue of responsibility also applies to theaters where Islamic groups were not involved in terrorist attacks, though these are beyond the purview of the present analysis.

Terrorist groups with Islamic leanings have aimed to separate Kashmir (i.e., the portion of it held by India) from its Indian moorings. Originally spawned by internal rebellion against the Indian state, the secessionist movement in Kashmir has, since the early 1990s, been superseded by powerful Pakistan-based groups seeking what they think of as a global Islamic order through a campaign of jihad (i.e., religious war). Their membership spans Afghans, Arabs, Chechens, and Pakistanis (Mehta and Schaffer 2002, 15). The best known among several groups operating in Kashmir and elsewhere in India include Lashkar-e-Taiba, Jaish-e-Mohammed, Harkat-ul-Mujahideen, and Hizbul Mujahideen (these names are spelled in various ways, depending on the writer). These and other groups have long found support from the Pakistani state, which has been able to use them as a low-cost instrument for applying pressure on India to part with the portion of Kashmir held by it, over which Islamabad claims full sovereignty (Fair 2018; Gall 2014; Hussain 2007; Kapur 2017; Riedel 2013; Siddiqa 2011). Apart from political turbulence in Kashmir, a key factor facilitating the strategy was Pakistan's acquisition of nuclear weapons capability—covertly in the mid-1980s, and overtly in 1998—which gave Islamabad a nuclear shield to deter the Indian military from a conventional riposte to its subconventional strategy. In addition, as acknowledged in an Indian ministerial report, the flow of cross-border terrorists was facilitated by the growing movement of illegal arms and narcotics between the two countries (Group of Ministers on National Security 2001, 12).

The portents for the Mumbai tragedy were plentiful. First, in the years preceding the event, major terrorist attacks in India occurred throughout the country in significant numbers, so there was good reason to be prepared. Between 1990, when terrorist assaults escalated, and 2007, the year before the Mumbai attack, as many as 42,393 terrorism-related deaths were recorded (calculated from South Asia Terrorism Portal n.d.–c). Hence, the 2008 incident was by no means a surprise. Second, commando-style attacks on civilian targets had occurred before, notably at Delhi's Red Fort in December 2000, on the Jammu and Kashmir legislature in October 2001, and on the Indian parliament in December 2001. Third, 2008 was marked by multiple terrorist attacks on urban targets: the May 13 Jaipur bomb explosions caused eighty fatalities; blasts in Bangalore on July 25 killed one person; the July 26 Ahmedabad bombings killed forty-five civilians; the September 13 New Delhi explosions killed thirty; and the October 30 bombings in Assam caused eighty-three deaths (Goswami 2013, 99, 101).

Fourth, Mumbai itself had been a regular target over the years. The 2008 attack was preceded by a fifteen-year-long chain of attacks dating back to a series of bombings in Mumbai in 1993. The 1993 bombings took a heavy toll: 257 persons died in the largest number of fatalities exacted by a single act of terrorism in Indian history (BBC News 2015). Between 1993 and 2006, Mumbai experienced twelve terrorist attacks that caused 518 deaths. While the largest toll was taken by the 1993 blasts, the multiple bombings of 2006 caused 181 deaths, which exceeded the fatalities in 2008 (South Asia Terrorism Portal n.d.–e).

INDIA'S POLICY RESPONSE: EXTERNAL TOUGHNESS, DOMESTIC TIGHTENING

Indian policymakers sought to counter the growing menace of cross-border terrorism by tackling both its external and internal facets. The former was deeply problematic, owing to Pakistan's ability to exploit the "stability/instability paradox" to impose strategic pressure on India. The concept was originally formulated to allow for the possibility of conventional war between nuclear-armed states rationally unable to risk crossing the nuclear threshold for fear of mutual destruction (Snyder 1965). A more recent modification holds that, fearing escalation, nuclear powers do not risk major conventional war either, so the paradox operates at a still lower level: marginal conflict and subconventional (including proxy) war (Krepon and Gagné 2001). Indian policymakers were aware of the Pakistani strategy since at least 1991, as a government-mandated report observes (Kargil Review Committee 2000, 197–99). They were also aware of the difficulty they faced in taking Islamabad to task. Yet they continued to focus inordinately on dissuading Pakistan from pursuing its strategy.

India's choices were limited. The option of conventional war against Pakistan was no longer feasible (Hagerty 2020, 46) owing to the risk of escalation to nuclear conflict. Military action was contemplated in the form of an unclear conception of "limited war," hot pursuit, air strikes against terrorist camps, and so on (Ladwig 2007–8; Menon 2018). But not much could be done for fear of setting off a catastrophic nuclear conflict. The high point was a massive military mobilization, accompanied by the threat of war, which was initiated by the government of Prime Minister Atal

Bihari Vajpayee in 2001–2 after a terrorist attack on the Indian Parliament in December 2001. India demanded that Pakistan cease support for cross-border terrorism once and for all or face the prospect of war. However, this compellence strategy produced only limited results by way of a temporary and partial backing down by Pakistan, which subsequently resumed its strategy (Basrur 2006, 80–101).

Given the constraints on action posed by nuclear weapons, India lacked control—that is, the capacity to act to carry out a threat of punishment. The crisis of 2001–2 represented a dual strategy of attempting to coerce Pakistan directly and also through the United States, which was expected to pressure Islamabad to back away from its subconventional strategy in order to prevent a nuclear conflagration. Given the context—the tragedy of the September 11, 2001, terrorist attacks on the United States had occurred just three months before the attack on India's Parliament—this appeared to be an opportune moment. But Washington's priorities did not coincide entirely with those of New Delhi. First, the predominant American objective was to destroy Al Qaeda and the Taliban in Afghanistan. The India-oriented terrorist groups supported by Pakistan were less important for Washington. Second, the United States needed Pakistan's assistance to carry out its counterterrorist campaign and did not want to alienate Islamabad by targeting its India-oriented assets (Farrow 2018, 44). Accordingly, the George W. Bush administration was willing to work with what US Central Intelligence Agency director Michael Hayden called "the ally from hell" (Farrow 2018, 43). By the time the 2008 attack took place, it was evident to Indian policymakers that their efforts were not working. Not surprisingly, though it was clear that the assault on Mumbai was carried out by Pakistan-based terrorists, the Indian government refrained from a military response, though thought was certainly given to it (Menon 2016, 61–64).

Since the lesson of 2001–2 was that limited war was not really a serious option and that Pakistan could not be restrained by military means, it was all the more incumbent on Indian policymakers to focus on the domestic realm to try and stem the flow of cross-border terrorism. The tightening of national security, including border management and intelligence, was a natural internal counterpart to the effort to counter Pakistan's support for cross-border terrorism (Gupta 2018). A series of reforms was set in motion as the incidence of terrorist attacks increased (Joshi 2014; Raghavan 2019).

But its implementation was uneven, and India's approach to counterterrorism remained overly ad hoc. The National Security Council appointed in 1990 met only once before falling into disuse. In 1998, a task force headed by a senior political figure, K. C. Pant, was established to consider reforms embracing a wide range of issues, from external threats to internal security. Accordingly, the government in April 1999 established the National Security Council under the prime minister, the Strategic Policy Group, the national security adviser (NSA), and the National Security Advisory Board. The National Security Council Secretariat—to assist the National Security Council, National Security Advisory Board, and Strategic Policy Group—was also created.

Within weeks the government was beset by the India–Pakistan Kargil crisis, when Pakistani forces in civilian garb occupied a substantial portion of territory under India's jurisdiction in Kashmir in 1999 (Chandran 2005). After the crisis—which involved costly but limited combat—had subsided, the government appointed a committee to deliberate on why and how it had happened. One outcome was intelligence reform. The Kargil Review Committee's (1999) report highlighted intelligence flaws as a cause of the onset of the crisis. Building on this, the Indian government tasked a Group of Ministers (GoM) to produce a comprehensive report on India's national security apparatus (Group of Ministers on National Security 2001). The GoM report encompassed four main areas of national security: intelligence (this section has been redacted from the publicly released version, but some information can be obtained from a secondary source: IDSA Task Force Report 2012), internal security, border management, and the management of defense. It recommended the establishment of the Multi-Agency Center in the capital and Subsidiary Multi-Agency Centers in the rest of the country.

Concomitantly, a process of police reform was also undertaken. In 2005, the central government appointed the Police Act Drafting Committee to draft a new model police law that could replace the colonial-era Police Act of 1861. Key features that the new legal framework sought to encourage were functional autonomy, professionalism, accountability, and improved service conditions (Chaturvedi 2017, 17). The Model Police Act was circulated to all the states in 2006 and was adopted by, among others, Maharashtra state (of which Mumbai is the capital), which enacted new laws or amended existing laws accordingly. Attention was also given to coastal security (Das 2009, 2013). India has a long coastline with numerous vulnerabilities, and smuggling has been a constant problem since independence. Major terrorist attacks, notably the Mumbai bombings of 1993, had been launched via the sea route. The government was also aware of the potential terrorist threat from the sea to offshore oil installations and coastal nuclear power plants (*Economic Times* 2007). Coastal security arrangements, it turned out, were critically important in 2008 because the terrorist team arrived by boat.

Following the 1993 Mumbai bombings, a multilayered system of coastal security management involving the Navy, the Coast Guard, and the police was established under Operation Swan. In 2005–6, the GoM-appointed Task Force on Border Management's recommendations resulted, among other things, in the centrally initiated Coastal Security Scheme for Maharashtra and Gujarat states, with funding assistance from New Delhi (Das 2009, 16–17). This plan involved setting up coastal police stations, strengthening Coast Guard patrolling, and creating an integrated system comprising the center, the state, and local fishermen's groups. For specific counterterrorism responses, the central government had previously created a commando force, the National Security Guard, in 1984.

None of these centrally pushed mechanisms to enhance security was opposed by the state government or subject to bureaucratic pressures when initiated. The problems, as will be seen, came to the fore later and were starkly manifested in Mumbai in 2008. For present purposes, it is pertinent to note that Maharashtra was in line with central policy reforms, though not always most efficiently. The state established an Anti-Terrorism Squad (ATS) in 1990, disbanded it in 1993, and recreated it in 2004. In the 1990s, it created one hundred flying squads, each with two motorcycle-borne commandos, to respond to threats from terrorists and organized crime (HLEC 2009, 17). The functions of the ATS included coordinating intelligence on terrorism, organized crime, and related activities with other agencies of the state and central governments (Badri-Maharaj 2009, 147–48).

The government's response to the rising threat was internal as well as external. Internally, there was no significant problem to obstruct the comprehensive reform that was set in motion. As in the preceding three chapters, the policy drift became manifest only when specific aspects of the general policy change came up for implementation.

THE MUMBAI ATTACK AND THE EXPOSURE OF DRIFT

When the attack on Mumbai occurred, Indian security forces at every level were caught woefully unprepared (Rabasa et al. 2009; Rath 2014; Unnithan 2014). A squad of ten men arrived by sea after hijacking an Indian fishing vessel, landed on the coast near the commercial heart of the city, and spread out in four teams to carry out commando-style assaults on several targets, the main ones being the Leopold Café, the Taj Mahal Hotel, the Oberoi Trident Hotel, the Chhatrapati Shivaji Maharaj Terminus (Mumbai's largest railway station), the Cama and Albless Hospital, and Nariman House, a Jewish synagogue and community center. The attack extended over a period of four days, from November 26 to 29, 2008—a time span that vividly illustrated the failure of Indian security forces to respond effectively. The chapter's next two subsections show how and why this happened. My focus is on both individuals and collectivities, as has been done in a comparable exercise on the Bhopal chemical disaster of December 1984 (Eckerman and Børsen 2018). But I hold that the responsibilities of agencies and other collectivities come down ultimately to the individuals—however many they may number—who make critical decisions.

As mentioned above, the identification of responsibility in this study picks up from the analysis by Robert Gregory (1998), who probes a very different incident, the collapse of a viewing platform for tourists in New Zealand in 1995, to assess the question of who was responsible. Gregory distinguishes between "backward" and "forward" mapping of an event to assign responsibility. In the present context, backward mapping relates to the failure of policymakers to make adequate preparation for an attack that was in the cards, considering the trend in terrorist attacks in Mumbai and elsewhere in India. Forward mapping demonstrates the ways in which the immediate response to the attack was flawed. The penultimate section of the chapter follows up by asking whether those responsible for both types of failings were held accountable, and, if so, to what extent.

Assigning Responsibility: Backward Mapping

Casting a historical net provides much of the explanation for why the response to the attack on Mumbai was in many ways subpar. The Indian state did not follow a single strategy to counter terrorists and insurgency.

Rather, it adopted three approaches (not always mutually exclusive): deal making, containment, and "total warfare" (Staniland 2018). The last was adopted against ethno-religious movements and groups that were thought to be the most threatening for the survival of the nation-state. Yet there appears to have been unclear thinking on the more specific direction of strategy. For instance, the terrain of the new movements, first in Punjab and later in Kashmir, was the urban landscape, for which Indian security forces were inadequately trained (Subramaniam 2012, 405). This mismatch could be traced to the distorted working of the higher national security leadership, with prime ministers and national security advisers failing to acquire a clear understanding on the changing context (Sood 2015, 340–41). Let me dwell on each major aspect of the poor performance displayed by Indian policy.

Command and Control

The National Security Council, the apex body on security matters, was inactive (Balachandran 2017, 211–17). Tellingly, one critic recalls, the council did not meet for as much as one month after the onset of the Kargil crisis in 1999 (Balachandran 2017, 212). Similarly, the Crisis Management Group chaired by the cabinet secretary was dysfunctional (Balachandran 2017, 217–20). And the GoM's recommendation that military and civilian leaders engage in politico-military war gaming was ignored (Unnithan 2014, 204). At the state level, the ATS was ambiguous in its command-and-control arrangement, with no clear lines of reporting and authority integrating its two wings, one of which was for Mumbai and the other for the rest of Maharashtra. The chain of command was disrupted by a senior police official who altered its channels of communication and authority by an executive order in violation of its original intent (HLEC 2009, 54). Moreover, the police did not function in an integrated manner. A short while before the Mumbai attack, a serious vulnerability in the security arrangement at the Taj Mahal Hotel was created by the removal by a senior police inspector, a relatively junior officer, of police guards posted at one entrance because they were needed at another location (HLEC 2009, 50).

Intelligence

India's intelligence apparatus had built-in flaws. Its colonial legacy had left it a bureaucratic organization geared to law and order and to spying on political rivals (Asthana 2010, 8). Improved intelligence coordination was recognized as a necessity and recommended by the GoM. But the creation and activation of the Multi-Agency Center in New Delhi and Subsidiary Multi-Agency Centers in the states, as recommended by the GoM, was laggardly; though the Multi-Agency Center had been established, its first meeting was called more than a month *after* the Mumbai attack (Rediff India Abroad 2009a). The GoM-mandated Intelligence Coordination Group, set up in 2001 and presided over by the NSA, was designed to fund allocations, optimize resource coordination, and exercise oversight, but was largely inactive (Datta 2005). Similarly, the National Security Council Staff, which should have given independent advice to the NSA, was bureaucratized and converted into the National Security Council Secretariat to reflect the deputy NSA's views (Jha 2009, 132). This was not just a "systemic" problem. There were periodic intelligence reports on potential threats to Mumbai. But the NSA and the officials below him had not established a coordinated response to assess information and preparation for action between the Intelligence Bureau and other agencies, such as the National Security Guard, at the center and between the center and the relevant agencies at the level of Maharashtra state (Datta 2018, 103). Veerappa Moily, chair of the central government's Administrative Reforms Commission, noted that the various intelligence agencies at the central and state levels were not networked (*Indian Express* 2008c).

Furthermore, the Special Protection Group team, tasked with protection of the prime minister—who was scheduled to attend a function at the Oberoi Trident three days later, on November 29—had undertaken a security survey of the hotel and left just a few minutes before the terrorists struck—all without being aware of the numerous intelligence alerts about a possible attack (George 2009, 103).

There were comparable difficulties at the state and local levels. Certainly, there were success stories too. A major plot to attack the Mumbai Stock Exchange was disrupted in 2004, and Maharashtra police intercepted a Lashkar-e-Taiba unit that had brought in large quantities of arms and explosives by sea (Fair 2009, 10). But the High-Level Enquiry Committee (HLEC)—commonly known as the Pradhan Committee, after its chairman, Ram Pradhan—appointed by the Maharashtra government in the aftermath of the attack found "total confusion in the processing of intelligence alerts at the level of State Government" (HLEC 1999, 7). The HLEC highlighted the "shocking revelation" that senior officials had not kept themselves fully informed of intelligence inputs, but blamed their junior-level desk officers for not briefing them (HLEC 1999, 7–8). Furthermore, the nodal officer for police intelligence in Mumbai, the State Intelligence Department's additional director-general of police, was not kept informed of intelligence reports from central government agencies. The information went instead to higher officials—the state's director-general of police and Mumbai city's commissioner of police—who had multiple responsibilities (HLEC 2009, para. 3.97). Astonishingly, the State Intelligence Department head was not aware of any of the numerous intelligence alerts on terrorist threats to Mumbai coming in before the attack (Balachandran 2017, 197)! Clearly, the problem was not the availability of intelligence but "action failure," that is, failure to channel it efficiently so as to act appropriately on it (Mahadevan 2012, 199–200).

Physical Response: The National Security Guard

The National Security Guard, the premier response team for the kind of terrorist attack that occurred in Mumbai, was in several ways unprepared for the crisis. First, the country's sole guard contingent was based at Manesar, about 40 kilometers from New Delhi, and had no presence in Mumbai or any other location. The agency had proposed four regional hubs in December 2006, partly because Delhi was frequently fog-bound in winter, which caused flight delays, but these had not been sanctioned (Unnithan 2014, 42). Second, the guard had no readily available transportation of the kind essential for a quick reaction force. The team had to drive to the Delhi airport in trucks because there were no helicopters available with night flying capability (Singh 2009, 102). The central government's Ministry of Home Affairs had not agreed to the request for its own fixed-wing aircraft (*Hindustan Times* 2009, 103). The guard depended on an intelligence agency aircraft, which was not kept ready at all times and was at this juncture located in Chandigarh, 200 kilometers away (Rabasa et al. 2009, 10). Hence, an alternative aircraft based in Delhi had to be refueled and its crew brought from home and transported to the Delhi airport, all of which took considerable time (Rabasa et al. 2009, 10; Unnithan 2014, 42). Moreover, the substitute aircraft was too small to accommodate the entire team and had to make three trips before the full contingent reached Mumbai (*The Wire* 2019). This was in spite of an old standing order by Prime Minister Rajiv

Gandhi expressly calling for full readiness to respond immediately in the event of a crisis (Balachandran 2017, 181). Further, there was poor preparation for the guard team's arrival at Mumbai airport. The only transportation made available was a number of commandeered local buses instead of helicopters, which further delayed them (*Economic Times* 2008a). As a result, the guard team took about 11 hours from the onset of the attack to come to the scene, by which time much of the killing had already occurred (Balachandran 2017, 180).

Third, the National Security Guard was not fully trained by means of simulation for terrorist attacks and hostage rescues (HLEC 2009, para. 35). Fourth, the guard lacked firing practice because of ammunition shortages. According to the HLEC, there had been no practice in firing since December 7, 2007 (HLEC 2009, para. 35). All the above points illustrate the serious lack of preparation for an event that was very much in the cards and would almost certainly have made a substantial difference in the number of lives lost in the attack.

Physical Response: State and Local Police

The Mumbai Police was an early responder, and its officers and men reached all the spots targeted by the terrorists quickly (Maria 2020, 402–6). Its alacrity and willingness to act despite being severely hampered by shortages of manpower, training, and equipment have been praised by the HLEC. But in contrast to the terrorists, the HLEC found, the police lacked adequate equipment and training for counterterrorist response (HLEC 2009, paras. 31–32.2). Police Commissioner Raymond Kelly of the New York Police Department subsequently testified before the US Senate Committee on Homeland Security and Government Affairs that, because the Mumbai police did not have the appropriate training and equipment, they did not engage the terrorists, which led to a high level of casualties (Sinha 2009).

The Mumbai police had a dedicated ATS, but its role was essentially intelligence-related and investigative (Interview 2012). For speedy response to emergencies, the police had created a small number of Quick Response Teams (QRTs). But these had received limited training, with no focus on terrorist attacks, and were poorly equipped. For instance, the HLEC found, there were only twenty-four bullet-proof helmets for eight officers and forty-eight men (HLEC 2009, para. 3.61). One member of the HLEC later wrote that, according to a secret report (never released) accompanying the public report, the QRTs were badly organized and trained (Balachandran 2017, 199). In addition, "Assault Mobiles" were posted at seven different locations in Mumbai, but their members were given limited training ("all weapons training" was provided for just seven days) and were posted in assault mobiles for only a year before being transferred (HLEC 2009, para. 3.65). There was also a Special Operations Squad with modern weapons—numbering only forty-one personnel, including four drivers—but it was tasked to protect investigators or raiding officers and had no front-line counterterrorist role (HLEC 2009, para. 3.66). The Maharashtra police had established one hundred flying squads of two policemen each for the state. But the commissioner of police in March 2006 reduced them to just seventy-five policemen with thirty motorcycles (HLEC 2009, para. 3.96). Of these, forty-six were stationed in Mumbai, but these were distributed around the city for diverse duties (HLEC 2009, para. 3.96).

Paucity of staff was a nationwide problem. At the time, the national police-to-population ratio was just 134 for every 100,000 persons, in stark contrast to the US ratio of 248 per 1,000 and the UK's ratio of 301 per 1,000 (Unnithan 2014, 214–15). At the state level, there was a severe shortage of police personnel; on the average, there were only 10,000 policemen on duty at police stations in the entire city, and vacancies for the critical position of assistant police inspector were as high as 35 percent (HLEC 2009, 55). More generally, the police in Mumbai—and indeed, in the rest of the country—were (and still are) suboptimal in their capabilities because they were poorly paid and housed, overworked, plagued by corruption, and regularly used by parties in power for their own political purposes (Gordon 2008, 111–24; Swami 2009).

At the state level, as one senior administrator put it, there was "some strange aversion" to the implementation of police reform (*Indian Express* 2008c). A national-level plan for police modernization with central government support was poorly implemented by the state government, as shown in a detailed report by the Comptroller and Auditor General of India (CAG n.d.). This report, which covers the financial years from 2000–1 to 2004–5, reveals significant failings with respect to police reform. First, the central government released substantially reduced funding to the state because of underspending by the latter. Second, of fifty-four residential quarters and other buildings for which funds were sanctioned, only seven were completed during this period. In the police stations checked by the CAG, half the personnel had not been provided with staff quarters. Of 568 replacement vehicles supplied to the state, only 30 percent were allotted to police stations, which received only 14 percent of 236 new vehicles. In 118 police stations checked, average response time with respect to reports of crimes was as much as 156 minutes. Of the police personnel targeted for training during 2000–4, only 69 percent were actually trained. And so on—the report is similarly reflective of the poor state of the Maharashtra police on other counts. (For the data in this paragraph, see CAG n.d., 111, 112, 114, 117–18.)

Police personnel were seriously lacking in equipment. Whereas the terrorists were well armed with pistols, AK-47 assault rifles, hand grenades, and RDX explosive, the mobile police units possessed only outdated .303 rifles, cane sticks, and gas guns for riot control. The weapons they did carry were not in good condition either. On at least three occasions they failed to fire (Unnithan 2014, 9, 11, 193). In addition, there were acute shortages of arms. For instance, less than 25 percent of the funding required for a period of five years was sanctioned (HLEC 2009, paras. 3.83, 3.84). The HLEC, on examining the record, found that the Maharashtra Home Department stated that substantial quantities of ammunition were received in the two financial years preceding the attack; but the director general of police, Maharashtra, stated that no ammunition was received for AK-47 rifles after 2005, and no ammunition at all was received after December 2006 (HLEC 2009, para. 3.86). Each policeman was supposed to fire forty rounds per year as practice, but this was not done because the paltry supplies were routed for other uses, such as the campaign against a left-wing insurgency far from Mumbai (HLEC 2009, para. 3.84). The city police also lacked good-quality communications equipment, so communication channels were clogged during the crisis (HLEC 2009, para. 56).

Bullet-proof jackets were short in supply, and those available were 15 years old and heavy, each weighing 10–12 kilograms (HLEC 2009, para. 3.89). One police officer complained that the body armor used by the Mumbai police had failed tests in 2001 and 2004 against bullets fired from AK-47 and AK-56 rifles (cited by Fair 2012, 152). ATS chief Hemant Karkare died during the Mumbai attack because terrorist bullets penetrated his bullet-proof vest (Rabasa et al. 2009, 10–11).

CHAPTER 5

Coastal Security

The *fidayeen* who attacked Mumbai came via the sea. This route was not only well known for smuggling but had also been used by the perpetrators of the 1993 Mumbai blasts. It was also known that eight terrorists had attempted to reach Mumbai in March 2007, had been intercepted by the Coast Guard, were let off (for reasons not known), and eventually rearrested on land (HLEC 2009, 50). The central government had stated repeatedly in Parliament and elsewhere that there was a real threat of a sea-based attack (Shourie 2008; Swami 2008). Coastal security requires a coordinated effort involving central forces: the Navy, which patrols waters beyond 200 nautical miles and the Coast Guard, which monitors waters from 12 to 200 miles; the state's marine police, which are responsible for the nearest 12 miles; and the city police, which, along with the state police, are responsible for the land area along the coast. But resources were inadequate despite the known threat. The Navy's call for a coordinating National Maritime Commission was not acceded to, and the Coast Guard remained underequipped. The Coast Guard had been authorized to operate a minimum of 106 vessels and 52 aircraft, but the actual numbers in operation were 80 and 45, respectively. Radar facilities were also inadequate (Pandit 2008a).

More damning still, the central agencies neglected coastal patrolling. The Indian Navy, which had agreed to provide eight vessels for patrolling the seas, decided to drop out of the arrangement in 2006 and instead establish QRTs at Murud and Ratnagiri, far from Mumbai (HLEC 2009, para. 2.9). A 2011 government report, which confirmed the severe shortage of equipment in the Coast Guard, also revealed that joint coastal patrolling had been discontinued by the Navy in 2005, while the Coast Guard never carried out "inner layer" patrols within its jurisdiction until December 2010 (*Indian Express* 2011).

At the state level, there were similar problems. In part, they were handed down from the center. The national government had promised to supply the state's marine police with 240 patrol boats in March 2006, but these had still not arrived when the attack took place (Pandit 2008a). Besides, the Mumbai police were given only rudimentary training by the Navy and the Coast Guard (HLEC 2009, para. 2.10.2). Conversely, according to a CAG report, the Maharashtra government failed to utilize additional resources offered by New Delhi. Funds provided by the center in 1995 were used to obtain four patrol boats, but these were left idle because the state was averse to bearing the cost of operation and maintenance. All four had to be scrapped in 2006 (Thakur 2008).

Preparedness at the organizational level was perfunctory, and the HLEC has observed that, despite six alerts, the state government made no effort to strengthen security: "Nothing other than convening meetings seems to have been achieved," and, even after the 2008 attack, "present arrangements are of a cosmetic nature" (HLEC 2009, paras. 3.81, 3.82). The HLEC also noted that though the Coast Guard, a central service, had in 2003 been designated the lead intelligence agency for coastal security by the Government of India, the state government had made no effort to interact regularly with it (HLEC 2009, section V). Despite a number of intelligence warnings, the state's Home Department did not arrange meetings to boost coastal security preparedness (Balachandran 2017, 179). The boats utilized by the state government were slow and did not have the capability to light up surrounding waters at night (Balachandran 2017, 171–72). No arrangements were made for identification of fishermen along a coast that had a history of terrorist infiltration (Balachandran 2017, 173).

Hotels

Although fingers have been pointed with good reason at government agencies, the private sector is not without culpability. It was well known that hotels elsewhere had recently been targeted by terrorists—for example, the Serena Hotel in Kabul in January 2008 and the Marriott Hotel in Islamabad in September 2008 (HLEC 2009, para. 3.76). In the United States, the American Hotel and Lodging Association took an active interest in tracking and responding to terrorist threats and had its own agency for security matters (HLEC 2009, para. 3.78; see also AHLA n.d.). The Marriott chain, which had been bombed just two months before the Mumbai attack, had developed an elaborate strategy involving awareness training, coded alerts, "target hardening," and interaction with stakeholders in response to the threat (Balachandran 2017, 176; Wernick and Glinow 2012).

The HLEC noted that the Taj Mahal Hotel and Oberoi Hotel were kept informed of security alerts, and police officers personally interacted with the managements of both hotels in the weeks preceding the attack (HLEC 2009, paras. 3.78, 11–13). However, the hotels did not appear to have taken the threat seriously, and neither requested an augmentation of security

(HLEC 2009, para. 14). This was confirmed by Ratan Tata, chairman of Tata Sons, which controls the Taj Hotels chain, who admitted that the Taj management had been warned and had tightened security but had reduced it shortly before the attack because it interfered with the flow of guests (Range 2008).

Assigning Responsibility: Forward Mapping

I now turn to the responses of the various actors involved at the time of the attack.

Command and Control

The most obvious deficiency in the response to the 2008 attack was in the initial management of the crisis. This was particularly apparent because of the high level of training and organization evident in the operations of the terrorists (Acharya and Marwah 2011). Indian authorities were, in contrast, disorganized and confused. In New Delhi, the government did not convene the National Crisis Management Committee but acted through the Ministry of Home Affairs (Unnithan 2014, 38–39). The National Security Guard received information of the attack a little over 20 minutes after the first shots were fired in Mumbai (Scott-Clark and Levy 2013, 284). But two and a half hours had passed since the onset of the attack before the guard was formally asked to mobilize (Nanjappa 2009; Singh 2009, 102). The commandos' late start was further delayed by nearly an hour because they had to wait for Home Minister Shivraj Patil to board the aircraft to accompany them from Delhi to Mumbai (Unnithan 2014, 80–81).

In Mumbai, there was no clear chain of command and control either. As reports of one incident after another came in, there was panic. The police Control Room (C/R) received as many as 1,365 calls between 9 p.m. on September 26 and 2 a.m. the next day, which led to haphazard deployment of police personnel (HLEC 2009, para. 30.1). The HLEC in its report observed that standard operating procedure was not followed by the police leadership: rather than take charge of the Command Center in the C/R, which would have optimized the response, the commissioner of police gave the responsibility to the joint commissioner of police–crime. The HLEC was particularly critical of the commissioner: it held that he should not only have assumed full command but should have been seen to be doing so

(HLEC 2009, para. 3.72). The commissioner set up an operational control center at the Trident, but for several hours there was no senior officer to organize forces outside the Taj Mahal Hotel (HLEC 2009, paras. 3.67–3.72). At the Cama Hospital, a large number of security forces were present, but no one seemed to know what to do except fire revolvers from a considerable distance (HLEC 2009, para. 3.37). At Nariman House, the gathering crowd nearly overwhelmed the security forces and was only held back by the sound of a stun grenade fired inside the building (Unnithan 2014, 201). The motorcycle-borne commandos of the Mumbai police were scattered at different locations in the city. The HLEC found they were not utilized during the attack (HLEC 2009, para. 3.96).

Intelligence

Aside from the structural weakness of the intelligence gathering and assessment system, there were significant problems with its functioning at the time of the crisis. The central government had sufficient indications from various reports that an attack was likely, that the Taj Mahal Hotel (among other hotels) was a target, and, most ominously on November 19, that there was a communication intercept stating that the "cargo" was on its way. But the pattern was not stitched together to generate coordinated action (Balachandran 2017, 194–95; Jha 2009, 128–30). The Maharashtra home minister made public some weeks after the attack that the Intelligence Bureau had intimated intelligence of an upcoming attack to the Navy, but not to the state government (Balachandran 2017, 193).

A still-more-astonishing example of bureaucratic incompetence was revealed a few weeks after the attack had ended. On November 21, 2008, just five days before the attack, the Intelligence Bureau received a secret note (the source has not been made public) with information that listed thirty-five cell phone numbers that were to be monitored and "information taken from these numbers regarding the contents of the conversation, current locations of the call detail records are required for further developing the information" (Baweja 2009). At least three of these numbers, it turned out, were used by the Mumbai attackers to communicate with their handlers in Pakistan. It was only after some hours—by which time dozens of people has been killed—that the Mumbai police were alerted and began to intercept the calls (Baweja 2009). Thereafter, the ATS recorded conversations spread over 12 hours and 33 minutes. But no attempt was made to jam the calls to try and minimize the toll wreaked by the terrorists by depriving them of guidance from their handlers, who conveyed up-to-date information to them on counterterrorist efforts (Rath 2014, 166–67).

Physical Response: Central Forces—the Naval Commandos and the National Security Guard

The Navy's Marcos (Marine Commandos) team, though one of the first central forces at the scene, was called late and, on arrival at the Taj Mahal Hotel, found no one there to brief it (*Economic Times* 2008b). The team engaged the terrorists at the Taj, but with little success as it had no knowledge of the layout of the hotels and the terrorists were constantly on the move (Rath 2014, 154; Trofimov et al. 2008). Years later, one member of the team recalled that he had thrown a grenade at the terrorists, but it did not explode (Mahadevan 2018). Part of the reason for the Marcos team's inability to flush out the terrorists while the National Security Guard was on its way may have been its lack of experience: its members were trained for special operations at sea and were not au fait with urban terrorism (Zee News 2009). The Army also did not play a central role, though it did provide helicopter support and manpower for security.

The National Security Guard, as shown above, arrived late because emergency protocols and resources were not in place. As also mentioned above, the home minister, wishing to accompany the commandos, further delayed their takeoff from the Delhi airport. The guard had sparse information about the attack; according to one report, when they arrived in Mumbai, they did not even know that two hotels were under attack or that one of them—the Taj Mahal—had two wings (Samanta 2009). At Nariman House, the National Security Guard team was compelled to borrow two army helicopters to attempt landing on the roof. But the communications systems used by the helicopters and the guard personnel were incompatible, creating confusion. The first chopper targeted the wrong building for dropping the commandos before urgent hand signals from below brought a correction (Datta 2014). At the Trident, the guard team innovated under difficult conditions to make up for its limited equipment. It used improvised Molotov cocktails—beer bottles filled with a mixture of fuel oil and gasoline—to attack the terrorists. The army did not play a significant role, other than cordoning off target areas (HLEC 2009, para. 3.22.2). On the whole, given the chaotic situation and their lack of the requisite training and equipment, the central security forces deployed in response to the crisis appear to have performed creditably.

Physical Response: State Level

The police response, as noted above, was not entirely flawless, as the commissioner of police had not swiftly assumed full command in the C/R. Nevertheless, the police acted quickly. One team reached the Leopold Café within minutes, and other units responded with alacrity (HLEC 2009, paras. 3.1–3.19). However, the HLEC has faulted the force generally for not keeping the C/R fully informed to enable the latter to build a clear composite picture of the action at various points (HLEC 2009, para. 3.33). The police, though poorly trained and equipped for the crisis, prevented the violence from spreading to a wider set of targets (Balachandran 2017, 180).

The Mumbai Fire Brigade also acted under difficult conditions, with terrorists throwing grenades, which fortunately did not explode, and firing at them (and missing) (*Hindustan Times* 2012). About a hundred firefighters were involved not only in putting out fires but also in rescuing hostages and rushing victims to hospital (*Hindustan Times* 2012; Thevar 2018). They had their share of problems: one snorkel ladder did not work, and they ran out of water and had to replenish from a well some distance away (HLEC 2009, para. 3.22.2). It is not clear why fresh supplies were not obtained in advance.

Coastal Security

The performance of both the Navy and the Coast Guard appears to have been below par. The central government had been regularly warning of a sea-based attack (Baweja 2008). The Navy and the Coast Guard did receive an Intelligence Bureau message on November 19 giving the precise coordinates of a suspected terrorist boat attempting to enter Indian waters (Unnithan 2014, xxvii–xxix). At the time, the two forces were engaged in a joint exercise. The Coast Guard immediately began a search operation but failed to find the boat, while the Navy's headquarters in New Delhi did not inform the Western Naval Command, whose ships continued with their routine exercise. A senior naval officer later claimed the Navy had not received "actionable intelligence" (Pandit 2016). The terrorist team, which arrived by means of a hijacked trawler, was able to slip through the security network because it was thin. A report from the CAG (2011, 49–59) reveals that, before the Mumbai attack, the Coast Guard was performing well below standards in conducting boarding operations, indicating laxity in its operations at the time. There was also a shortfall in the number of coastal police stations set up under the centrally mandated Operation Swan.

Media Handling

The Indian media, as keen as their counterparts anywhere else, have been criticized by no less than the Supreme Court of India for their eagerness to be au courant with the action. The Court observed while deliberating on a legal aspect of the crisis some years later that detailed descriptions of counterterrorist operations in live television broadcasts actually helped the perpetrators, who obtained useful information through their handlers in Pakistan who were watching the broadcasts (Ali 2012). But it was not just TV stations that disseminated information the attackers could obtain. Social media—Facebook and Twitter—were heavily used by onlookers, and details of the action were being circulated widely (Mirchandani 2019). The BBC's Twitter image gave away the location of Indian forces storming Nariman House from the roof, which enabled the terrorists in the building to launch a counterattack (Kelly and Rizvi 2015, 4). In addition, the HLEC noted, there was no systematic briefing of the media by the police (HLEC 2009, para. 43).

With no clear media handling guidelines in place, television reporters and sometimes members of the public were able to approach the scene of the crisis. According to one analyst, reporters even "stood alongside National Security Guard chief J. K. Dutt as he directed operations" (Mirchandani 2019). The rot began earlier, when Home Minister Shivraj Patil, before leaving Delhi with the guard team, informed the press that he was flying to Mumbai along with a force of 250 commandos (Datta 2018, 110). Poor media handling was a serious impediment to the conduct of counterterrorist operations and reflected the lack of a standard operating procedure for such crises at the national, state, and local levels.

EXPLAINING DRIFT: THE PROBLEM OF ACCOUNTABILITY

The brief analysis above leads to the inescapable conclusion that India's practical failings in the face of the terrorist onslaught in Mumbai were not simply "material" realities. The tragedy was only possible because multiple actors failed to shoulder their responsibilities appropriately. As stressed in chapter 1, this responsibility deficit is a persistent problem and lies at the root of repeated costly crises when the ethical aspect is not addressed. Here, I look at this aspect of the problem.

I have focused on the Indian response to the threat of cross-border terrorism and asked whether it was adequate and responsible. That is, the allocation of responsibility in the present context relates not to identifying the origins of the Mumbai attack but to whose actions or lack of them led to the enormity of the pain inflicted on the victims. As shown, India's options for tackling the source of the attack—that is, Pakistan—were, and still are, very limited, owing to Pakistan's possession of nuclear weapons. Because Indian policymakers lacked control on this aspect of the problem, they cannot be held responsible for the persistence of cross-border terrorist activity. Arguably, India could do the same thing to Pakistan—that is, arm rebels who target the Pakistani state and its citizens. This might force Pakistan to back off or, alternatively, exacerbate matters by weakening a nuclear-armed state that is itself subject to terrorist attacks. Former foreign secretary Shyam Saran, arguing that Indian leaders "lack a toolkit of options," has suggested something similar: that pressure could be put on Pakistan-controlled Gilgit and Baltistan, over which India has claims (Saran 2017, 98). Pakistan has long accused India of aiding insurgents in its Balochistan Province, but there is no known evidence for this. From a social contract perspective, it is a moot point whether India's citizens would actually gain in security. It may not be a good idea to encourage internal turbulence in an unstable nuclear-armed state already afflicted with violent jihadi groups, which may explain why India's leaders have avoided this course of action. The issue of responsibility thus boils down to what the Indian state has done in the area where it does have control (i.e., the domestic realm). And here, as is clear from the evidence presented, the Indian state was seriously wanting in meeting its responsibility.

The distinction between forward- and backward-mapping is useful in ascertaining responsibility. A backward-mapping analysis reveals a high level of culpability, most of it traceable to those holding bureaucratic and political office at the central and state levels. At the central level, there were multiple failures of organization, command and control, intelligence, and coastal security. The HLEC, appointed by the State of Maharashtra, had no jurisdiction over the central government and hence could not consider the critically important questions relating to these matters. But V. Balachandran, one of the two members of the HLEC, later highlighted these, and many of the lapses he identifies have been noted above. On January 9, 2009, the Maharashtra government wrote to the central government to inform them of the constitution of the HLEC and asked for cooperation, but little was forthcoming. Balachandran notes that senior central intelligence officers personally told him that they were unable to participate in the inquiry or share intelligence reports (Balachandran 2017, 184–85).

The new home minister, P. Chidambaram, obfuscated when he told Parliament on November 30, 2008, that there were two kinds of lapses: "systemic mistakes" and "indecision" (quoted by Balachandran 2017, 192). Balachandran pointedly asks: "Whose indecision was he talking about?" (Balachandran 2017, 192). That is a question the Indian government clearly had no desire to answer. The national government was evasive on the opposition demand for an inquiry commission into the whole episode. Chidambaram told Parliament that there was no need for it, because the state government had already appointed a committee, which begged the question of how the HLEC, whose remit was confined to the state of Maharashtra, could unveil issues pertaining to the center (NDTV 2009).

It is evident that both the Coast Guard, which was generally lax, as shown by the CAG's (2011) report on its functioning, and the Navy were responsible for letting the terrorists slip through their security cordon. Both are accountable for failing to carry out their assigned patrolling duties, which created gaps in the already challenging task of coastal surveillance. Navy chief Admiral Sureesh Mehta's explanation for not following up an intelligence warning of a sea-based threat—that it was "not actionable"—was no more than a prevarication (Pandit 2016), but he was not—so far as we know—asked to explain why. Neither he nor his deputies were held accountable for this serious failure.

Above all, the state and central governments may be held accountable for poor planning and lax implementation of such plans as were made to ensure both the capacity to prevent the attack and the capability to respond competently to an attack. The veteran journalist Prem Shankar Jha homes in on top decision-makers. For the failure of intelligence, he argues (Jha 2009, 130), "The fault lies in the chain of command that stretches from those whose business it is to collect the intelligence to those whose business it is to collate and analyze it, and recommend the appropriate course of action. The entire function, and the Secretariat that performs it, is located in the Prime Minister's Office, and is presided over by the National Security Adviser."

At the state level, as the HLEC points out, the failure of senior officials to make themselves aware of critically important intelligence inputs led them to be ignorant of numerous intelligence reports that, if they had been put together coherently, could have led the government to respond more effectively to a clear and immediate threat. Realizing that their culpability might be exposed, state government policymakers decided—somewhat late in the day—to make the HLEC's report a classified document (Balachandran 2017, 202). But the report was leaked anyway and became freely available on the internet.

From the standpoint of forward-mapping, senior government functionaries failed to respond in a coordinated way through apex national security institutions designed precisely for crises. The home minister further delayed the response by making the National Security Guard team wait for an hour before departing from Delhi. The most egregious failures were those of intelligence officials who (1) failed to intercept the cell phones used by terrorists despite knowing the numbers and being forewarned; and (2) when they did intercept the numbers during the actual attack, failed to jam the cellphones of the terrorists. The senior Navy official who ignored the intelligence warning that a boat was attempting to infiltrate coastal waters was also responsible for a serious error of judgment that did not take into account the specificity of the warning and the context in which it was given. The culpability of the commissioner of police for unsatisfactory handling of the crisis, itself a matter of controversy, is far less in comparison.

Holding individuals accountable is a key principle in a democratic state, both for moral reasons (failure to exercise responsibility properly) and because a society that does not punish a defaulter is likely to experience the default again. The Indian state has shown ample evidence of being one that allows such recurrences because very few, if any, pay a personal price for the kinds of failures that were manifest in 2008. Let us review the political fallout from the event.

In the central government, the prime minister and his cabinet did not acknowledge collective responsibility. Home Minister Shivraj Patil resigned immediately after the Mumbai attack. But in 2010, he was appointed to the powerful position of governor of the state of Punjab. Defense Minister A.

K. Anthony offered to resign, but the offer was not accepted. Likewise, NSA M. K. Narayanan, a key figure in the central government's response, gave his resignation, but it too was rejected. The Prime Minister's Office, which is normally the focal point of major policy decisions and actions, was not held responsible. According to a newspaper report, the central government came "close to sacking" top officials of the Intelligence Bureau and the Research and Analysis Wing (the agency responsible for external intelligence), but they were let off because they were due to retire within a short period (Baweja 2012). No action was taken against the Navy's officials for ignoring the warning on intrusion by a suspicious vessel.

At the level of Maharashtra State, Chief Minister Vilasrao Deshmukh resigned soon after the attack. However, a few months later, in May 2009, he was appointed minister of heavy industries and public enterprises in the central government. Home Minister Raosaheb Ramrao Patil, who held charge of the state's intelligence and police, initially tried to pass off the attacks as a minor incident, eliciting public outrage. He, too, was compelled to resign in December 2008, but was back as Maharashtra's home minister in slightly less than a year, in November 2009 (Kuber 2009). Mumbai's commissioner of police, Hasan Gafoor, who was criticized for a number of lapses by the HLEC, was removed from his post in June 2009 but was promoted to director-general of the state's Anti-Corruption Bureau.

It is far from clear, then, that any one was held responsible other than in a temporary and limited, face-saving way to minimize criticism. In short, no one paid the price for India's poor preparedness and inadequate response to the attack, which paved the way for similar occurrences in the future. The picture across the board is dispiriting. Fatalities caused by terrorist attacks have certainly been reduced over the years compared with the high numbers at the turn of the century, but they have remained substantial since the Mumbai attacks and persist today (South Asia Terrorism Portal n.d.–b).

It appears that if many individuals are responsible for an event, accountability becomes diffused and the individual is lost in the crowd. This enables leaders to evade moral culpability and pass off a failure as a "systemic" problem for which no one is held accountable. The same reasoning as Chidambaram's was applied by the Kargil Review Committee's Report to explain the intelligence failure that produced that particular crisis, as a critic has noted (Bedi 2000, 1429). This is a typical example of evasion of responsibility of the kind that has occurred elsewhere, for instance, with respect to the sorry state of electric power management in India (Chatterjee 2012). Studies show that diffusion of responsibility produces increased risk taking (Beyer et al. 2017; Chou and Nordgren 2017). Nevertheless, membership in a collective does not give individuals the right to evade responsibility (Narveson 2002). We may differ on the extent to which specific individuals are responsible in a specific case. We may also differ on the quantum of punishment that should properly be meted out to that individual. But the principle of accountability does not exempt individuals who are responsible for acts of commission or omission. In the present case, no one was held fully accountable and punished for failing to act in a responsible way.

There is one more culpable "agent" that I have not touched on above, and that is the "principal" itself—the people. In a democracy, as I have noted in chapter 1, the people, who elect the government as their agent, may have relatively limited control over the latter on an everyday basis, but they are ultimately accountable to themselves. Each society may have different mechanisms—such as referendums, recalls, and elections—by which the principal (the public) controls its agents (elected leaders and unelected officials). But this responsibility—of holding leaders and through them officials accountable—does exist, though there are arguably qualifications to the degree of responsibility (Pasternak 2011). In this sense, the public cannot escape from the responsibilities that accompany freedom.

As it happened, the citizenry did not exercise its ultimate power through democratic elections to hold those in political office accountable for their failings. Election data show that the ruling party in the national Parliament as well as the Maharashtra legislative assembly—the Congress in both cases—remained unaffected by the Mumbai disaster. At the national level, in the Lok Sabha elections of 2009, the Congress obtained the highest number of seats—206 of 543—though still needing to form a coalition, while in the Maharashtra assembly, it achieved the same rank with 82 seats of 288, again sufficient to form a coalition government (*Indiavotes* n.d.). The need to form coalition governments was not unusual because the Congress had been in a similar position before the 2008 attack. In short, the ruling party at both the central and state levels was not held accountable or punished electorally for its poor performance in 2008. By reelecting them, the citizenry as principal abdicated its responsibility to itself.

The thrust of my argument is that many contemporary scholars, though providing valuable understandings of diverse phenomena in international relations, may miss something important if they ignore the normative element. In the present case, India's failure to respond properly to the Mumbai terrorist attack could have been analyzed by focusing on "objective" factors, such as inadequate state capacity, corruption, institutional weakness, and bureaucratic politics (e.g., Basrur 2009; Ganguly and Thompson 2016; Mukherji 2016; Thompson 2018). But that would have lost sight of a key explanation for why states sometimes fail to provide security to their people. The focus on responsibility here subsumes "objective" explanations, and yet it empirically identifies the essential cause of an important phenomenon—the state's failure to protect its people—which is ultimately a moral failure.

The Mumbai attack produced a relatively serious upheaval in the Indian approach to counterterrorism. Policymakers were galvanized into action, and a flurry of reforms was set in motion. At the national level, the Unlawful Activities (Prevention) Act was passed in December 2008, and the National Investigative Agency was established. The National Security Guard was doubled in size, and hubs were established in Ahmedabad, Chennai, Hyderabad, Kolkata, and Mumbai. The intelligence apparatus was tightened; the Multi-Agency Center in the capital and Subsidiary Multi-Agency Centers were activated, and the National Intelligence Board was created, with the prime minister as its head. A mechanism was created to issue identity cards to all fishermen (Karve 2018).

But there were still numerous inadequacies in the system. The National Counter-Terrorism Center, mooted by the Congress-led United Progressive Alliance government in 2012, was abandoned by the Narendra Modi government (Shekhar 2020). This might appear to be a structural problem because the Bharatiya Janata Party did not have a majority in the Rajya Sabha, which would need to approve the law establishing the Counter-Terrorism Center, but the real problem is the lack of trust that plagues center–state relations. States resist the expansion of central power because they are not consulted (Interview 2012). The National Security Guard remained a body without a specialized cadre and depended on personnel deputed from other departments (Unnithan 2014, 216). Intelligence oversight was still inadequate (Joshi 2014, 6). Lacunae in coastal security remained, such as the absence of a standing body to "strategize, plan, oversee, and coordinate maritime security from a wider context (beyond coastal security)" (Das

2018, 112). State marine police remained poorly funded and underequipped (Karve 2018).

Did material factors shape policy drift? Prima facie, there may appear to be reason to make an argument along this line. First, governmental politics may have produced policy failings because both central and state governments had a role to play in the Mumbai disaster. In particular, terrorism was a national concern, but a primary line of action—both prevention and response—was through the state police and home departments. There have certainly been regular tensions between the center and the states over the former's encroachment on the latter's jurisdiction. But the Mumbai attack occurred when the ruling party at both central and state levels was the same, and there is no evidence of any tension between the center and the state at this time. Second, there is ample evidence in the pages above of poor bureaucratic coordination between various agencies at the center, at the state level, and between the center and the state. But such inefficiency would not have occurred if there had been adequate supervision by policymakers from the highest level down the line. And it would not have been sustained if responsibility and accountability had been practiced routinely. Third, organizational pathologies abounded, ranging from a lack of adequate equipment and training to leadership in several agencies. But these only underline the lack of responsibility and accountability that allowed the functioning of sub-optimal policy, because no one made the kinds of decisions required and undertook appropriate follow-up actions that might have mitigated the problem.

Why did the responsibility deficit remain as substantial as it did? Three major reasons may be adduced. First, the national government was able to successfully focus on the external source of cross-border terrorism (Pakistan) and in effect minimize its own responsibility for the domestic aspect. There is a considerable literature on the diversionary theory of conflict showing how governments facing domestic difficulties at home try to transfer the burden of responsibility to other states (Butcher and Maru 2018; Gelpi 1997; Kagotani, Kimura, and Weber 2014). Though much of it looks at domestic problems as the source of external tension, the picture given in this chapter is somewhat different. Though Pakistan *was* the source of the cross-border problem, successive Indian governments were able to depict it as the *sole* source of its costly effects and thereby minimize their own responsibility for the cost imposed on their society.

Second, the appearance of action both against Pakistan through bilateral and multilateral pressure and at home via changes in the national security apparatus showed the government to be doing something, which somewhat diminished the negative image that might have been conveyed by inaction. As I noted in chapter 1, there is a difference between complete failure and policy drift, and the evidence given above demonstrates the latter rather than the former.

Third, in the aftermath of the series of terrorist attacks that had taken place over the years—both in Mumbai and elsewhere in the country—there was no major political upheaval, hence the political costs to policymakers were, in a sense, bearable. Both factors discussed above were repeated ad nauseam, producing temporary anger and a flurry of externally directed and internal actions before the system lapsed into routine inertia.

In the end, we may deduce, the cost/benefit calculation of policymakers has inclined them toward drift. The cost of ineffectiveness has been politically tolerable. In contrast, the cost of actually producing an effective domestic response would be substantial. It would involve, among other things, restructuring and properly activating the national security apparatus; optimizing the organization of intelligence and counterterrorism responses at both the central and state levels; allocating funds for raising national security standards through investment in equipment and training; and, perhaps the most difficult and politically arduous task, tackling the pervasive corruption that has allowed substantial cross-border terrorist and criminal activity to persist.

The most obvious but difficult path to countering cross-border terrorism—negotiating a political solution to political disaffection within Indian-held Kashmir—has barely been attempted. The national government—no matter who is in charge—has tended to concentrate too much of its attention pertaining to the problem of cross-border terrorism on its external dimension. Even domestically, an excessive focus on the military option—the deployment of large numbers of military and paramilitary forces in Kashmir—has not worked. The Indian government has expended much less effort than it might have done in trying to arrive at a political solution to the Kashmir issue, which offers space to externally based terrorists (International Crisis Group 2020; Navlakha 2009). The scope for terrorists to obtain assistance within India depends on the extent to which they can draw on local support. The secessionist movement for "Khalistan" in

India's Punjab province in the 1980s was tackled effectively by means of a concerted police response, combined with a political solution that weaned local support away from the movement (Jamwal 2003). But this has not been attempted with tenacity and commitment in Kashmir. Arguably, the domestic aspect of India's Kashmir "problem" is a complex one that requires a more nuanced approach rather than the simple, security-driven one that has been adopted by successive national governments (Chowdhary 2015). As A. S. Dulat, a former intelligence chief, has argued (quoted by Haidar 2018): "Delhi needs to do much more. There are two standard excuses from the establishment in Delhi. One is, who do we talk to in Pakistan, and the other, what is the point of speaking to anyone in Kashmir if they are controlled by Pakistan? It's a negative way of thinking. You need to find people to speak with in Pakistan and in Kashmir."

CONCLUSION

As in the preceding three chapters, India's policymaking is shown in this one to have been characterized by prolonged drift. The shock that sparked a move to tackle cross-border terrorism was not a single one (though the 1993 Mumbai blasts should have been sufficient), but a series of damaging attacks by means of bombings and commando-style assaults that in fact began with the violent Punjab secessionist movement in the 1980s and continued into the 1990s in Kashmir, Delhi, Mumbai, and elsewhere. Though much of its energy was focused on a futile effort to deter Pakistan from backing jihadis based on its soil, the Indian leadership nevertheless did try to reorganize its internal security capabilities. None of the major moves it undertook faced significant domestic opposition.

Yet the whole process of security reform failed to develop much drive. The reason for this, we have seen, was not structural: the domestic distribution of power—unlike in the India-US and India–Sri Lanka cases—was not a factor in setting a laggardly and inefficient pace or causing the whole process to meander ineffectively to culminate in the shock of the Mumbai attack. As systematically demonstrated through a backward- and forward-mapping analysis, the Mumbai disaster was the outcome of multiple abdications of responsibility, topped with a failure to pin the faults unequivocally on those who had caused the failure and hold them accountable. Because the rot had set in from the top, no one was punished. And because no one had to pay a significant price, the responsibility deficit remains in place and the problem continues to fester.

In 2020, for instance, a government audit pertaining to the national capital, New Delhi—where security is higher than in most other Indian cities—identified a number of serious flaws in preparedness. Even as crimes rose sharply by 275 percent between 2013 and 2019, the proportion of functional CCTV cameras remained "abysmally low," the police communication system continued to be obsolete, the number of wireless systems was woefully inadequate, and thousands of approved posts in the Delhi Police lay vacant (*Tribune* 2020). The responsibility deficit could not be starker, illustrating a classic example of how normative failure facilitates security disasters.

6

CONSIDERATIONS FOR POLICY AND THEORY

The main objective of this book has been to explain why Indian foreign policy has often been characterized by multiple hesitations, delays, and diversions. Underlying the question of recurrent policy uncertainty is the larger question of whether India—as many policymakers, scholars, media persons, and members of the public have long considered inevitable—will achieve the promise of major power status and capacity in the foreseeable future. It would seem that a chronic inability to make and implement decisive policy constrains the capacity to attain major power status. At the time of writing (spring 2022), the prospects seem challenging as, despite signs of recovery, India still reels from the crushing blow of the COVID-19 pandemic and its associated economic costs. But it is important to recall that, in the aftermath of independence, India's very survival was thought to be a daunting task by even the most optimistic. Those "dangerous decades" (Harrison 1960) are a dim memory, having been overlaid by an optimistic script written by a "rising power" seeking its place in the sun in the new millennium. But the downturn in India's economic fortunes over the past decade has revived the pessimism of those who have constantly drawn attention to India's limitations, its inefficiencies and its corruption, and the sheer magnitude of the tasks before its multitudinous peoples and fragmented society in a world characterized by unpredictable change.

LOOKING BACK

I have attempted in these pages to explain why India, after attaining a positive trajectory in the post–Cold War years, has periodically stumbled or appeared to lose control over the reins of its potential. Most analysts have sought to highlight the difficulties posed by its tumultuous politics and the sheer enormity of the tasks its policymakers face. But these same conditions did not prevent India from performing with unprecedented success once it had shed much of its historical baggage and embarked on a period of accelerated growth and recognition as a major power in the making. The latest version of the palimpsest has caused much dismay, but one that has not been adequately understood, not least because the "rising power" has harbored inherent contradictions that have come to leash it. I have tried to provide a measure of systematic understanding of the complexity of the process through an inquiry that transcends the limitations of materialist analysis.

The four cases explored in this book demonstrate that there are two basic types of explanation for India's indecision on crucial issues. In every instance of policy drift, Indian policymakers have sought to put in place substantial alterations in broad policy to adapt to systemic incentives. They have been able to do this without too much difficulty, though they have subsequently faltered on crucial specifics of policy. As chapter 2 shows, they have tried to respond to looming isolation and stagnation by opening up the economy and establishing unprecedented strategic linkages with the predominant power of the post–Cold War era, the United States. Chapter 3 shows how policymakers have tried to stave off a looming threat from China by strengthening relations with a small neighbor, Sri Lanka, which sought Indian assistance in its civil war. Chapter 4 illustrates how Indian leaders have responded to the perceived threat from two closely connected nuclear powers—China and Pakistan—as well as the nuclear nonproliferation regime by shedding their past reluctance to adopt nuclear weapons as formal instruments of national security. And in chapter 5, we see how they have sought to counter the relentless tide of terrorist attacks from across India's western border by pressuring Pakistan as well as revamping their domestic security apparatus.

All these efforts have struggled to achieve success. Although the broad policy changes introduced have not been difficult to put in place, their translation into specifics has wobbled and lost momentum. The main focus of this book has been to assess the reasons for the policy drift that has been visible in each case after the initial reformulation of policy. In two cases, the source of India's uncertainty in implementing desired policy was material. The India-US nuclear agreement, discussed in chapter 2, was the cornerstone of a transformed relationship that would give Indian security a major boost. Though there was no serious opposition to the initial reframing of the India-US relationship, the implementation of its centerpiece—the nuclear deal—soon floundered and nearly fell through owing to domestic political opposition. Political groups with diverse priorities, many with little interest in the nuclear deal itself, exploited the weakness of a coalition government that struggled to maintain a firm policy path for three years and nearly collapsed before managing to squeak through.

Chapter 3 shows how the government tried to nip China's strategic ambitions in the bud by assisting Sri Lanka in its civil war with the Liberation Tigers of Tamil Eelam and bolstering Colombo's military capabilities. But the policy sailed into choppy waters as domestic resistance stemming from state-level politics in Tamil Nadu gathered sufficient momentum to thwart the national government, which was once again constrained by the weakness of its coalition, this time exploited by both allied and opposition parties. In both cases, the distribution of domestic political power severely hampered the central government's capacity to carry out a major policy change already in motion.

Material factors have not been central to policy drift with respect to two other critically important policies. Chapter 4 demonstrates that the formal adoption of nuclear weapons as a pillar of national security strategy was a dramatic policy shift that was not met with serious opposition. The devil lurked in the details. The new strategic framework was accompanied by a doctrinal preference for nuclear minimalism as the underpinning of nuclear strategy. But, despite the absence of material constraints, it soon ran into difficulty and split into divergent trajectories, one minimalist and one tending toward the maximalist. The difference between the two, yet to be reconciled, has been due to ideational confusion: the foundational concept of minimum deterrence—based on a clear understanding of how deterrence has worked historically—has not been properly understood, which has allowed doctrine and posture to incorporate serious contradictions. The source of the problem, I argue, has been the political leadership's reluctance to exercise its responsibility for optimizing a strategy that was always under its control and the consequent emergence of an increasingly dissonant policy framework.

India's most urgent and costly problem—cross-border terrorism emanating from Pakistan—has similarly been ineffectively dealt with. Chapter 5, giving due recognition to India's inability to coerce a nuclear-armed

Pakistan to desist from backing jihadis targeting it, focuses on the domestic dimension of policy, which *was* under policymakers' control. A comprehensive revamping of the national security apparatus in response to the sustained subconventional threat from across the border (there were also similar internal threats) was set in motion and faced no significant difficulties; yet the horrific assault on Mumbai, like many bombings and attacks before it, happened. The failures to prevent it and, when it occurred, to respond adequately to it, were due not to material constraints but—as in the preceding case—to an unquestionable responsibility deficit. Policymakers repeatedly failed to put a recharged policy fully in place and to hold those responsible for its recurring setbacks accountable. These two chapters underscore the material effects of ethical failings: the recurrence of responsibility deficits produces practical effects of a negative character because unproductive policy remains in situ and continues to produce suboptimal results.

Conceptually, the analysis makes a critical distinction between two types of policy drift. Involuntary drift occurs when policymakers lack adequate control over the levers of policy implementation owing to material factors (in the two cases discussed, the distribution of domestic political power). Voluntary drift occurs when policymakers do have control (though there may be some material constraints) but do not exercise this control properly, partly because they lack the political will to do so and partly because they are able to get way with limited action that makes the outcome, however costly it might be, politically tolerable. The distinction between the two types of drift is an important conceptual contribution of this volume because it opens the door to accommodating both material and ideational explanations for suboptimal policy outcomes.

My argument recognizes that factors outside those considered in these pages do regularly hinder the making of effective policy. Here are three noteworthy examples.

OTHER SOURCES OF DRIFT

Not all instances of drift relating to important policy issues can be attributed to the domestic failings of governments. India's inability to make progress on a number of policies related to national security may be explained by external factors or by conscious choices aimed at avoiding costs. Three examples are briefly considered here.

The Enduring Rivalry of India and Pakistan

The India-Pakistan conflict is a tale of continual tensions from the moment the two parted bitterly at the time of independence from British rule in 1947 (Basrur 2008; Cohen 2013; Ganguly 2002; Paul 2005). The contest over largely Muslim-populated Kashmir, which acceded to India upon Partition, has been central to the acrimony, with Muslim-majority Pakistan claiming possession of the territory and predominantly Hindu India averring its secular composite identity as a basis for retaining it. The first war between them (1947–49) left Kashmir divided, with about a third wrested by Pakistan. Since then, there have been more wars, in 1965 and 1971; rising tensions, with the covert and later overt nuclearization of the two states (between the mid-1980s and 1998); armed combat bringing them close to war in 1999; and a series of crises—including a near-war in 2001–2—that have periodically threatened to unleash a nuclear conflagration on the subcontinent (Basrur 2008; Chari, Cheema, and Cohen 2007; Ganguly and Hagerty 2005; Paul 2005).

Why have the two states been pitted against each other for so long? Though numerous reasons have been adduced for the continuing struggle, the chief ones have been the centrality of Kashmir to their national identities and the dominance of Pakistan's domestic politics by a military with a vested interest in perpetuating the conflict in order to stay in power (Cohen 2013; Paul 2014; Varshney 1991). Domestic politics on the Indian side has been an exacerbating cause because making concessions to Pakistan has always been fraught with peril for policymakers. Nonetheless, the potential for arriving at some sort of sustained détente, or perhaps even resolution, was revealed in the mid-2000s, when the two states began to think out of the box.

Two factors played a significant role in this new willingness to come to terms. First, the nuclearization of the subcontinent after matching nuclear tests in 1998 was followed by the outbreak of major crises. In 1999, fierce but limited combat took place along the icy Himalayan heights of Kargil; and in 2001–2, both sides mobilized extensively for a major war after an attack on India's Parliament by Pakistan-based terrorists. The lesson of the two crises was that the risk of war was unaffordable and a negotiated compromise had to be found. Second, the end of the Cold War amid the increasing integration brought by economic globalization highlighted the cost of continuing military confrontation and the potential benefits of economic cooperation in a fast-changing world (Friedman 2002). Prime Minister Manmohan Singh of India and general-turned-president Pervez Musharraf of Pakistan agreed to soften the Line of Control (LoC) that separated their armies in Kashmir by enhancing trade and travel across it and engaged in back-channel negotiations that had the potential to transform the LoC into a formal border over time (Coll 2009; Parashar 2011). However, the prospect of a breakthrough disintegrated as Musharraf's domestic position went into a tailspin and compelled him to step down. In the end, Pakistan returned to the hybrid system Musharraf had earlier overthrown—a formal democracy with the military exercising veto power—and the deal was aborted. The Pakistani military then backtracked on its assent to the compromise on the LoC and continued to exploit nuclear deterrence to engage in asymmetric conflict (Jervis 1999).

This episode not only showed that the Kashmir issue is not as impervious to conciliation as it has seemed but also suggested that a solution to the enduring imbroglio is unlikely to be found as long as Pakistan's army needs continuing conflict to ensure its hold on the reins of power. The troubled relationship has certainly exhibited elements of the security dilemma (Glaser 1997; Jervis 1978)—for instance, in the conventional and nuclear arms competition between them. But, at bottom, though India has been relatively status quo–ist, Pakistan has been a consistently revisionist state determined to wrest Kashmir in one way or another (Ganguly 2016). In short, this is a problem that is fundamentally beyond India's capacity to resolve and not a case of policy drift on its part.

Persistent Tensions between India and China

The conflict between India and China has displayed a similar pattern. At its root lies their dispute over a long border stretching about 3,500 kilometers. Both polities were uncertain of their position in the postwar years: India struggled to meet the promise of independence; China was treated as a pariah by the United States and much of the world after the communist revolution in 1949. Strains between them began early and, despite efforts to come to an understanding, the relationship took on the character of an enduring rivalry (Egreteau 2012; Garver 2001; Guyot-Réchard 2019; Huchet 2008; Malik 2010; Ogden 2017; Paul 2018). War broke out in 1962 over a border that still remains disputed, followed by brief clashes in 1967, a prolonged face-off in 1986–87, and repeated confrontations over the so-called Line of Actual Control (LAC) that should separate their forces but is a source of constant friction because they cannot agree on demarcating it.

Recurring military confrontations have occurred over the LAC, and these have grown frequent and more violent. Between 2003 and 2014, there were thirty incidents along the LAC (Bhonsale 2018). In 2017 and 2020, major faceoffs took place at Doklam at the India–Bhutan–China trijunction and in Eastern Ladakh on the India–China border respectively. In the latter case, India acknowledged losing twenty men in one incident and one more in another, while China did not admit to any losses (Ganguly 2018b; Maini 2020), though evidence later emerged that a number of Chinese troops had also been killed (Yang, Chen, and Liu 2021). The prolonged and rising tension between the two nations stems partly from domestic factors. Both sides have been reluctant to come to a compromise because border concessions tend to have political repercussions. This particularly applies to populated areas, of which the Indian state of Arunachal Pradesh—claimed by China—is a prominent example. India's Modi and China's Xi—because they are populist strongmen inclined to be tough on opponents—may have also exacerbated rising tensions. But they are relatively new leaders and, as in the India–Pakistan relationship, the friction-filled relationship has shown potential for compromise.

The two states have been able to manage their rivalry since the late 1980s by establishing military confidence-building measures, employing mechanisms for political negotiation on their differences, and engaging in a substantial trade and investment relationship (Diehl 2018; Ganguly and Scobell 2018; Shankar 2018). The rising friction between them has transcended changes in leadership on both sides. A negative turning point can be traced to the rapid warming of India-US relations (discussed in chapter 2), which exacerbated the tensions between New Delhi and Beijing and generated a balancing game that had hitherto been moderated by their mutual willingness to focus on positives.

The aggravation of tensions has been marked by a pattern of interaction typical of balancing behavior between rival states. The balance-of-power dynamic has been a complex one linking India, China, and the United States (and other countries) in a strategic chain (Einhorn and Sidhu 2017; Pant 2019). China and India are not in any sense at a comparable level of material power, other than in size and population. China, which considers itself as being on the same level as the United States, is a challenger to American primacy in the global system. To a considerable degree, the tensions between the United States and China carry the features of a growing security dilemma. Each views the other as a threat and responds with, among other things, the modernization of its military capabilities. A much weaker but rising India, viewing China's growing military strength as a threat to itself, has responded with a similar effort to build a more robust military force. This cascading security dilemma has sharpened antagonisms considerably. India has sought to establish strategic partnerships with China's rivals—notably the United States, Japan, and Vietnam—while China has tightened its linkage with Pakistan. In a maritime dimension to the security dilemma, China has expanded into the Indian Ocean, while India has become more active in the Western Pacific (Koh 2016, 2019).

Although the persistence of the India–China rivalry has been sustained partly by domestic factors in both states with respect to the potential fallout of a compromise, the cascading security dilemma that links the United States with China and with India is the main driver. The latter is not attributable to Indian domestic politics, and therefore the drift in the relationship does not fall clearly within the purview of neoclassical realist analysis, at least of the Type I category employed here. There is still a case for the view that Indian policymakers have neglected China's threat potential in the past, but a more energetic policy would not have reduced the drift. The main cause of their continuing hostility has been balance-of-power politics.

Limited Progress with Status Markers

Status, an important concept in world politics, is an indicator of a state's image (and self-image) and of its actual or potential influence, and thus complements its security (Freedman 2015; Paul, Larson, and Wohlforth 2017; Volgy et al. 2011a). India's leadership has since independence sought to attain high status in the world of states (Basrur and de Estrada 2017; Nayar and Paul 2003; Paul and Shankar 2014). In the early postindependence years, Nehru played an active role in diplomacy at the global level, helping to pull together the developing postcolonial world into what became the nonaligned movement, which pressed the major powers to disarm, decolonize, and dismantle apartheid. But India under Nehru and his successors lacked the power to command more than limited influence and to bring about real change in the global political order.

India's status began to grow from the early 1990s, when it revised its worldview and made the two watershed decisions alluded to in chapter 1. First, it discarded its autarkic approach to the world economy, seeking the integration it had previously shunned by expanding external trade and inviting large-scale foreign direct investment. This brought it the sobriquet of an "emerging market" or "emerging economy" (Eichengreen, Gupta, and Kumar 2010; Panagariya 2008; Shamsi et al. 2014). Second, after a long period of hesitation on nuclear weapons—unutilized capability after 1974 and a covert and underdeveloped arsenal from the late 1980s—India went public with a series of tests and declared itself a nuclear power in 1998. This brought it the label of a "rising" or "emerging" power, which further elevated its status (Cohen 2001; Narlikar 2013; Pant 2009; Pardesi 2015; Scott 2009).

The attainment of eminent status is illustrated by a wide range of possible markers, such as relative material (economic and military) capabilities, the number of embassies a state attracts, the number and frequency of high-level visitors it receives, its association with major powers through alliances or partnerships, and its membership of and positions in exclusive "clubs" of nations (Volgy 2011b; Ward 2017). India's post–Cold War search for status has notched up several of these markers. Its economic capabilities have grown (in constant 2010 dollars), with its gross domestic product rising from $512.92 billion in 1991 to $2.96 trillion in 2019 (World Bank n.d.–c). In the same time frame, its military spending has also grown (in current dollars), from $8.62 billion to $66.51 billion (World Bank, n.d.–d). It has obtained membership in several global clubs, such as the Group of Twenty; the Quadrilateral Security Dialogue (Australia, India, Japan, and the United States); BRICS (Brazil, Russia, India, China, and South Africa); IBSA (India, Brazil, and South Africa); and institutional components of the nuclear nonproliferation regime, such as the Missile Technology Control Regime and the Wassenaar Arrangement (though not the Nuclear Suppliers Group). It has also signed strategic partnerships—defense linkages, short of alliances—with major powers like France, Japan, Russia, and the United States, plus several with other powers. These give it impressive credentials and considerable status gains.

But the flurry of successes has not been sustained and India has experienced a slowdown, much of it owing to factors beyond the control of its policymakers. Its growth rate has been sluggish, dropping from 8.25 percent in 2016 to 5.04 percent in 2019 (World Bank n.d.–c). But this is not simply a reflection of domestic failure. A quick glance at the World Bank's gross domestic product growth graph shows that India's growth trend roughly parallels that of the world economy, broadly starting in 1999, but closely after 2016. The precipitous contraction of the Indian economy by 24 percent during the period April–June 2020 reflects the calamitous effects of the COVID-19 pandemic (Gulati, Jose, and Singh 2021) and is hardly unusual: similar declines have been experienced by other countries. During the same period, the US economy declined by 32.9 percent (Cox 2020), the United Kingdom's by 20.4 percent (Smith 2020), and Japan's by 11.3 percent (*Japan Times* 2020). Doubtless, India's position as a rising power and its security generally have been adversely affected by its economic woes, but—regardless of its own limitations in responding to them—the origins of these woes appear to lie in substantial part outside its borders.

In addition, there are important global institutions India has not obtained access to. One is the Nuclear Suppliers Group, membership in which has been denied to it owing to Chinese opposition (Rajagopalan 2016b; Rajagopalan and Biswas 2016; Weigold 2016). India has also pressed for permanent membership in a redesigned United Nations Security Council but has not made any significant progress, partly because of opposition from China—which is also firmly opposed to another claimant, Japan—and some smaller states. Besides, major powers that have been formally more supportive have shown little interest in undertaking UN reform (Hosli and Dörfler 2019; Kumar 2017). As with India's economic difficulties, its inability to acquire a seat at key tables is not the consequence of domestic factors.

India has also held itself back by refraining from one form of strategic behavior that major powers have characteristically displayed throughout history: military intervention. Since the early 1990s, it has eschewed employing military force outside its borders, despite opportunities and even invitations to do so. It is worth keeping in mind that India had been an interventionist state as a regional power until about 1990. It interceded in the civil war between East Pakistan and West Pakistan in 1971, and helped in the emergence of an independent Bangladesh (Marwah 1979); militarily asserted its control over New Moore / Talpatty Island—disputed with Bangladesh—in the Bay of Bengal in 1981 (Mitra 1981); prepared (though it eventually did not deploy) its Navy for a countercoup in Mauritius in 1983 (Brewster and Rai 2013b); sent the Indian Navy to help avert a coup in the Seychelles in 1986 (Brewster and Rai 2013a); intervened in Sri Lanka's civil war in 1987 to try and subdue the Liberation Tigers of Tamil Eelam (Kadian 1990); and overturned a coup d'état in the Maldives in 1988 (Singh 2016b).

In contrast, India has eschewed intervention and kept a low profile in the post–Cold War era. It has turned down a US invitation to send a peacekeeping force to Iraq in 2003 (Thakur 2003); contemplated but desisted from military action in Afghanistan, or even the extension of extensive defense assistance to it (Destradi 2014; Krishnan 2017); stayed away from active military support for Sri Lanka's government in its civil war (as seen in chapter 4); ignored a plea for intervention from the Maldives—then under threat from Islamist forces—in 2012 (Chellaney 2018); and disregarded domestic pressure to intervene militarily against an unstable and unfriendly government in the Maldives (Kazmin 2018). The potential gains from status have been outweighed by the potential costs of intervention, a lesson learned from India's failed intervention in Sri Lanka in 1987. Indian caution reveals a preference for avoiding suboptimal outcomes that might arise from imitating traditional great power behavior. There is perhaps a societal basis for Indian leaders' willingness to take their time. The quest for collective upward status mobility, deeply rooted in India's caste-dominated Hindu society, has historically been carried on through a process known as "Sanskritization" (Srinivas 1966, 1–48). A key facet of this is knowing that the acquisition of higher status takes time, usually "a generation or two" (Srinivas 1966, 6), which may explain the lack of impatience on the part of Indian leaders to ensure they have arrived.

The examples of drift identified here are not the consequences of domestic factors, but of impediments to policy that stem from the actions of—and interactions with—other nations, and, in the last case, partly from a prudent reluctance to incur excessive costs in order to attain higher status.

CHAPTER 6

POLICY DRIFT AND INDIA'S MAJOR POWER PROSPECTS

Has India's quest for major power status been bogged down by its domestic failures? Its capacity to implement vital policies is under question, not only because of the specific negativities associated with the cases examined here but also more generally given the shadow they cast over the ability of the Indian state to surmount domestic obstacles in pursuit of its interests as a potential major power.

The near failure of the nuclear deal with Washington demonstrates how close New Delhi came to losing the plot, so to speak, on building a relationship that has benefited it immensely in several ways: (1) adding to security through the acquisition of a wide range of sophisticated conventional arms and through greatly increased bilateral cooperation on a range of issues, from counterterrorism to regional stability; (2) paving the way for a major new strategic partnership with Japan as well as enhanced partnerships with France, Germany, and the United Kingdom; (3) setting in motion the building of a strong strategic network, in the form of the Quad; (4) triggering a range of new strategic partnerships with regional powers, such as Indonesia and Singapore in Southeast Asia and Israel, Saudi Arabia, and the United Arab Emirates in the Middle East; and (5) enhancing India's security position as well as status by altering the rules of the nuclear nonproliferation regime to make an exception for India by facilitating its membership in several of its components (the Nuclear Suppliers Group excepted). Much of this might not have happened, or at least would have been significantly slowed down, but for the successful culmination of the nuclear deal. The case harkens to the uncertainty over India's future as a major power arising from domestic constraints at pivotal junctures.

In the India–Sri Lanka case, India's strategic position not only in that country but also in the region would have been much stronger if a defense arrangement of the kind Colombo wanted had been worked out because it would have had rippling effects. It would have forged the kind of close relationship with Sri Lanka that India has been able to build with Bangladesh, kept China at bay, and facilitated similar close linkages with other neighboring states, such as the Maldives and Nepal, though not Pakistan.

A more effectual nuclear strategy would have allowed India to complement its moderate posture with restrained investment in capabilities that do not add to deterrence. The resources conserved could have been allocated to more urgent security areas that have received less attention than they might have, notably cybersecurity, in which India has vulnerabilities across the board (Bischoff 2020; Madhavan 2019; Voo et al. 2020). To be fair, however, it could reasonably be argued against this that India's image as a rising power has been enhanced by the symbolic power of nuclear weapons.

Finally, India's failure to prevent repeated and costly terrorist attacks such as the Mumbai assault has laid bare the shallowness of its claims to be a leading power and a net security provider. A state that cannot protect its own people does not have much of a foundation on which to build a major power reputation. Besides, the lopsided Pakistan-centric policy on cross-border terrorism has also revealed the weakness of the oft-repeated claim to India's status as the world's largest democracy because it has not shown the determination to work out a political solution to the issue of Kashmir through the democratic process.

The overall picture is that India's potential for achieving major power status stands on a relatively weak foundation, owing to its inability to follow through on those policies that are crucial to its security. Of the two sources of uncertainty, involuntary drift may possibly be temporary, but voluntary drift is a more debilitating long-term problem.

REFINING THEORY

The analysis of world politics today has been characterized by the revival of the realist approach owing to a number of factors. First, power politics has come to the forefront again with the rise of China and its challenge to American hegemony, and Russia's invasion of Ukraine in February 2022, which has intensified the sense that the optimism of the post–Cold War era was an aberration. Second, growing competitiveness in the world economy signifies the return of elements of mercantilist sentiment and interstate economic competition that cannot be fully understood without due regard to the realist perspective. Third, the rising tensions produced by the COVID-19 pandemic—with its pattern of interstate frictions over responsibility for its origins and over measures to mitigate it—have underscored the relevance of realism as an explanatory framework in international politics (Basrur and Kliem 2021; Walt 2020). These developments draw attention to the prominent role of conflicting national interests and power differentials in shaping the contemporary world but also to the role of intrastate factors in generating interstate antipathies and competitive policies.

The interplay between interstate and intrastate dynamics in the examples described above is conducive to explanation by Type III neoclassical realism, which looks at how systemic factors affect domestic politics and these in turn produce systemic effects. Though neoclassical realism (NCR) has moved on from its early focus on the domestic political sources of suboptimal outcomes, this book makes the point that there is still much to be gained from the application of Type I NCR theory. The application of this approach shows how crucial aspects of India's national security have been adversely affected by domestic politics. In the first two cases—the India-US nuclear deal and India's role in the Sri Lankan civil war—the preferences of policymakers were faced with major domestic roadblocks, which impeded their ability to craft appropriate policy. In the other two—the devising of nuclear deterrence doctrine and posture and the implementation of policy to counter cross-border terrorism—the efficacy of policy was and continues to be hindered by the leadership's failure to assume full responsibility for it. In only one of the four cases—that relating to the India-US nuclear agreement—was the intended policy eventually put in place. But even here, India came close to shooting itself in the foot on a critically important policy change.

Two of the other three cases represent costly setbacks. India's inability to play a major role in Sri Lanka's civil war allowed China to step in and establish a strategic foothold in that country. Since then, India has experienced the constant uneasiness that comes with a hostile state from the north gaining purchase to its south. The most damaging example of policy drift has been the inability to act decisively in responding to the internal security requirements of cross-border terrorism. In addition to the price paid in lives and injuries, it has left India struggling to fulfil its promise as a net security provider to its neighborhood and beyond (Mukherjee 2014), a claim that hardly stands much scrutiny when it is unable to put its own house in order. In comparison, the confusion relating to India's thinking and practice of nuclear deterrence has not produced an unmitigated failure. On the negative side, it has led to muddled strategy and the misallocation of scarce resources that might have been better spent on other security requirements pertaining to high technology, such as cyber defense and defense-related artificial intelligence. Conversely, there have been prestige gains—not to be dismissed lightly—accruing from the development of nuclear weapons as symbols of power. That said, the four case studies highlight the continuing relevance of NCR's Type I approach as critical to our understanding of the pathologies of international political life today.

The analysis in these pages calls for the qualification of neoclassical realism's established view that suboptimal outcomes are more likely under "normal" conditions, whereas structurally driven policy responses are the norm when threats to security are high. In three of the cases, there have been serious concerns driven by national security. The most serious ones pertain to cross-border terrorism, which has taken a severe toll on human life in India. The India-US nuclear deal was also propelled by a major national security concern: India's sudden isolation in the post–Cold War world and the rapid rise of an antagonistic China as a major power. The Chinese threat was accentuated by its military assistance to Sri Lanka, which has long been a critical security concern for India. Policy drift nevertheless did take place on all these issues.

It is worth reiterating the point I made in chapter 1 that the criticism of Type I NCR theory—that it sets arbitrary standards for deviation from the norm in trying to explain suboptimal outcomes (Narizny 2017)—does not apply here. In all the cases discussed in these pages, the standard from which deviation is evident was explicitly set by policymakers themselves. They envisioned a breakthrough with the United States, a significantly strengthened defense relationship with Sri Lanka, fortified national security underpinned by a minimalist nuclear strategy, and a revamped internal security apparatus in response to escalating cross-border terrorism. In each case, the broad outlines of the policy were put in place, but they then tended to become bogged down in political resistance and inertia. There is no place for scholarly bias here.

Perhaps the most notable contribution of this book—and the one most likely to be contested—is its expansion of the ambit of neoclassical realism to the normative sphere. The distinction I have made between involuntary and voluntary drift—based on the control (or lack of it) that decision-makers have over their policy environment—opens up a wider conceptual space for the accommodation of responsibility and accountability, which tends to be ignored or downplayed in most materialist analyses. Not all suboptimal outcomes can be explained by material factors. Two of the cases discussed—nuclear strategy and cross-border terrorism—exemplify the abdication of responsibility—that is, policymakers have done something, but not enough to produce effective policies. In the former, accountability has been difficult because the subject of policy is abstruse and beyond the reach of most nonspecialists. In the latter, that is not the case, and it is clear that a wide range of irresponsible agents have not been held to account by principals, the latter ultimately including the citizens of the country. This has resulted in the perpetuation of both problems.

The melding of material and nonmaterial factors in this work has been possible because of the inextricable linkage between the two. The concepts of responsibility and accountability are not outside the bounds of empirical analysis because the effects of failure in this regard are practical effects. Failure to exercise responsibility has reinforced negative trends in both cases: the inconsistent trajectories taken by nuclear strategy continue to be manifest; and the costs of not strengthening domestic responses adequately to externally based terrorist threats continue to be substantial. The persistence of suboptimal policies tends also to be sustained over time—two decades and more in the cases examined here. The integrated, materialist-ethical analysis of this book expands the scope of neoclassical realism and strengthens its capacity to better grasp Type I cases.

LOOKING AHEAD

The approach adopted here offers much scope for the study of unproductive policies in other spheres. With respect to Indian foreign policy, for instance, a Type I, NCR-based analysis would be useful in teasing out the skein of strategic neglect with respect to India's China policy. Though the antagonism between the two states may, as seen above, be attributed to external drivers, the question remains whether Indian policymakers have tended to allow their responses to the threat to be driven by occasional flurries of activity driven by crises, only to become more lackadaisical when tensions recede. A focused study of the relationship is likely to produce a nuanced picture.

There is also room for a deeper NCR-based understanding of the domestic politics of the India–Bangladesh relationship. Why, for instance, has a powerful political leader like Narendra Modi avoided an agreement on sharing river water? This does not, at first glance, seem to fit into the category of involuntary drift, as it did under previous coalition governments, since Modi has led a majority government (Ashraf 2020; Ranjan 2017). Appraisals might also be made of India's prolonged resistance and eventual refusal to join the Regional Comprehensive Economic Partnership with Australia, China, Japan, New Zealand, South Korea, and all ten members of the Association of Southeast Asian Nations, in a classic case of policy drift (Palit 2019; Verma 2020).

There is a case for the view that the inability of the Indian government to respond speedily and effectively to the COVID-19 pandemic, which produced severe domestic economic fallout and massive casualties, was a case of voluntary drift. Even in the narrow context of India's quest for power and status, its policy performance threatened to diminish its power, interests, and international image as a provider of public goods (Ganguly 2020; Taneja and Bali 2021). However, in this respect, it may be too early to make a clear judgment vis-à-vis the international dimension of Indian policy because (1) India's performance in the context of an extraordinary and unprecedented crisis was not notably different from that of many other states with far better resources; and (2) the problem was exacerbated by factors outside the control of Indian policymakers: the mutation of COVID-19 into a more malevolent form and the impact of external factors such as weak coordination of national responses, interstate competition for scarce resources (medical equipment and vaccines), and the disruption of supply chains.

Policies in other states, both small and large, may be examined similarly: for instance, the prolonged crisis over the United Kingdom's exit from the European Union and the worldwide phenomenon of erratic responses to the COVID-19 pandemic. The analysis of India's nuclear strategy in chapter 4 points the way to the need for a similar critique—invoking the problem of voluntary drift—of nuclear strategy in other states and indeed in the expert community as well, because the latter is sorely lacking in a balanced understanding of how deterrence actually works. A compelling case for analytically prioritizing voluntary drift and the abdication of political responsibility could be made with respect to policies on international trafficking in narcotics, arms, and humans, though all these also have substantial material elements.

More generally, the major thrust of this book is to encourage a nuanced understanding of impaired policies by categorizing those that cannot be controlled, which requires the analyst to examine material factors, and those that can be, which calls for a closer look at responsibility and accountability. Though I have not attempted to do so, a study in depth of any single policy issue would likely gain from examining *both* involuntary and voluntary sources of policy drift where we can discern elements of control and elements of the lack of it. For instance, the failure of states to respond effectively to climate change can be traced to involuntary drift (the problem of cost sharing for obtaining collective goods and resistance from powerful interests) but also to voluntary drift (a lack of initiative and interest from leaders as well as publics).

Realism has deeply embedded itself in the minds of both practitioners and scholars. As noted in chapter 1, the revival of interest in classical realism and its focus on the moral dimension generate a degree of optimism about the capacity of realism to become a more comprehensive paradigm. NCR has helped it cross the analytical boundaries between the external and domestic realms of states in a rigorous fashion. Conceivably, this book might help to take this further by juxtaposing the material and ethical aspects of theory on practical policy issues. A key question is: how might the realists' focus on material power and interest better incorporate ethics today? This remains a task that both materialist and ideational theorists might usefully pursue with a view to bridging paradigmatic gaps in the discipline. The tendency toward binary material/ethical explanations of why things happen in international politics needs to be corrected. I am optimistic that this book can help to do that.

REFERENCES

Abb, Pascal. 2013. "What Drives Interstate Balancing? Estimations of Domestic and Systemic Factors," Working Paper 238, March, German Institute of Global and Area Studies, Hamburg. www.giga-hamburg.de/en/system/files/publications/wp238_abb.pdf.

Abraham, Itty. 1998. *The Making of the Indian Atomic Bomb: Science, Secrecy and the Postcolonial State.* London: Zed Books.

Acharya, Arabinda, and Sonal Marwah. 2011. "*Nizam, la Tanzim* (System, Not Organization): Do Organizations Matter in Terrorism Today? A Study of the November 2008 Mumbai Attacks." *Studies in Conflict and Terrorism* 34, no. 1: 1–16.

Acharya, Shankar. 2002. "India: Crisis, Reforms and Growth in the Nineties." Stanford Center for International Development, Stanford, CA. http://citeseerx.ist.psu.edu/viewdoc/download?doi=10.1.1.572.4558&rep=rep1&type=pdf.

Agarwal, O. P., and T. V. Somanathan. 2005. "Public Policy Making in India: Issues and Remedies." Centre for Policy Research, New Delhi. https://pdfs.semanticscholar.org/0d04/1dfc528024776570 68b3381ecae5e025e052.pdf.

AHLA (American Hotel and Lodging Association). No date. "Emergency Planning and Preparedness." www.ahla.com/resources/emergency-planning-and-preparedness.

Ahluwalia, Montek Singh. No date. "Economic Reforms in India since 1991: Has Gradualism Worked?" Planning Commission of India. http://planningcommission.nic.in/aboutus/speech/spemsa/msa008.pdf.

Ahmed, Ali. 2009. "India's Thermonuclear Test: Bombed?" Institute of Peace and Conflict Studies, August 29. www.ipcs.org/comm_select.php?articleNo=2959.

AidData. No date. "China Eximbank Provides $306.7 Million Buyer's Credit Loan for Phase I of Hambantota Port Development Project." https://china.aiddata.org/projects/33256/.

Alden, Chris, and Klaus Brummer. 2019. "Foreign Policy Analysis and the Study of Indian Foreign Policy: A Pathway for Theoretical Innovation?" *India Review* 18, no. 5: 471–84.

Ali, S. Ahmed. 2012. "26/11 Attack: Media Pulled by Supreme Court for Its Role." *Times of India*, August 3. https://timesofindia.indiatimes.com/city/mumbai/26/11-attack-Media-pulled-by-Supreme-Court-for-its-role/articleshow/16054201.cms.

Ali, S. Mahmud. 1999. *Cold War in the High Himalayas: The USA, China, and South Asia in the 1950s.* New York: St. Martin's Press.

Anand, Y. P., ed. 1998. *What Mahatma Gandhi Said about the Bomb.* New Delhi: National Gandhi Museum.

Aneja, Atul. 2000. "Naval Exercise on East Coast." *The Hindu*, May 13. www.thehindu.com/thehindu/2000/05/13/stories/01130002.htm.

Ansari, Javed M. 2008. "How U-Turns and No-Shows Helped." *Daily News and Analysis*, July 23. www.dnaindia.com/report.asp?newsid=1179258.

Appadorai, A. 1981. *The Domestic Roots of India's Foreign Policy*, 1947–1972. Delhi: Oxford University Press.

Aroor, Shiv. 2013. "New Chief of India's Military Research Complex Reveals Brave New Mandate." *India Today*, July 3. www.indiatoday.in/india/story/indias-nuclear-counterstrike-response-time-to-be-in-minutes-drdo-chief-169019-2013-07-03.

Ashraf, Tamanna. 2020. "Bangladesh and India: The Domestic and International Repercussions of Asymmetric and Securitized Hydro-politics." PhD diss. https://digitalcommons.fiu.edu/etd/4430.

Asthana, Vandana. 2010. *Cross-Border Terrorism in India: Counterterrorism Strategies and Challenges*. ACDIS Occasional Paper. Champaign: Program in Arms Control, Disarmament, and International Security, University of Illinois at Urbana-Champaign.

Badri-Maharaj, Sanjay. 2009. "The Mumbai Attacks: Lessons to Be Learnt from the Police Response." *Journal of Defence Studies* 3, no. 2: 145–56.

Bagla, Pallava. 2006. "US Shifting Goalpost on Nuclear Deal: Atomic Energy Chief." *Indian Express*, February 6. http://archive.indianexpress.com/oldStory/87388/.

Bain, William. 2000. "Deconfusing Morgenthau: Moral Inquiry and Classical Realism Reconsidered." *Review of International Studies* 26, no. 3 (July): 445–64.

Bajoria, Jayshree, and Esther Pan. 2010. "The US-India Nuclear Deal." Council on Foreign Relations, New York, November 5. www.cfr.org/backgrounder/us-india-nuclear-deal.

Bajpai, K. Shankar. 2006. "A New Clear Deal." *Hindustan Times*, December 16. www.hindustantimes.com/india/a-new-clear-deal/story-eU2JI2R1ZvXBSuV9fWuyrK.html.

Bajpai, Kanti. 2009. "The BJP and the Bomb." In *Inside Nuclear South Asia*, edited by Scott D. Sagan. Stanford, CA: Stanford University Press, 2009.

———. 2014. "Indian Grand Strategy: Six Schools of Thought." In *India's Grand Strategy: History, Theory, Cases*, edited by Kanti Bajpai, Saria Basit, and V. Krishnappa. New Delhi: Routledge.

Bajpai, Kanti, and Byron Chong. 2019. "India's Foreign Policy Capacity." *Policy Design and Practice* 2, no. 2: 137–62.

Balachandran, Vappala. 2017. *Keeping India Safe: The Dilemma of Internal Security*. Noida: HarperCollins.

Balakrishnan, Bhaskar. 2014. "India's Vote on Sri Lanka: A Responsible Choice." *E-International Relations*, April 10. www.e-ir.info/2014/04/10/indias-vote-on-sri-lanka-a-responsible-choice/.

Balmer, Brian. 1997. "The Drift of Biological Weapons Policy in the UK 1945–1965," *Journal of Strategic Studies* 20, no. 4: 115–45.

Bandarage, Asoka. 2009. *The Separatist Conflict in Sri Lanka: Terrorism, Ethnicity, Political Economy*. Bloomington, IN: Author's Choice Press.

Bandhyopadhyaya, Jayantanuja. 2003. *The Making of India's Foreign Policy*, 3rd ed. Mumbai: Allied.

Banerji, Devika, and Rishi Shah. 2012. "India Overtakes Japan to Become Third-Largest Economy in Purchasing Power Parity." *Economic Times*, April 19. https://economictimes.indiatimes.com/news/economy/indicators/india-overtakes-japan-to-become-third-largest-economy-in-purchasing-power-parity/articleshow/12722921.cms.

Baru, Sanjaya. 2006. *Strategic Consequences of India's Economic Performance*. New Delhi: Academic Foundation.

———. 2013. "Decoding Manmohan's Red Lines." *The Hindu*, January 23. www.thehindu.com/opinion/lead/Decoding-Manmohan-Singh%E2%80%99s-red-lines/article12316646.ece.

———. 2014. *The Accidental Prime Minister: The Making and Unmaking of Manmohan Singh*. Gurgaon: Viking.

Baruah, Amit. 2004. "India Will Step Up Defense Ties with Sri Lanka: Natwar Singh." *The Hindu*, June 1. www.thehindu.com/2004/06/01/stories/2004060108370100.htm.

———. 2006. "Manmohan Allays Fears of Scientists." *The Hindu*, August 26. www.thehindu.com/todays-paper/manmohan-allays-fears-of-scientists/article3096645.ece.

Basrur, Rajesh M. 2001. "Nuclear Weapons and Indian Strategic Culture" *Journal of Peace Research* 38, no. 2: 181–98.

———. 2006. *Minimum Deterrence and India's Nuclear Security*. Stanford, CA: Stanford University Press.

———. 2008. *South Asia's Cold War: Nuclear Weapons and Conflict in Comparative Perspective*. New York: Routledge.

———, ed. 2009. *Challenges to Indian Democracy*. New Delhi: Oxford University Press.

———. 2013. "China, India and Pakistan: Models for an Intermediate Stage toward Disarmament?" *Australian Journal of International Affairs* 67, no. 2: 176–89.

———. 2019. "India and China: A Managed Nuclear Rivalry?" *Washington Quarterly* 42, no. 3: 151–70.

Basrur, Rajesh, Timothy Hoyt, Rifaat Hussain, and Sujoyini Mandal. 2009. *The 2008 Mumbai Terrorist Attacks: Strategic Fallout*. Singapore: S. Rajaratnam School of International Studies.

Basrur, Rajesh, and Frederick Kliem. 2021. "COVID-19 and International Cooperation: IR Paradigms at Odds," *SN Social Sciences* 1, no. 1: 7. DOI: 10.1007/s43545-020-00006-4.

Basrur, Rajesh, and Kate Sullivan de Estrada. 2017. *Rising India: Status and Power*. New York: Routledge.

Baweja, Harinder. 2008. "A Mindset of Insecurity." *Tehelka*, December 20. http://tehelka.com/a-mindset-of-insecurity/.

———. 2009. "More Evidence of Lashkar Role, More Evidence of Our Bungling." *Tehelka*, January 17. http://tehelka.com/more-evidence-of-lashkar-role-more-evidence-of-our-bungling/.

———. 2012. "IB, R&AW Brass Almost Got the Sack." *Hindustan Times*, June 17. www.pressreader.com/india/hindustan-times-patiala/20120717/282114928690727.

BBC News. 2002. "Impact of a Nuclear Strike." May 29. http://news.bbc.co.uk/2/hi/south_asia/2012543.stm.

———. 2010. "China to Build New International Airport in Sri Lanka." March 10. http://news.bbc.co.uk/2/hi/8560544.stm.

———. 2015. "How the 1993 Blasts Changed Mumbai Forever." July 30. www.bbc.com/news/world-asia-india-33713846.

Bedi, Rahul. 2000. "Kargil Report: More Questions Raised Than Answered." *Economic & Political Weekly* 35, no. 17: 1429–31.

Behuria, Ashok K., and Gulbin Sultana. 2013. "Mahinda Rajapaksa's India Policy: Engage and Countervail." *Strategic Analysis* 37, no. 1: 84–100.

Béland, Daniel, and Martin Powell. 2016. "Continuity and Change in Social Policy." *Social Policy and Administration* 50, no. 2: 129–47.

Béland, Daniel, Philip Rocco, and Alex Waddan. 2016. "Reassessing Policy Drift." *Social Policy and Administration* 50, no. 2 (March): 201–18.

Bergenwall, Samuel. 2016. "Assessing India's Rise and the Road Ahead." *Strategic Analysis* 50, no. 5: 386–404.

Berlin, Don. 2011. "The Rise of India and the Indian Ocean." *Journal of the Indian Ocean Region* 7, no. 1: 1–31.

Berwick, Elissa, and Fotini Christia. 2018. "State Capacity Redux: Integrating Classical and Experimental Contributions to an Enduring Debate." *Annual Review of Political Science* 21: 71–91.

Betz, Joachim. 2010. "India: The Interaction of Internal and External Foreign Policy." In *Regional Leadership in the Global System*, edited by Daniel Flemes. Burlington, VT: Ashgate.

———. 2012. "India's Turn in Climate Policy: Assessing the Interplay of Domestic and International Policy Change," Working Paper 190. German Institute of Global and Area Studies, Hamburg. http://repec.giga-hamburg.de/pdf/giga_12_wp190_betz.pdf.

Betz, Joachim, and Melanie Hanif. 2010. "The Formation of Preferences in Two-Level Games: An Analysis of India's Domestic and Foreign Energy Policy," Working Paper 142. German Institute of Global and Area Studies, Hamburg. www.giga-hamburg.de/en/system/files/publications/wp142_betz-hanif.pdf.

Beyer, Frederike, Nura Sidarus, Sofia Bonicalzi, and Patrick Haggard. 2017. "Beyond Self-Serving Bias: Diffusion of Responsibility Reduces Sense of Agency and Outcome Monitoring." *Social Cognitive and Affective Neuroscience* 12, no. 1: 138–45.

Bhatia, Vandana. 2012. "Change in the US Nuclear Nonproliferation Policy toward India (1998–2005): Accommodating the Anomaly." PhD thesis, University of Alberta, Edmonton. https://era.library.ualberta.ca/items/bfd0036b-8187-44e9-8983-a99dbd4b6944.

Bhatt, Arunkumar. 2006. "Don't Concede Right to Test: Scientists." *The Hindu*, December 16. www.thehindu.com/todays-paper/dont-concede-right-to-tests-scientists/article3034263.ece.

Bhaumik, Saba Naqvi, and Harish Gupta. 1998. "Pokhran Nuclear Tests: BJP Euphoric, Opposition Responds with Stunned Confusion." *India Today*, June 1 (updated March 20, 2013). www.indiatoday.in/magazine/nation/story/19980601-pokhran-nuclear-tests-bjp-euphoric-opposition-responds-with-stunned-confusion-826491-1998-06-01.

Bhonsale, Mihir. 2018. *Understanding Sino-Indian Border Issues: An Analysis of Incidents Reported in the Indian Media*. New Delhi: Observer Research Foundation. www.orfonline.org/wp-content/uploads/2018/02/ORF_Occasional_Paper_143_India-China.pdf.

Bidwai, Praful. 2005. "Charter of Dependence?" Rediff.com, July 19. www.rediff.com/news/2005/jul/19bidwai.htm.

Bischoff, Paul. 2020. "Which Countries Have the Best (and Worst) Cybersecurity)?" Comparitech, Maidstone, UK, March 3. www.comparitech.com/blog/vpn-privacy/cybersecurity-by-country/.

Blackett, P. M. S. 1948. "A Report to the Hon'ble the Defence Minister on Scientific Problems of Defence in Relation to the Needs of the Indian Armed Forces, New Delhi, 10 September." Archives of the Royal Society, London, document PB/7/1/1/2 G4.

———. 1961. "Critique of Some Contemporary Defence Thinking." *Encounter*, April, 9–17.

Blackwill, Robert D. 2005. "The India Imperative." *National Interest* 80 (Summer): 9–17.

Blackwill, Robert D., and Naresh Chandra, chairs. 2011. "The United States and India: A Shared Strategic Future." Council on Foreign Relations, New York, and Aspen Institute India, New Delhi, September.

Blank, Stephen. 2007. "The Geopolitical Implications of the Indo-American Strategic Partnership." *India Review* 6, no. 1: 1–24.

Blarel, Nicolas. 2017. "Inside Out? Assessing the Domestic Determinants of India's External Behavior." In *Theorizing Indian Foreign Policy*, edited by Mischa Hansel, Raphaëlle Khan, and Melissa Levaillant. New York: Routledge.

Blarel, Nicolas. 2019. "Coalition Politics and the Making of Indian Foreign Policy: A New Research Program," *India Review* 18, no. 5: 582–95.

Blarel, Nicolas, and Jayita Sarkar. 2019. "Substate Organizations as Foreign Policy Agents: New Evidence and Theory from India, Israel, and France," *Foreign Policy Analysis* 15, no. 3: 413–31.

Blarel, Nicolas, and Niels Van Willigen. 2021. "How Do Regional Parties Influence Foreign Policy? Insights from Multilevel Coalitional Bargaining in India." *European Journal of International Relations* 27, no. 2: 478–500.

Bloomfield, Alan. 2021. "The India-China Bilateral Relationship: A 'Serious and Enduring Rivalry.'" *Journal of the Indian Ocean Region*, March 13. DOI: 10.1080/19480881.2021.1878580.

Bobb, Dilip. 1983. "Tensions Grow in South Asia as India Assumes a Global Role Neglecting Its Neighbors." *India Today*, October 15 (updated June 24, 2014). www.indiatoday.in/magazine/cover-story/story/19831015-tensions-grow-in-south-asia-as-india-assumes-a-global-role-neglecting-its-neighbours-771105-2013-07-15.

Boucher, David, and Paul Kelly, eds. 1994. *The Social Contract from Hobbes to Rawls.* London: Routledge.

Bovens, Mark, and Paul 't Hart. 1996. *Understanding Policy Fiascoes.* London: Transaction.

———. 2016. "Revisiting the Study of Policy Failures." *Journal of European Public Policy* 23, no. 5: 653–66.

Brawley, Mark R. 2009. *Political Economy and Grand Strategy: A Neoclassical Realist View.* Abingdon, UK: Routledge.

Brewster, David, and Ranjit Rai. 2013a. "Flowers Are Blooming: The Story of the Indian Navy's Secret Operation in the Seychelles." *Naval Review* 99, no. 1: 58–62, www.academia.edu/7698363/Flowers_Are_Blooming_the_story_of_the_India_Navys_secret_operation_in_the_Seychelles.

———. 2013b. "Operation Lal Dora: India's Aborted Military Intervention in Mauritius." *Asian Security* 9, no. 1: 62–74.

Bueno de Mesquita, Bruce. 2002. "Domestic Politics and International Relations." *International Studies Quarterly* 46, no. 1 (March): 1–9.

Bullion, Alan J. 1995. *India, Sri Lanka and the Tamil Crisis, 1976–1994: An International Perspective.* London: Pinter.

Burns, R. Nicholas. 2007. "America's Strategic Opportunity with India: The New US-India Partnership," *Foreign Affairs* 86, no. 6 (November–December): 131–46.

Business Standard. 2008. "Nuke Deal: UNPA Talks Its Own Separation Plan." July 4 (updated January 29, 2013). www.business-standard.com/article/economy-policy/nuke-deal-unpa-talks-its-own-separation-plan-108070401070_1.html.

Butcher, Charity, and Makda Maru. 2018. "Diversionary Tactics and the Ethiopia-Eritrea War (1998–2000)." *Small Wars and Insurgencies* 29, no. 1: 68–90.

Cabinet Committee on Security. 2003. "The Cabinet Committee on Security Reviews Operationalization of India's Nuclear Security Doctrine." Ministry of External Affairs, Government of India, New Delhi. www.mea.gov.in/press-releases.htm?dtl/20131/The+Cabinet+Committee+on+Security+Reviews+perationalization+of+Indias+Nuclear+Doctrine.

Cadier, David, and Margot Light, eds. 2015. *Russia's Foreign Policy: Ideas, Domestic Politics and External Relations.* New York: Palgrave Macmillan.

CAG (Comptroller and Auditor General of India). No date. "Compendium of Performance Audit Reviews on Modernization of Police Force." https://

cag.gov.in/sites/default/files/cag_pdf/Compendium_Performance_Audit_Reviews_Modernisation_Police_Force.pdf.

———. 2011. "Performance Audit on the Role and Functioning of the Indian Coast Guard: Report No. 7 of 2010–11." https://cag.gov.in/sites/default/files/audit_report_files/Union_Performance_Defence_Services_Role_and_Functioning_Indian_Coast_guard_7_2011.pdf.

Carlsnaes, Walter. 2013. "Foreign Policy." In *Handbook of International Relations*, edited by Walter Carlsnaes, Thomas Risse, and Beth Simmons. London: Sage.

Carter, Ashton B. 2006. *Testimony Before the Committee on Foreign Relations, United States Senate*, April 26. US Senate, Washington, DC.

Cha, Victor D. 2000. "Abandonment, Entrapment, and Neoclassical Realism in Asia: The United States, Japan, and Korea." *International Studies Quarterly* 44, no. 2 (June): 261–91.

Chadda, Maya. 2019. "Explaining India's Foreign Policy: Theoretical Explorations." *India Review* 18, no. 5: 485–502.

Chakma, Bhumitra. 2011. "Introduction." In *The Politics of Nuclear Weapons in South Asia*, edited by Bhumitra Chakma. Burlington, VT: Ashgate.

Chakrabarty, Bidyut. 2008. *Indian Politics and Society since Independence*. Abingdon, UK: Routledge.

Chakravarthi, Rekha. 2009. "Internal Roadblocks to the Indo-US Nuclear Deal." In *Indo-US Nuclear Deal: Seeking Synergy in Bilateralism*, edited by P. R. Chari. New Delhi: Routledge.

Chalmers, Malcolm, Andrew Somerville, and Andrea Berger, eds. 2011. *Small Nuclear Forces: Five Perspectives*. London: Royal United Services Institute for Defence and Security Studies.

Chanda, Nayan. 2007. "The US and India: Nuclear Bonding." *Yale Global Online*, August 2. https://yaleglobal.yale.edu/content/us-and-india-nuclear-bonding.

Chandran, D. Suba. 2005. *Limited War: Revisiting Kargil in the Indo-Pak Conflict*. New Delhi: India Research Press.

Chang, Gordon. 1990. *Friends and Enemies: The United States, China, and the Soviet Union, 1948–1972*. Stanford, CA: Stanford University Press.

Chari, P. R. 2006. "Implementing the Indo-US Nuclear Deal: A Pyrrhic Struggle," *IDSA Comment*, Institute of Defence Studies and Analyses, January 5. https://idsa.in/idsastrategiccomments/ImplementingtheIndoUSNuclearDeal_PRChari_050106.

———. 2007. *Indo-US Nuclear Deal: Unending Drama in Many Acts*. New Delhi: Institute of Peace and Conflict Studies.

———, ed. 2009. *Indo-US Nuclear Deal: Seeking Synergy in Bilateralism*. New Delhi: Routledge.

———. 2012. "Defence Reforms after 1962: Much Ado About Nothing." *Journal of Defence Studies* 6, no. 4 (October): 171–88.

———. 2014. "India's Nuclear Doctrine: Stirrings of Change." Carnegie

Endowment for International Peace, Washington, DC, June 4. http://m.ceip.org/2014/06/04/india-s-nuclear-doctrine-stirrings-of-change/hckt&lang=en.

Chari, P. R., Pervaiz Iqbal Cheema, and Stephen P. Cohen. 2007. *Four Crises and a Peace Process: American Engagement in South Asia.* Washington, DC: Brookings Institution Press.

Chatterjee, Elizabeth. 2012. "Dissipated Energy: Indian Electric Power and the Politics of Blame." *Contemporary South Asia* 20, no. 1: 91–103.

Chaturvedi, Anviti. 2017. *Police Reform in India.* New Delhi: PRS Legislative Research.

Chaudhuri, Rudra. 2014. *Forged in Crisis: India and the United States since 1947.* New York: Oxford University Press.

Chawla, Prabhu. 1998. "We Live in a World where India Is Surrounded by Nuclear Weaponry: Atal Bihari Vajpayee" (interview). *India Today*, May 25. www.indiatoday.in/magazine/cover-story/story/19980525-we-live-in-a-world-where-india-is-surrounded-by-nuclear-weaponry-atal-bihari-vajpayee-828210-1998-05-25.

———. 2008a. "The Day of the Dealmaker." *India Today*, July 17. http://indiatoday.intoday.in/site/Story/11527/Cover%20Story/The+day+of+the+dealmaker.html.

———. 2008b. "Mayawati, Modi, Advani More Lethal than Bush." *India Today*, July 17. http://indiatoday.intoday.in/site/Story/11529/Interview/'Mayawati,+Modi,+Advani+more+lethal+than+Bush'.html.

Chellaney, Brahma. 2018. "India's Choice in the Maldives." *Strategist*, February 21. www.aspistrategist.org.au/indias-choice-maldives/.

Chen, Jian. 2001. *Mao's China and the Cold War.* Chapel Hill: University of North Carolina Press.

Cherian, John. 2000. "A Reassuring Mission." *The Hindu Frontline*, June 24–July 7. https://frontline.thehindu.com/magazine/archive/.

Chengappa, Raj. 2000. *Weapons of Peace: The Secret Story of India's Quest to Be a Nuclear Power.* New Delhi: HarperCollins.

Chinoy, Kamal Mitra, and Anuradha Chinoy. 2007. *Economic and Political Weekly* 42, no. 35 (September 1–7): 3547–54.

Chou, Eileen Y., and Loran F. Nordgren. 2017. "Safety in Numbers: Why the Mere Physical Presence of Others Affects Risk-Taking Behaviors." *Journal of Behavioral Decisionmaking* 30, no. 3: 671–82.

Chowdhary, Rekha. 2015. *Jammu and Kashmir: Politics of Identity and Separatism.* New Delhi: Routledge India.

Christensen, Thomas J. 1996. *Useful Adversaries: Grand Strategy, Domestic Mobilization, and Sino-American Conflict, 1947–1958.* Princeton, NJ: Princeton University Press.

Chung, Chien-peng. 2004. *Domestic Politics, International Bargaining, and China's Territorial Disputes.* London: RoutledgeCurzon.

Clary, Christopher, and Vipin Narang. 2018/19. "India's Counterforce Temptations: Strategic Dilemmas, Doctrine, and Capabilities." *International Security* 43, no. 3: 7–52.

CNN. 2005. "Tsunami Death Toll." February 22. http://edition.cnn.com/2004/WORLD/asiapcf/12/28/tsunami.deaths/.

Cohen, Stephen P. 2001. *India: Emerging Power*. Washington, DC: Brookings Institution Press.

———. 2013. *Shooting for a Century: The India-Pakistan Conundrum*. Washington, DC: Brookings Institution Press.

Cohen, Stephen P., and Sunil Dasgupta. 2010. *Arming Without Aiming: India's Military Modernization*. New Delhi: Penguin.

Coll, Steve. 2009. "The Back Channel: India and Pakistan's Secret Kashmir Talks." *New Yorker*, February 23. www.newyorker.com/magazine/2009/03/02/the-back-channel.

Congressional Record. 2001. Volume 147, November 8–28, US Congress. https://books.google.com.sg/books?id=MuBNGjy506AC&pg=PA21992&lpg=PA21992&dq=2001+vajpayee+offered+Bush+military+bases&source=bl&ots=TCHdYltZtx&sig=egQBkqUOrdCtRYnBodAAInCMiq8&hl=en&sa=X&ved=2ahUKEwjo44acw7DeAhWJbysKHcRGDlo4ChDoATACegQIBxAB#v=onepage&q=2001%20vajpayee%20offered%20Bush%20military%20bases&f=false.

Copley, Gregory. 1988. "Inevitable India, Inevitable Power." *Defense and Foreign Affairs* 16, no. 12 (December): 29, 52.

Cortright, David, and Amitabh Mattoo, eds. 1996. *India and the Bomb: Public Opinion and Nuclear Options*. Notre Dame, IN: University of Notre Dame Press.

Cox, Jeff. 2020. "Second-Quarter GDP Plunged by Worst-Ever 32.9% Amid Virus-Induced Shutdown." CNBC, July 30, www.cnbc.com/2020/07/30/us-gdp-q2-2020-first-reading.html.

Cozette, Muriel. 2008. "What Lies Ahead: Classical Realism on the Future of International Relations." *International Studies Review* 10, no. 4 (December): 667–79.

Cumings, Bruce. 2003. "Wrong Again." *London Review of Books* 25, no. 23 (December 4), www.lrb.co.uk/the-paper/v25/n23/bruce-cumings/wrong-again.

Dabhade, Manish S. 2017. *India's Pursuit of United Nations Security Council Reforms*. Observer Research Foundation, New Delhi. https://orfonline.org/wp-content/uploads/2017/12/ORF_Occasional_Paper_131_UNSC_Dabhade.pdf.

Daily News and Analysis. 2008. "Two Indians Hurt in LTTE Air Strike, 22 killed." September 9. www.dnaindia.com/world/report-two-indians-hurt-in-ltte-air strike-22-killed-1188921.

Das, Ajaya Kumar. 2015. "India-US Relations; Assessing India's Soft Power." PhD thesis, S. Rajaratnam School of International Studies, Nanyang Technological University, Singapore.

Das, Pushpita. 2009. *Coastal Security Arrangement: A Case Study of Gujarat and Maharashtra Coasts*. New Delhi: Institute for Defence Studies and Analyses.

———. 2013. *Coastal Security: The Indian Experience*. New Delhi: Institute for Defence Studies and Analyses.

Dasgupta, Sunil. 2008. "The Indian Army and the Problem of Military Change."

In *Security and South Asia: Ideas, Institutions, and Initiatives*, edited by Swarna Rajagopalan. New Delhi: Routledge.

Datta, Saikat. 2018. "Intelligence, Strategic Assessment, and Decision Process Deficits: The Absence of Indian Learning from Crisis to Crisis." In *Investigating Crises: South Asia's Lessons, Evolving Dynamics, and Trajectories*, edited by Hannah Haegeland, Michael Krepon, Sameer Lalwani, and Yun Sun. Washington, DC: Henry L. Stimson Center.

Dawn. 2008. "Pakistan Proposes Defence Deal with Sri Lanka." August 1. www.dawn.com/news/415012.

Deng, Francis M. 2010. "From Sovereignty as Responsibility to the Responsibility to Protect." *Global Responsibility to Protect* 2, no. 4: 353–70.

Deshpande, Rajeev, and Srinivas Laxman. 2006. "PM Wins over Top Scientists to N-Deal." *Times of India*, August 26. https://timesofindia.indiatimes.com/india/PM-wins-over-top-scientists-to-N-deal/articleshow/1929494.cms.

de Silva, K. M. 1999. "Sri Lanka: The Security Problems of a Small State." *Defence and Peace Economics* 10, no. 4: 361–81.

———. 2012. *Sri Lanka and the Defeat of the LTTE*. New Delhi: Penguin.

Dessler, David. 1989. "What's at Stake in the Agent-Structure Debate?" *International Organization* 43, no. 3: 441–73.

Destradi, Sandra. 2010. "India and the Civil War in Sri Lanka: On the Failures of Regional Conflict Management in South Asia." Working Paper 154, German Institute of Global and Area Studies, Hamburg. http://hdl.handle.net/10419/47768.

———. 2014. "India: A Reluctant Partner for Afghanistan." *Washington Quarterly* 37, no. 2: 103–17.

DeVotta, Neil. 2003. "Is India Over-Extended? When Domestic Disorder Precludes Regional Intervention." *Contemporary South Asia* 12, no. 3 (September): 365–80.

———. 2010. "When Individuals, States, and Systems Collide: India's Foreign Policy towards Sri Lanka." In *India's Foreign Policy: Retrospect and Prospect*, edited by Sumit Ganguly. New Delhi: Oxford University Press.

Diehl, Paul F. 2018. "Whither Rivalry or Withered Rivalry?" In *The China-India Rivalry in the Globalization Era*, edited by T. V. Paul. Washington, DC: Georgetown University Press.

Dikshit, Sandeep. 2005. "India Gives Two Radars to Sri Lanka." *The Hindu*, December 28. www.thehindu.com/2005/12/28/stories/2005122804511300.htm.

Dixit, J. N. 1998. *Assignment Colombo*. New Delhi: Konark.

Doty, Paul. 2009. "The Minimum Deterrent and Beyond." *Daedalus* 138, no. 4: 130–39.

Doyle, Michael. 1997. *Ways of War and Peace*. New York: W. W. Norton.

Dyson, Stephen Benedict. 2009. *The Blair Identity: Leadership and Foreign Policy*. Manchester: Manchester University Press.

Eckerman, Ingrid, and Tom Børsen. 2018. "Corporate and Governmental Responsibilities for Preventing Chemical Disasters: Lessons from Bhopal." *Hyle: International Journal for Philosophy of Chemistry* 24, no. 1: 29–53.

Economic Times. 2007. "Advani Debunks 'Course Correction,' Says BJP Always Opposed Nuke Deal." August 31. https://economictimes.indiatimes.com/news/politics-and-nation/advani-debunks-course-correction-says-bjp-always-opposed-nuke-deal/articleshow/2324636.cms.

Economic Times. 2008a. "Why Did NSG Take 10 Hours to Arrive?" November 30. https://economictimes.indiatimes.com/news/politics-and-nation/why-did-nsg-take-10-hours-to-arrive/articleshow/3775099.cms.

———. 2008b. "Deadly Delay in Calling the Marine Commandos," November 30. https://economictimes.indiatimes.com/news/politics-and-nation/deadly-delay-in-calling-the-marine-commandos/articleshow/3774354.cms?from=mdr.

Effendi, Maria Saifuddin. 2007. *Role of a Third Party in Conflict Resolution: A Case Study of India and Norway in Sri Lanka*. Colombo: Regional Centre for Strategic Studies.

Egreteau, Renaud. 2012. "The China–India Rivalry Reconceptualized." *Asian Journal of Political Science* 20, no. 1: 1–22.

Eichengreen, Barry, Poonam Gupta, and Rajeev Kumar, eds. 2010. *Emerging Giants: China and India in the World Economy*. New York: Oxford University Press.

Einhorn, Robert, and W. P. S. Sidhu. 2017. *The Strategic Chain: Linking Pakistan, India, China, and the United States*. Washington, DC: Brookings Institution Press.

Election Commission of India. 2004. "Performance of National Parties Vis-à-Vis Others." Statistical Report on General Elections. https://eci.nic.in/eci_main/SR_KeyHighLights/LS_2004/Vol_I_LS_2004.pdf.

Elman, Miriam Fendius. 2000. "Unpacking Democracy: Presidentialism, Parliamentarism, and Theories of Democratic Peace." *Security Studies* 9, no. 4 (Summer): 91–126.

Erskine, Toni. 2008. "Locating Responsibility: The Problem of Moral Agency in International Relations." In *The Oxford Handbook of International Relations*, edited by Christian Reus-Smit and Duncan Snidal. New York: Oxford University Press.

Fair, C. Christine. 2009. "Antecedents and Implications of the November 2008 Lashkar-e-Taiba (LeT) Attack upon Several Targets in the Indian Mega-City of Mumbai." Testimony presented before the House Homeland Security Committee, Subcommittee on Transportation Security and Infrastructure Protection, March 11, 2009. Santa Monica, CA: RAND Corporation. www.rand.org/content/dam/rand/pubs/testimonies/2009/RAND_CT320.pdf.

———. 2012. "Prospects for Effective Internal Security Reforms in India." *Commonwealth and Comparative Politics* 50, no. 2: 145–70.

———. 2018. *In Their Own Words: Understanding Lashkar-e-Tayyaba*. London: Hurst.

Farrow, Ronan. 2018. *War on Peace: The End of Diplomacy and the Decline of Influence*. New York: W. W. Norton.

Fearon, James. 1998. "Domestic Politics, Foreign Policy, and Theories of International Relations." *Annual Review of Political Science* 1, no. 1: 298–313.

Fernando, Tyronne. 2002. *Alien Winds across Paradise: A New Look at Sri Lanka's Foreign Relations through the Ages.* New Delhi: Vikas.

Fiammenghi, Davide. 2011. "The Security Curve and the Structure of International Politics." *International Security* 35, no. 4 (Spring): 126–54.

Finnemore, Martha. 1996. *National Interests in International Society.* Ithaca, NY: Cornell University Press.

FitzGerald, Cathal, Eoin O'Malley, and Deiric Ó Broin. 2019. "Policy Success / Policy Failure: A Framework for Understanding Policy Choices." *Administration* 67, no. 2: 1–24.

Forsyth, James Wood, Jr. 2016. "The Common Sense of Small Nuclear Arsenals." *Strategic Studies Quarterly* 10, no. 5: 43–61.

Freedman, Joshua. 2015. "Status Insecurity and Temporality in World Politics." *European Journal of International Relations* 22, no. 4: 797–822.

Friedman, Thomas L. 2002. "India, Pakistan and G.E." *New York Times*, August 11. http://query.nytimes.com/gst/fullpage.html? res=940CEED9153AF932A2575BC0A9649C8B6.

Gaddis, John Lewis. 1992–93. "International Relations Theory and the End of the Cold War," *International Security* 17, no. 3 (Winter): 5–58.

Gailmard, Ian. 2014. "Accountability and Principal–Agent Theory." In *The Oxford Handbook of Accountability*, edited by Mark Bovens, Robert E. Goodin, and Thomas Schillemans. Oxford: Oxford University Press. DOI: 10.1093/oxfordhb/9780199641253.013.0016.

Gall, Carlotta. 2014. *The Wrong Enemy: America in Afghanistan, 2001–2014.* Boston: Houghton Mifflin Harcourt.

Gamage, Rajni Nayanthara. 2017. "Balancing and Bandwagoning: Explaining Shifts in Sri Lankan Foreign Policy." *Journal of the Indian Ocean Region* 13, no. 2: 1–22.

Ganguly, Rajat. 1998. *Kin State Interventions in Ethnic Conflicts: Lessons for South Asia.* New Delhi: Sage.

Ganguly, Sumit. 1999. "India's Pathway to Pokhran II." *International Security* 23, no. 4: 148–77.

———. 2002. *Conflict Unending: India–Pakistan Tensions since 1947.* New Delhi: Oxford University Press.

———. 2008. "India Held Back." *Current History* 107, no. 712 (November): 369–74.

———. 2012. "Think Again: India's Rise." *Foreign Policy*, July 5. http://foreignpolicy.com/2012/07/05/think-again-indias-rise/.

———. 2016. *Deadly Impasse: Indo-Pakistani Relations at the Dawn of a New Century.* Cambridge: Cambridge University Press.

———.2015. *Hindu Nationalism and the Foreign Policy of India's Bharatiya Janata Party.* Washington, DC: Transatlantic Academy.

———. 2018a. "Ending the Sri Lankan Civil War," *Daedalus* 147, no. 1: 78–89.

———. 2018b. "India and China: On a Collision Course?" *Pacific Affairs* 91, no. 2: 231–44.

———. 2018c. "India's National Security: A Neo-classical Realist Account." In *The*

Oxford Handbook of India's National Security, edited by Sumit Ganguly, Nicolas Blarel, and Manjeet S. Pardesi. New Delhi: Oxford University Press.

———. 2020. "Mangling the COVID Crisis: India's Response to the Pandemic." *Washington Quarterly* 43, no. 4: 105–20.

Ganguly, Sumit, and Devin T. Hagerty. 2005. *Fearful Symmetry: India-Pakistan Crises in the Shadow of Nuclear Weapons.* New Delhi: Oxford University Press.

Ganguly, Sumit, and Michael R. Kraig. 2005. "The 2001–2002 Indo-Pakistani Crisis: Exposing the Limits of Coercive Diplomacy." *Security Studies* 14, no. 2: 290–324.

Ganguly, Sumit, and Dinshaw Mistry. 2006. "The US-India Nuclear Pact: A Good Deal." *Current History* 105, no. 694 (November): 375–78.

Ganguly, Sumit, and Manjeet Pardesi. 2009. "Explaining Sixty Years of India's Foreign Policy." *India Review* 8, no. 1 (January): 4–49.

Ganguly, Sumit, and Andrew Scobell. 2018. "The Himalayan Impasse: Sino-Indian Rivalry in the Wake of Doklam." *Washington Quarterly* 41, no. 3: 177–90.

Ganguly, Sumit, and William R. Thompson. 2016. *Ascending India and Its State Capacity: Extraction, Violence, and Legitimacy*. New Haven, CT: Yale University Press.

Gardner, Hannah. 2009. "China's Aid Revealed in Sri Lanka's Victory Parade." *The National*, June 9. www.thenational.ae/world/asia/china-s-aid-revealed-in-sri-lanka-s-victory-parade-1.556125.

Garver, John W. 2001. *Protracted Contest: Sino-Indian Rivalry in the 20th Century.* Seattle: University of Washington Press.

Gelb, Leslie H. 2009. "Necessity, Choice, and Common Sense: A Policy for a Bewildering World." *Foreign Affairs*, May–June. www.foreignaffairs.com/articles/2009-05-01/necessity-choice-and-common-sense.

Gelman, Harry. 1982. *The Soviet Far East Buildup and Soviet Risk-Taking against China.* Santa Monica, CA: RAND Corporation.

Gelpi, Christopher. 1997. "Democratic Diversions: Governmental Structure and the Externalization of Domestic Conflict." *Journal of Conflict Resolution* 42, no. 2: 255–82.

George, Varghese K. 2007. "RSS Backs Advani on Nuke Deal." *Indian Express*, August 28, http://archive.indianexpress.com/news/ties-with-us-in-our-national-interest-deal-ok-if-home-law-changed-advani/213221/.

———. 2009. In *26/11: The Attack on Mumbai by Hindustan Times*. 2009. New Delhi: Penguin.

Ghoshal, Debalina. 2016. "India's Recessed Deterrence Posture: Prospects and Implications." *Washington Quarterly* 39, no. 1: 159–70.

Gilpin, Robert. 1981. *War and Change in World Politics.* New York: Cambridge University Press.

———. 1984. "The Richness of the Tradition of Political Realism." *International Organization* 38, no. 2 (Spring): 287–304.

Giridharadas, Anand. 2008. "Land of Gandhi Asserts Itself as Global Military

Power." *New York Times*, September 22. www.nytimes.com/2008/09/22/world/asia/22india.html?ref-world/.

Glaser, Charles L. 1996. "Realists as Optimists: Cooperation as Self-Help." In *Realism: Restatements and Renewal*, edited by Benjamin Frankel. London: Frank Cass.

———. 1997. "The Security Dilemma Revisited." *World Politics* 50, no. 1: 171–201.

Glenn, R. 2015. *Rethinking Western Approaches to Counterinsurgency: Lessons from Postcolonial Conflict.* New York: Routledge.

Gokhale, Nitin A. 2009. *Sri Lanka: From War to Peace.* New Delhi: Har-Anand.

Goldstein, Lyle J. 2003. "When China Was a 'Rogue' State: The Impact of China's Nuclear Weapons Program on US-China Relations during the 1960s." *Journal of Contemporary China* 12, no. 37: 739–64.

Goodheart, Michael. 2014. "Accountable International Relations." In *The Oxford Handbook of Accountability*, edited by Mark Bovens, Robert E. Goodin, and Thomas Schillemans. Oxford: Oxford University Press. DOI: 10.1093/oxfordhb/9780199641253.013.0028.

Gooneratne, John. 1996. "India's Management of Sri Lanka's Ethnic Conflict." In *Diplomacy and Domestic Politics in South Asia*, edited by Baladas Ghoshal. Delhi: Konark.

Gopalan, T. N. 2002. "'Tamils' and Tamil Nadu." In *Towards Peace in Sri Lanka.* New Delhi: Observer Research Foundation.

Gordon, Sandy. 2008. "Policing Terrorism in India." *Crime Law and Social Change* 50, nos. 1–2: 111–24.

Goswami, Namrata. 2013. *India's Internal Security Situation: Present Realities and Future Pathways.* New Delhi: Institute of Defence Studies and Analyses.

Gourevitch, P. 2002. "Domestic Politics and International Relations." In *Handbook of International Relations*, edited by Walter Carlsnaes, Thomas Risse, and Beth A. Simmons. London: Sage.

Gregory, Robert. 1998. "Political Responsibility for Bureaucratic Incompetence." *Public Administration* 76, no. 3: 519–38.

Grewal, Kairvy. 2020. "How Will RCEP Benefit Member Nations and What Does India's Exit from the Trade Pact Mean?" *The Print*, November 17. https://theprint.in/theprint-essential/how-will-rcep-benefit-member-nations-and-what-does-indias-exit-from-the-trade-pact-mean/545701/.

Group of Ministers on National Security. 2001. *Reforming the National Security System: Report of the Group of Ministers on National Security.* New Delhi: Government of India.

The Guardian. 2011. "US Embassy Cables: Indian MPs 'Paid Off by Congress Party' Ahead of Nuclear Vote." March 18. www.theguardian.com/world/us-embassy-cables-documents/162458.

Gujral, I. K. 1997. "Aspects of India's Foreign Policy." Speech delivered at Bandaranaike Center for International Studies, Colombo, January 20. Text available as "The Gujral Doctrine," Henry L. Stimson Center, Washington, DC. www.stimson.org/the-gujral-doctrine.

Gulati, Ashok, Shyma Jose, and B. B. Singh, 2021. *COVID-19: Emergence, Spread and Its Impact on the Indian Economy and Migrant Workers*. Working Paper. Bonn: Center for Development Research, University of Bonn.

Gülmez, Seçkin Barış. 2020. "From Indifference to Independence: Turkey's Shifting Cyprus Policy in the 1950s." *Middle Eastern Studies* 56, no. 5: 744–58.

Gupta, Arvind. 2018. *How India Manages Its National Security*. Gurgaon: Penguin/Viking.

Gupta, Rakesh. 2001. "India: Towards a Political Economy of Intra-State Conflicts." *Faultlines*, no. 5. www.satp.org/satporgtp/publication/faultlines/volume5/Fault5-9rgupta.htm.

Gupta, Shekhar. 1984. "Large Number of Sri Lankan Tamil Rebels Acquires Training in Obscure Parts of Tamil Nadu." *India Today*, March 31 (updated April 11, 2014). www.indiatoday.in/magazine/investigation/story/19840331-large-number-of-sri-lankan-tamil-rebels-acquires-training-in-obscure-parts-of-tamil-nadu-802910-1984-03-31.

Gupta, Shishir, and C. Raja Mohan. 2005. "This Means a Cap on Our N-Arsenal, Says Brajesh Mishra; Facts Show Otherwise." *Indian Express*, July 20. http://archive.indianexpress.com/oldStory/74767/.

Guyot-Réchard, Bérénice. 2019. "The Fear of Being Compared: State-Shadowing in the Himalayas, 1910–62." *Political Geography* 75, no. 102050 (November). https://doi.org/10.1016/j.polgeo.2019.102050.

Haelig, Carlton G. 2017. "The Sri Lankan Civil War: Turning COIN on Its Head and Learning to Adapt." *Small Wars Journal*, September 9. https://smallwarsjournal.com/jrnl/art/the-sri-lankan-civil-war-turning-coin-on-its-head-and-learning-to-adapt.

Hagerty, Devin T. 1991. "India's Regional Security Doctrine." *Asian Survey* 31, no. 4 (April): 351–63.

———. 2020. *Nuclear Weapons and Deterrence Stability in South Asia*. Cham, UK: Palgrave.

Haidar, Suhasini. 2018. "Pakistan Is a Neighbor You Can't Wish Away: A. S. Dulat." *The Hindu*, June 6. www.thehindu.com/opinion/interview/pakistan-is-a-neighbour-you-cant-wish-away/article24089836.ece.

Hall, Ian. 2019. *Modi and the Reinvention of Indian Foreign Policy*. Bristol: Bristol University Press.

Hansel, Mischa, Raphaëlle Khan, and Melissa Levaillant, eds. 2017. *Theorizing Indian Foreign Policy*. New York: Routledge.

Hargreaves, Caroline, Martin Karlsson, Surabhi Agrawal, Jonathan Hootnick, and Katharine Tengtio. No date. "International Dimensions of the Sri Lankan Conflict." Center for Peace and Conflict Studies, University of St. Andrews, St. Andrews, Scotland. www.academia.edu/1565798/International_Dimensions_of_the_Sri_Lankan_Conflict.

Harris, Nigel. 1987. *The End of the Third World: Newly Industrializing Countries and the Decline of an Ideology*. London: Penguin.

Harrison, Selig S. 1960. *India: The Most Dangerous Decades*. Princeton, NJ: Princeton University Press.

Hasan, Zoya. 2012. *Congress after Indira: Policy, Power, Political Change (1984–2009)*. New Delhi: Oxford University Press. DOI: 10.1093/acprof:oso/9780195685978.001.0001.

Hashim, Ahmed S. 2013. *When Counterinsurgency Wins: Sri Lanka's Defeat of the Tamil Tigers*. Philadelphia: University of Pennsylvania Press.

Hayes, Jarrod. 2013. *Constructing National Security: US Relations with India and China*. Cambridge: Cambridge University Press.

He, Kai. 2017. "Explaining United States–China Relations: Neoclassical Realism and the Nexus of Threat-Interest Perceptions." *Pacific Review* 30, no. 2: 133–51.

Hein, Patrick. 2017. "Riding with the Devils: China's Role in the Cambodian and Sri Lankan Conflicts." *India Quarterly* 73, no. 1: 77–98.

Hershberg, Jim. 1995. "Anatomy of a Controversy: Anatoly F. Dobrynin's Meeting with Robert F. Kennedy, Saturday, 27 October 1962." National Security Archive, George Washington University, no date; reproduced from *Cold War International History Bulletin*, no. 5, https://nsarchive2.gwu.edu/nsa/cuba_mis_cri/moment.htm.

Heyman, Steven J. 1991. "The First Duty of Government: Protection, Liberty and the Fourteenth Amendment." *Duke Law Journal* 41, no. 3 (December): 507–71.

The Hindu. 1999. "India Not to Engage in a Nuclear Arms Race: Jaswant" (interview). November 29.

———. 2004a. "India-Sri Lanka Defence Agreement." October 26. www.thehindu.com/2004/10/26/stories/2004102602761000.htm.

———. 2004b. "Vajpayee Opposed Move to Resume Nuclear Programme in 1979: Congress." April 3. www.thehindu.com/todays-paper/tp-national/vajpayee-opposed-move-to-resume-nuclear-programme-in-1979-congress/article27592030.ece.

———. 2005a. "'India Made a Junior Partner of the US.'" August 4. www.thehindu.com/2005/08/04/stories/2005080414611200.htm.

———. 2005b. "It Is a Blunder, Charges NDA." August 5. www.thehindu.com/2005/08/05/stories/2005080500251200.htm.

———. 2005c. "Left Attacks Joint Statement." July 22. www.thehindu.com/2005/07/22/stories/2005072206731400.htm.

———. 2006a. "Brajesh Mishra Trashes India, US Nuclear Agreement." February 1. www.thehindu.com/todays-paper/tp-national/brajesh-mishra-trashes-india-us-nuclear-agreement/article3172457.ece.

———. 2006b. "Experts Express Concern over Nuclear Deal with US." July 3. www.thehindu.com/todays-paper/tp-national/experts-express-concern-over-nuclear-deal-with-us/article3099534.ece.

———. 2006c. "Hyde Act and Nuclear Scientists' Note." December 16. www.thehindu.com/todays-paper/tp-opinion/hyde-act-and-nuclear-scientists-note/article3034446.ece.

———. 2006d. "Natwar Singh Mobilising Parties against the Nuclear Deal between India and US." August 6. www.thehindu.com/todays-paper/tp-national/natwar-singh-mobilising-parties-against-the-nuclear-deal-between-india-and-us/article3086360.ece.

———. 2006e. "No Arms to Sri Lanka for Use against Civilians." December 16. www.thehindu.com/todays-paper/tp-national/No-arms-to-Sri-Lanka-for-use-against-civilians/article15728137.ece.

———. 2006f. "Review Nuclear Deal: Rajnath." July 20. www.thehindu.com/todays-paper/tp-national/review-nuclear-deal-rajnath/article3107801.ece.

———. 2006g. "Set Ground Rules on Nuclear Deal." August 15. www.thehindu.comtodays-paper/set-ground-rules-on-nuclear-deal/article3090634.ece.

———. 2007a. "CPI (M) Polit Bureau Statement on Nuclear Deal." August 19. www.thehindu.com/todays-paper/tp-national/CPI-M-Polit-Bureau-statement-on-nuclear-deal/article14818878.ece.

———. 2007b. "Left 'Unable to Accept' 123 Agreement." August 8. www.thehindu.com/todays-paper/Left-lsquounable-to-acceptrsquo-123-agreement/article14811827.ece.

———. 2007c. "'No Truck with a Pro-imperialist Party like BJP.'" August 20. www.thehindu.com/todays-paper/tp-national/ldquoNo-truck-with-a-pro-imperialist-party-like-BJPrdquo/article14819454.ece.

———. 2008. "Patil Expresses Concern over LTTE's 'Air Capability.'" May 14. www.thehindu.com/todays-paper/tp-national/Patil-expresses-concern-over-LTTErsquos-lsquoair-capabilityrsquo/article15222421.ece.

Hindustan Times. 2009. *26/11: The Attack on Mumbai*. New Delhi: Penguin.

———. 2012. "26/11 Terror Attacks Redefined the Role of the Fire Brigade." November 26. www.hindustantimes.com/india/26-11-terror-attacks-redefined-the-role-of-the-fire-brigade/story-mSP9pl1cbp6Uad3F2qO9CO.html.

HLEC (High-Level Enquiry Committee). 2009. "Report of the High-Level Inquiry Committee (HLEC) on 26/11, Government of Maharashtra, India." Available at "Full Text: What the High-Level Inquiry Committee on the 26/11 Attacks Had to Say," *The Wire*, November 26, 2019, https://thewire.in/security/26-11-mumbai-terror-attack-inquiry-committee.

Hoeber, Francis P. 1978–79. "How Little Is Enough?" *International Security* 3, no. 3: 53–73.

Hosli, Madeleine O., and Thomas Dörfler. 2019. "Why Is Change So Slow? Assessing Prospects for United Nations Security Council Reform." *Journal of Economic Policy Reform* 22, no. 1: 35–50.

Howard, Michael. 1991. *Makers of Nuclear Strategy*, edited by John Baylis and John Garnett. London: Pinter.

Huchet, Jean-François. 2008. "Between Geostrategic Rivalry and Economic Competition: Emergence of a Pragmatic India-China Relationship." *China Perspectives*, no. 3. http://journals.openedition.org/chinaperspectives/4073.

Hudson, Valerie M. 2005. "Foreign Policy Analysis: Actor-Specific Theory and the Ground of International Relations." *Foreign Policy Analysis* 1, no. 1: 1–30.

Huemer, Michael. 2013. *The Problem of Political Authority: An Examination of the Right to Coerce and the Duty to Obey*. New York: Palgrave Macmillan.

Hurrell, Andrew, and Terry Macdonald. 2013. "Ethics and Norms in International Relations." In *Handbook of International Relations*, edited by Walter Carlsnaes, Thomas Risse, and Beth A. Simmons. London: Sage. https://dx.doi.org/10.4135/9781446247587.n3.

Hussain, Zahid. 2007. *Frontline Pakistan: The Struggle with Militant Islam*. New York: Columbia University Press.

IDSA (Institute for Defence Studies and Analyses). 2012. *A Case for Intelligence Reform in India*. Task Force Report. New Delhi: IDSA.

India, Ministry of Home Affairs. 2018–19. *Annual Report 2018–19*. New Delhi: Ministry of Home Affairs.

India, Ministry of External Affairs. 2005. "Joint Press Conference by External Affairs Minister Shri Natwar Singh and Foreign Minister of Sri Lanka Mr. Lakshman Kadirgamar," June 10. www.mea.gov.in/media-briefings.htm?dtl/3910/Joint+Press+Conference+by+External+Affairs+Minister+Shri+Natwar+Singh+and+Foreign+Minister+of+Sri+Lanka+Mr+Lakshman+Kadirgamar.

India Today. 2009. "Karunanidhi Joins 'Eelam' Bandwagon." May 7. www.indiatoday.in/election-news/story/karunanidhi-joins-eelam-bandwagon-46747-2009-05-07.

Indian Express. 2003. "LTTE Gun Running Stalled by Secret Indian Assistance." June 16. http://archive.indianexpress.com/oldStory/25836/.

———. 2005. "Pokharan's PM Slams Deal: Not On." www.indianexpress.com/full_story.php?content_id=74780.

———. 2008a. "India Must Intervene in Lanka Crisis." October 21. http://archive.indianexpress.com/news/-india-must-intervene-in-lanka-crisis-/375815/.

———. 2008b. "Lanka Row: Karunanidhi Withdraws Pullout Threat." October 26. http://archive.indianexpress.com/news/lanka-row-karunanidhi-withdraws-pullout-thr/378161/.

———. 2008c. "RAW, IB Pass the Buck: Moily." December 3. http://archive.indianexpress.com/news/raw-ib-pass-the-buck-moily/393417/.

———. 2008d. "Tamil Cause: Ally DMK Steps on Gas, 14 MPs 'Put In' Papers." October 18. http://archive.indianexpress.com/news/tamil-cause-ally-dmk-steps-on-gas-14-mps--/374802/.

———. 2008e. "Won't Stop Military Cooperation with Lanka: Pranab." October 24. http://archive.indianexpress.com/news/won-t-stop-military-cooperation-with -lanka-pranab/377216/.

———. 2009. "Third Suicide in Chennai Over Lanka." February 8. http://archive.indianexpress.com/news/third-suicide-in-chennai-over-lanka/420557/.

———. 2011. "26/11: Coast Guard, Navy Caught Napping." August 6. www.indianexpress.com/news/26-11-coast-guard-navy-caught-napping/827967/.

———. 2013a. "Legacy and Sanctions Made Narasimha Rao Decide against Nuke

Tests: Reports." February 23. www.indianexpress.com/news/legacy-and-sanctions-made-narasimha-rao-decide-against-nuke-tests-reports/1078588.

———. 2013b. "UPA Govt Policy Paralysis Led to Economic Slowdown, Says BJP." March 14. http://archive.indianexpress.com/news/rbi-cuts-interest-rate-by-25-bps/1090138/.

Indiavotes. No date. www.indiavotes.com/.

International Crisis Group. 2010. *War Crimes in Sri Lanka*. Asia Report 191. https://d2071andvipowj.cloudfront.net/191-war-crimes-in-sri-lanka.pdf.

———. 2020. *Raising the Stakes in Jammu and Kashmir*. Asia Report 310. www.crisisgroup.org/asia/south-asia/kashmir/310-raising-stakes-jammu-and-kashmir.

International Monetary Fund. No date. *Direction of Trade Statistics*. http://data.imf.org/regular.aspx?key=61013712.

Interview. 2004. Former Sri Lankan minister, May 15.

Interview. 2012. Retired Mumbai commissioner of police, April 2.

Interview. 2017. Former Sri Lankan minister, April 10.

Interview. 2019. "Scientific Advisor to the Defense Minister and Director General DRDO, Padmashri Dr. V. K. Saraswat." *Force*, March 28. http://forceindia.net/scientific-advisor-to-the-defence-minister-and-director-general-defence-research-and-development-organisation-padmashri-dr-v-k-saraswat/.

Iyengar, P. K. 2007. "Controversy over the Nuclear Deal." *The Hindu*, May 31. www.thehindu.com/todays-paper/tp-opinion/Controversy-over-the-nuclear-deal/article14770956.ece.

———. 2009. *Briefings on Nuclear Technology in India*. New Delhi: Rupa.

Jabbar, Zacki, 2010. "Enhanced Sri Lanka–Pakistan Defense Cooperation Likely." *Island*, November 19. www.island.lk/index.php?page_cat=article-details&page=article-details&code_title=11642.

Jacob, Cecilia, and Alistair D. B. Cook, eds. 2016. *Civilian Protection in the Twenty-First Century: Governance and Responsibility in a Fragmented World*. New Delhi: Oxford University Press.

Jacob, Happymon. 2010. "Neoclassical Realism and Indian Foreign Policy." In *Shaping India's Foreign Policies: People, Politics and Places*, edited by Amitabh Mattoo and Happymon Jacob. New Delhi: Har-Anand.

Jacobsen, John Kurt. 1996. "Are All Politics Domestic? Perspectives on the Integration of Comparative Politics and International Relations Theories." *Comparative Politics* 29, no. 1 (October): 93–115.

Jaipal, Rikhi. 1977. "The Indian Nuclear Explosion." *International Security* 1, no. 4: 44–51.

Jaishankar, Dhruva. 2017. "Decoding India's Nuclear Status." *The Wire*, March 4. https://thewire.in/120800//decoding-India-nuclear-status/.

Jaishankar, S. 2015. "India, the United States and China." IISS-Fullerton Lecture, July 20, International Institute for Strategic Studies, Singapore. www.iiss.org/en/events/events/archive/2015-f463/july-636f/fullerton-lecture-jaishankar-f64e.

Jamwal, N. S. 2003. "Counter Terrorism Strategy." *Strategic Analysis* 27, no. 1: 56–78.

Japan Times. 2020. "Japan's Record GDP Drop Seen Even Worse Than Preliminary 27.8%." September 2. www.japantimes.co.jp/news/2020/09/02/business/economy-business/japan-gdp-drop-record/#:~:text=Japan's%20April%2DJune%20gross%20domestic,post%2DWorld%20War%20II%20period.&text=The%20Cabinet%20Office%20will%20announce%20revised%20April%2DJune%20GDP%20data%20Tuesday.

Jervis, Robert. 1978. "Cooperation Under the Security Dilemma." *World Politics* 30, no. 2: 167–214.

———. 2009. "Kargil Deterrence and International Relations Theory." In *Asymmetric Warfare in South Asia: The Causes and Consequences of the Kargil Conflict*, edited by Peter R. Lavoy. Cambridge: Cambridge University Press.

———. 2013. "Do Leaders Matter and How Do We Know?" *Security Studies* 22, no. 2 (April): 153–79.

Jha, Prem Shankar. 2000. "Peril from Sri Lanka." *Outlook*, May 15. www.outlookindia.com/magazine/story/peril-from-sri-lanka/209387.

———. 2009. "How a Plot Was Lost." In *26/11: The Attack on Mumbai* by Hindustan Times. New Delhi: Penguin: 128–32.

Jha, Sanjay K. 2007. "Advani Ammo for Nuclear Deal Distance from Left, Signal to Sangh" *Telegraph*, August 28. www.telegraphindia.com/india/advani-ammo-for-nuclear-deal-distance-from-left-signal-to-sangh/cid/1569954.

Joint Statement. 2003. "Joint Statement on the Visit of Honorable Prime Minister Ranil Wickremesinghe to India, October 19–21, 2003." Sri Lankan Embassy to the United States, October 21. www.slembassyusa.org/statements/2003/SL_India_joint_stmnt_21oct03.html.

Joshi, Manoj. 1997a. "Jain Commission: 'Justice Jain's Unthinking Approach Could Harm National Interests.'" *India Today*, December 8. www.indiatoday.in/magazine/cover-story/story/19971208-jain-commission-justice-jains-unthinking-approach-could-harm-national-interests-831040-1997-12-08.

———. 1997b. "Jain Commission Opens Up Old Wounds India Inflicted upon Itself." *India Today*, December 1. www.indiatoday.in/magazine/cover-story/story/19971201-jain-commission-opens-up-old-wounds-india-inflicted-upon-itself-831009-1997-12-01.

———. 2014. *The Unending Quest to Reform India's National Security System*. Singapore: S. Rajaratnam School of International Studies, Nanyang Technological University.

———. 2017. *Doklam: To Start at the Very Beginning*. New Delhi: Observer Research Foundation. www.orfonline.org/wp-content/uploads/2017/08/ORF_SpecialReport_40_Doklam.pdf.

Joshi, Murli Manohar. 2005. "The US-India Agreement: Victory for Whom?" October 22. www.thehindu.com/2005/10/22/stories/2005102202701000.htm.

Joshi, Yogesh. 2015. *The Imagined Arsenal: India's Nuclear Decision-Making, 1973–76*. Washington, DC: Nuclear Proliferation International History Project, Woodrow Wilson International Center for Scholars.

———. 2019. "*Samudra*: India's Convoluted Path to Undersea Nuclear Weapons." *Nonproliferation Review* 26, nos. 5–6: 481–97.

Joshi, Yogesh, and Frank O'Donnell. 2019. *India and Nuclear Asia: Forces, Doctrine, and Dangers*. Washington, DC: Georgetown University Press.

Juneau, Thomas. 2015. *Squandered Opportunity: Neoclassical Realism and Iranian Foreign Policy*. Stanford, CA: Stanford University Press.

Kaarbo, Juliet. 2015. "A Foreign Policy Analysis Perspective on the Domestic Politics Turn in International Relations Theory." *International Studies Review* 17, no. 2 (June): 189–216.

Kabir, Mohammad Humayun. 1996. *The India Factor in Sri Lanka's Foreign and Security Policy*. Colombo: Bandaranaike Centre for International Studies.

Kadian, Rajesh. 1990. *India's Sri Lanka Fiasco: Peace Keepers at War*. New Delhi: Vision Books.

Kagotani, Koji, Kan Kimura, and Jeffrey R. Weber. 2014. "Democracy and Diversionary Incentives in Japan–South Korea Disputes." *International Relations of the Asia-Pacific* 14, no. 1: 33–58.

Kailash, K. K., and Balveer Arora. 2016. "Federal Coalitions in India: Strategic Calculations and Revolving-Door Partners." *Studies in Indian Politics* 4, no. 1: 63–76.

Kale, Sunila. 2009. "Inside Out: India's Global Reorientation." *India Review* 8, no. 1 (January–March): 43–62.

Kampani, Gaurav. 2014a. "Is the Indian Nuclear Tiger Changing Its Stripes?" *Nonproliferation Review* 21, nos. 3–4: 383–98.

———. 2014b. "New Delhi's Long Nuclear Journey: How Secrecy and Institutional Roadblocks Delayed India's Weaponization." *International Security* 38, no. 4: 79–114.

Kapur, Ashok. 1976. *India's Nuclear Option: Atomic Diplomacy and Decision Making*. New York: Praeger.

———. 1998. "Indian Strategy: The Dilemmas about Enmities, the Nature of Power and the Pattern of Relations." In *India: Fifty Years of Democracy and Development*, edited by Yogendra K. Malik and Ashok Kapur. New Delhi: APH.

———. 2006. *India: From Regional to World Power*. New York: Routledge.

Kapur, S. Paul, and Sumit Ganguly. 2007. "The Transformation of U.S.–India Relations: An Explanation for the Rapprochement and Prospects for the Future." *Asian Survey* 47, no. 4: 642–56.

Kapur, S. Paul. 2017. *Jihad as Grand Strategy: Islamist Militancy, National Security, and the Pakistani State*. New York: Oxford University Press.

Karat, Prakash. 2007. "Why the CPI(M) and the Left Oppose the Nuclear Deal." *The Hindu*, August 20. www.thehindu.com/todays-paper/tp-opinion/Why-the-CPIM-and-the-Left-oppose-the-nuclear-deal/article14819399.ece.

Kargil Review Committee. 2000. *From Surprise to Reckoning: The Kargil Review Committee Report*. New Delhi: Sage.

Karnad, Bharat. 2008. *India's Nuclear Policy*. New Delhi: ABC-CLIO.

Karunakaran, C. K. 1960. "Atoms and Man." *Sainik Samachar*, July 17. Archives of the Royal Society, London, document PB/8/27/ H 53-56.

Karve, Abhay Raghunath. 2018. "Maritime Security: A Decade after 26/11." Gateway House, November 29. www.gatewayhouse.in/maritime-security-after-2611/#:~:text=The%20Indian%20Navy%20was%20made,directorate%20immediately%20after%2026%2F11.

Kautilya. *The Arthashastra*. 1992. Edited by L. N. Rangarajan. New Delhi: Penguin.

Kazmin, Amy. 2018. "Maldives Lashes Out at Calls for India Military Intervention." *Financial Times*, February 14. www.ft.com/content/332a5b1a-1155-11e8-8cb6-b9ccc4c4dbbb.

Kelly, Joshua L., and Shahrzad Rizvi. 2015. "The Continued Relevance of the November, 2008, Mumbai Terrorist Attack: Countering New Attacks with Old Lessons." *Homeland Security Affairs* 11, no. 6 (June). www.hsaj.org/articles/4541.

Kennedy, Paul. 2009. "American Power Is on the Wane." *Wall Street Journal*, January 14. http://online.wsj.com/article/SB123189377673479433.html.

Keohane, Robert, and Joseph S. Nye. 1977. *Power and Interdependence: World Politics in Transition*. Boston: Little, Brown.

Kile, Shannon N., and Hans M. Kristensen. 2017. *Trends in World Nuclear Forces*. Stockholm: Stockholm International Peace Research Institute. www.sipri.org/sites/default/files/2017-06/fs_1707_wnf.pdf.

Koh Swee Lean, Collin. 2016. "'New Normal' in the Indo-Pacific: Sino-Indian Maritime Security Dilemma." In *India's Naval Strategy and Asian Security*, edited by Anit Mukherjee and C. Raja Mohan. New York: Routledge.

———. 2019. "China-India Rivalry at Sea: Capability, Trends and Challenges." In *India-China Maritime Competition: The Security Dilemma at Sea*, edited by Rajesh Basrur, Anit Mukherjee, and T. V. Paul. New York: Routledge.

Koithara, Verghese. 2005. "India-US Defence Cooperation: Expectations and Prospects." *Economic and Political Weekly* 40, no. 32 (August 6): 3585–88.

———. 2012. *Managing India's Nuclear Forces*. New Delhi: Routledge.

Kolappan, B. 2009. "Vaiko Warns of Bloodbath in Tamil Nadu." *The Hindu*, April 9. www.thehindu.com/todays-paper/Vaiko-warns-of-bloodbath-in-Tamil-Nadu/article16612222.ece.

Krepon, Michael, and Chris Gagné, eds. 2001. *The Stability-Instability Paradox: Nuclear Weapons and Brinkmanship in South Asia*. Washington, DC: Henry L. Stimson Center.

Krishna, Gopal. 1984. "India and the International Order: Retreat from Idealism." In *The Expansion of International Society*, edited by Hedley Bull and Adam Watson. Oxford: Clarendon Press.

Krishna, Sankaran. 1999. *Postcolonial Insecurities: India, Sri Lanka, and the Question of Nationhood*. Minneapolis: University of Minnesota Press.

———. 2001. *India's Role in Sri Lanka's Ethnic Conflict*. Colombo: Marga Institute.

Krishnan, Murali. 2017. "Why Is India Reluctant to Send Troops to Afghanistan?"

Deutsche Welle, September 27. www.dw.com/en/why-is-india-reluctant-to-send-troops-to-afghanistan/a-40706506.

Kristensen, Hans M., and Matt Korda. 2020. *Status of World Nuclear Forces.* Washington, DC: Federation of American Scientists. https://fas.org/issues/nuclear-weapons/status-world-nuclear-forces/.

Kroenig, Matthew. 2018. *The Logic of American Nuclear Strategy: Why Strategic Superiority Matters.* New York: Oxford University Press.

Kropatcheva, Elena. 2012. "Russian Foreign Policy in the Realm of European Security through the Lens of Neoclassical Realism." *Journal of Eurasian Studies* 3, no. 1 (January): 30–40.

Kuber, Girish. 2009. "R. R. Patil of 26/11 'Fame' Is Back." *Economic Times*, November 10. https://economictimes.indiatimes.com/news/politics-and-nation/r-r-patil-of-26/11-fame-is-back/articleshow/5214152.cms?from=mdr.

Kumar, Anand. 2013. "Impact of West Bengal Politics on India-Bangladesh Relations." *Strategic Analysis* 37, no. 3: 338–52.

Kumar, Rajeesh. 2017. "Waiting for Godot: India and United Nations Security Council Reform." *Strategic Analysis* 41, no. 6: 546–58.

Kundra, Swati. 2014. "Unhappy." *Hindustan Times*, February 16. www.pressreader.com/india/hindustan-times-delhi/20140216/281582353531486.

Kux, Dennis. 1993. *India and the United States: Estranged Democracies, 1941–1991.* Washington, DC: National Defense University Press.

Ladwig, Walter C., III. 2007–8. "A Cold Start for Hot Wars? The Indian Army's New Limited War Doctrine." *International Security* 32, no. 3: 158–90.

———. 2010. "India and Military Power Projection: Will the Land of Gandhi Become a Conventional Great Power?" *Asian Survey* 50, no. 6 (November–December): 1162–83.

Ladwig, Walter C., III, and Anit Mukherjee. 2019. "India and the United States: The Contours of an Asian Partnership." *Asia Policy* 14, no. 1: 3–18.

Lalwani, Sameer, and Hannah Haegeland. 2017. "The Debate over Indian Nuclear Strategy Is Heating Up." *War on the Rocks*, April 5. https://warontherocks.com/2017/04/the-debate-over-indian-nuclear-strategy-is-heating-up/.

Lapid, Yosef. 1989. "The Third Debate: On the Prospects of International Theory in a Post-Positivist Era." *International Studies Quarterly* 33, no. 3 (September): 235–54.

Lavoy, Peter R. 2002. "Fighting Terrorism, Avoiding War: The Indo-Pakistani Situation." *Joint Forces Quarterly*, no. 32 (Autumn): 27–34.

Laxman, Srinivas. 2006. "Sticky Deal, Say Critics." *Times of India*, June 29. https://timesofindia.indiatimes.com/india/Sticky-deal-say-critics/articleshow/1689104.cms.

Layne, Christopher. 2012. "This Time It's Real: The End of Unipolarity and the Pax Americana." *International Studies Quarterly* 56, no. 1 (March): 203–13.

Lebow, Richard Ned. 2003. *The Tragic Vision of Politics: Ethics, Interests and Orders.* Cambridge: Cambridge University Press.

Lebow, Richard Ned, and Janice Gross Stein. 1994. *We All Lost the Cold War*. Princeton, NJ: Princeton University Press.

Lee, John. 2010. *Unrealised Potential: India's Soft Power Ambition in Asia*. Sydney: Centre for Independent Studies. www.cis.org.au/app/uploads/2015/07/fpa4.pdf.

Legro, Jeffrey. 2005. *Rethinking the World: Great Power Strategies and International Order*. Ithaca, NY: Cornell University Press.

Legro, Jeffrey W., and Andrew Moravcsik. 1999. "Is Anybody Still a Realist?" *International Security* 24, no. 2 (Fall): 5–55.

Levering, Ralph. 2005. *The Cold War: A Post–Cold War History*, 2nd ed. Wheeling, IL: Harlan Davidson.

Levi, Michael, and Charles D. Ferguson. 2006. *US-India Nuclear Cooperation: A Strategy for Moving Forward*. New York: Council on Foreign Relations.

Lewis, John Wilson, and Xue Litai. 1988. *China Builds the Bomb*. Stanford, CA: Stanford University Press.

Lieber, Keir A. 2007. "The New History of World War I and What It Means for International Relations Theory." *International Security* 32, no. 2: 155–91.

Lieber, Keir A., and Daryl G. Press. 2006. "The End of MAD? The Nuclear Dimension of US Primacy." *International Security* 30, no. 4: 7–44.

Lewis, John Wilson, and Xue Litai. 2006. *Imagined Enemies: China Prepares for Uncertain War*. Stanford, CA: Stanford University Press.

Lobell, Steven E., Norrin M. Ripsman, and Jeffrey W. Taliaferro, eds. 2009. *Neoclassical Realism, the State, and Foreign Policy*. Cambridge: Cambridge University Press.

MacInnis, Laura. 2009. "UN Rights Body Backs Sri Lankan Resolution on War." Reuters, May 28. https://in.reuters.com/article/idINIndia-39926020090528.

Mack, Andrew. 1975. "Why Big Nations Lose Small Wars: The Politics of Asymmetric Commitment." *World Politics* 27, No. 2 (January): 175–200.

Madhavan, N. 2019. "Is India Cyber Security Ready?" *The Hindu Business Line*, November 7. www.thehindubusinessline.com/opinion/columns/is-india-cyber-security-ready/article29911679.ece.

Magcamit, Michael. 2020. "The Duterte Method: A Neoclassical Realist Guide to Understanding a Small Power's Foreign Policy and Strategic Behavior in the Asia-Pacific." *Asian Journal of Comparative Politics* 5, no. 4: 416–36.

Mahadevan, Asha. 2018. "26/11 Hero Praveen Teotia Remembers the Attack on the Taj Hotel: 'If My Grenade Had Burst, the Terrorists Would Have Been Killed on the First Night Itself.'" *Mumbai Mirror*, November 26. https://mumbaimirror.indiatimes.com/mumbai/other/26/11-hero-praveen-teotia-remembers-the-attack-on-the-taj-hotel-if-my-grenade-had-burst-the-terrorists-would-have-been-killed-on-the-first-night-itself/articleshow/66794562.cms.

Mahadevan, Prem. 2012. *The Politics of Counterterrorism in India: Strategic Intelligence and National Security in South Asia*. London: I. B. Tauris.

Mahoney, James, and Richard Snyder. 1999. "Rethinking Agency and Structure in the Study of Regime Change." *Studies in Comparative International Development* 34, no. 3 (June): 3–32.

Mahoney, James, and Kathleen Thelen. 2010. "A Theory of Gradual Institutional Change." In *Explaining Institutional Change: Ambiguity, Agency, and Power*, edited by James Mahoney and Kathleen Thelen. Cambridge: Cambridge University Press.

Maini, Tridivesh Singh. 2020. *China, India and the Galwan Valley Clashes: What Can India Do?* Nedlands, Australia: Future Directions International. www.futuredirections.org.au/wp-content/uploads/2020/06/China-India-and-the-Galwan-Valley-Clashes-What-Can-India-Do.pdf.

Malik, J. Mohan. 1998. "India Goes Nuclear: Rationale, Benefits, Costs and Implications." *Contemporary Southeast Asia* 20, no. 2: 191–215.

Malik, Priyanjali. 2010. *India's Nuclear Debate: Exceptionalism and the Bomb.* New Delhi: Routledge.

Malone, David M., C. Raja Mohan, and Srinath Raghavan, eds. 2015. *The Oxford Handbook of Indian Foreign Policy.* Oxford: Oxford University Press.

Mandelbaum, Michael. 1988. *The Fate of Nations.* New York: Cambridge University Press.

———. 2010. *The Frugal Superpower: America's Global Leadership in a Cash-Strapped Era.* New York: PublicAffairs.

Manning, Robert A. 2002. "United States–North Korean Relations: From Welfare to Workfare?" In *North Korea and Northeast Asia*, edited by Samuel S. Kim and Tai Hwan Lee. Lanham, MD: Rowman and Littlefield.

Mansingh, Surjit. 1984. *India's Search for Power: Indira Gandhi's Foreign Policy, 1966–1982.* New Delhi: Sage.

March, Kevin. 2012. "Managing Relative Decline: A Neoclassical Realist Analysis of the 2012 US Defense Strategic Guidance." *Contemporary Security Policy* 33, no. 3 (December): 487–511.

Maria, Rakesh. 2020. *Let Me Say It Now.* Chennai: Westland.

Markey, Daniel. 2009. "Developing India's Foreign Policy 'Software.'" *Asia Policy*, no. 8 (July): 73–96.

Marshall, Larry. 2009. "Winners and Losers in Sri Lanka's Long War." CETRI (Le Centre Tricontinental / Tricontinental Center), Louvain-la-Neuve, Belgium, December 4. https://www.cetri.be/Winners-and-losers-in-Sri-Lanka-s?lang=fr.

Marwah, Omkar. 1979. "India's Military Intervention in East Pakistan, 1971–1972." *Modern South Asian Studies* 13, no. 4: 549–80.

Matthijs, Matthias. 2016. "The Euro's 'Winner-Take-All' Political Economy: Institutional Choices, Policy Drift, and Diverging Patterns." *Politics and Society* 44, no. 3: 393–422.

Mattoo, Amitabh, and Happymon Jacob. 2010. "Foreign Relations of India: The Federal Challenge." In *Shaping India's Foreign Policy: People, Politics and Places*, edited by Amitabh Mattoo and Happymon Jacob. New Delhi: Har-Anand.

Mazarr, Michael J. 2007. "The Long Road to Pyongyang: A Case Study in Policy-making without Direction." *Foreign Affairs* 86, no. 5: 75–94.

McConnell, Allan. 2016. "A Public Policy Approach to Understanding the Nature and Causes of Foreign Policy Failure." *Journal of European Public Policy* 23, no. 5: 667–84.

———. 2017. "Policy Success and Failure." *Oxford Research Encyclopedia of Politics*, May 21. https://doi.org/10.1093/acrefore/9780190228637.013.137.

McCormick, Thomas J. 1982. "Drift or Mastery? A Corporatist Synthesis for American Diplomatic History," *Reviews in American History* 10, no. 4 (December): 318–30.

McGarr, Paul M. 2013. *The Cold War in South Asia: Britain, the United States, and the Indian Subcontinent.* New York: Cambridge University Press.

McLean, Wayne. 2016. "Neoclassical Realism and Australian Foreign Policy: Understanding How Security Elites Frame Domestic Discourses." *Global Change, Peace and Security* 28, no. 1: 1–15.

McMahon, Robert J. 1988. "United States Cold War Strategy in South Asia: Making a Military Commitment to Pakistan." *Journal of American History* 57, no. 3 (December): 812–40.

———. 1994. *The Cold War on the Periphery: The United States, India, and Pakistan.* New York: Columbia University Press.

Mearsheimer, John J. 2001. *The Tragedy of Great Power Politics.* New York: W. W. Norton.

Mehta, Mandavi, and Teresita Schaffer. 2002. *Islam in Pakistan: Unity and Contradictions.* Washington, DC: Center for Strategic and International Studies.

Menon, Prakash. 2012. Interview, New Delhi, March 30.

———. 2018. *The Strategy Trap: India and Pakistan under the Nuclear Shadow.* New Delhi: Wisdom Tree.

———. 2019. Interview, Bengaluru, November 3.

Menon, Prakash, and Anirudh Kanisetti. 2021. *China, India and Doklam in 2020.* Bengaluru: Takshashila Institution. https://takshashila.org.in/takshashila-strategic-assessment -china-india-and-doklam-in-2020/.

Menon, Shivshankar. 2014. Speech by Shri Shivshankar Menon at NDC on "The Role of Force in Strategic Affairs," Ministry of External Affairs, Government of India, New Delhi. www.mea.gov.in/Speeches-Statements.htm?dtl/798/Speech+by+NSA+Shri+Shivshankar+Menon+at+NDC+on+The+Role+of+Force+in+Strategic+Affairs.

———. 2016. *Choices: Inside the Making of India's Foreign Policy.* Washington, DC: Brookings Institution Press.

Mian, Zia, and M. V. Ramana. 2006. "Wrong Ends, Means, and Needs: Behind the US Nuclear Deal with India." *Arms Control Today*, January–February. www.armscontrol.org/act/2006_01-02/JANFEB-IndiaFeature.

Milhollin, Gary. 2006. "The US-India Nuclear Pact: Bad for Security." *Current History* 105, no. 694 (November): 371–74.

Miller, Manjari Chatterjee, and Kate Sullivan de Estrada. 2017. "Pragmatism in Indian Foreign Policy: How Ideas Constrain Modi." *International Affairs* 93, no. 1: 27–49.

Mir, Amir. 2009. "Pakistan's Crucial Role in the Death of Tamil Tigers." *Pakistan Defence*, May 20. https://defence.pk/pdf/threads/pakistans-crucial-role-in-the-death-of-tamil-tigers.26946/.

Mirchandani, Maya. 2019. "26/11 and the Media: Where Were the Protocols?" *The Wire*, November 26. https://thewire.in/media/26-11-mumbai-attack-media-coverage.

Mistry, Dinshaw. 2004. "A Theoretical and Empirical Assessment of India as an Emerging Power." *India Review* 3, no. 1 (January): 64–87.

———. 2014. *The US–India Nuclear Agreement: Diplomacy and Domestic Politics.* Delhi: Cambridge University Press.

Mitra, Devirupa. 2017. "As UNHRC Session Draws to a Close, Here's How India Voted on Key Resolutions." *The Wire*, March 27. https://thewire.in/diplomacy/unhrc-vote-india-myanmar.

Mitra, Subrata K. 2003. "The Reluctant Hegemon: India's Self-Perception and the South Asian Strategic Environment." *Contemporary South Asia* 12, no. 3 (September): 399–417.

Mitra, Subrata K., and Michael Liebic. 2017. *Kautilya's Arthashastra: An Intellectual Portrait.* New Delhi: Rupa.

Mitra, Sumit. 1981. "India, Bangladesh at Loggerheads over New Moore Island." *India Today*, June 15 (republished September 19, 2014). www.indiatoday.in/magazine/special-report/story/19810615-india-bangladesh-at-loggerheads-over-new-moore-island-805968-2014-02-22.

Mkhwanazi, Ezekiel. 2013. "To Be Human Is to Be Responsible to the Other: A Critical Analysis of Levinas' Conception of Responsibility." *Phronimon* 14, no. 1 (2013): 133–49.

Mohan, Gopu. 2008. "Lanka Battle Gives New Ammo to Parties in TN." *Indian Express*, October 17. http://archive.indianexpress.com/news/lanka-battle-gives-new-ammo-to-parties-in-tn/374395/.

Montgomery, Evan Braden. 2006. "Breaking Out of the Security Dilemma: Realism, Reassurance, and the Problem of Uncertainty." *International Security* 31, no. 2 (Fall): 151–85.

Moorcraft, Paul. 2012. *The Destruction of the Tamil Tigers: The Rare Victory of Sri Lanka's Long War.* Barnsley, UK: Pen and Sword Military.

Moorthy, N. Sathiya. 2011. "Sri Lanka: Trans-border Consequences of An Internal Conflict." In *Conflict in Sri Lanka: Internal and External Consequences*, edited by V. R. Raghavan. New Delhi: Vij Books.

Moravcsik, Andrew. 1997. "Taking Preferences Seriously: A Liberal Theory of International Politics." *International Organization* 51, no. 4 (Autumn): 513–53.

Morgan, Iwan. 2019. "Make America Great Again: Ronald Reagan and Donald Trump." In *The Trump Presidency*, edited by Mara Oliva and Mark Shanahan. London: Palgrave Macmillan. https://doi.org/10.1007/978-3-319-96325-9_4.

Morgenthau, Hans. 1962. *The Decline of Democratic Politics*. Chicago: University of Chicago Press.

———. 2006. *Politics among Nations: The Struggle for Power and Peace*, 7th edition. Revised by Kenneth W. Thompson and W. David Clinton. Boston: McGraw Hill.

Morrow, Daniel, and Michael Carriere. 1999. "The Economic Impacts of the 1998 Sanctions on India and Pakistan." *Nonproliferation Review* 6, no. 4: 1–16.

Mukherjee, Anit. 2014. *India as a Net Security Provider: Concept and Impediments*. Singapore: S. Rajaratnam School of International Studies, Nanyang Technological University. www.rsis.edu.sg/wp-content/uploads/2014/09/PB_140903_India-Net-Security.pdf.

———. 2020. *The Absent Dialogue: Politicians, Bureaucrats, and the Military in India*. New York: Oxford University Press.

Mukherjee, Rohan. 2020. "Chaos as Opportunity: The United States and World Order in India's Grand Strategy." *Contemporary Politics* 26, no. 4: 426–38.

Mukherjee, Rohan, and Rahul Sagar. 2018. "Pragmatism in Indian Strategic Thought: Evidence from the Indian Strategic Debate of the 1960s." *India Review* 17, no. 1: 12–32.

Mukherji, Rahul. 2010. "Political Economy of Reforms." In *The Oxford Companion to Politics in India*, edited by Neerja G. Jayal and Pratap Bhanu Mehta. New Delhi: Oxford University Press.

———. 2014. *Globalization and Deregulation: Ideas, Interests and Institutional Change in India*. New Delhi: Oxford University Press.

———. 2016. "Governance Reform in a Weak State: Thirty Years of Indian Experience." *Wiley Governance*, September 29. www.uni-heidelberg.de/md/sai/pol/team/mukherji-2016-governance.pdf.

Muni, S. D. 1993. *Pangs of Proximity: India and Sri Lanka's Ethnic Crisis*. New Delhi: Sage.

———. 2004. "Sri Lanka's Peace Process: Donors as Peace Makers." In *Federalism and Conflict Resolution in Sri Lanka*, edited by V. R. Raghavan and Volker Bauer. New Delhi: Lancer.

Munro, Ross. 1989. "Superpower Rising." *Time*, April 3, 6–13.

Munton, Don, and David A. Welch. 2007. *The Cuban Missile Crisis: A Concise History*. Oxford: Oxford University Press.

Murari, S. 2009a. "Partial Strike in Tamil Nadu on Sri Lanka." Reuters, February 4. www.reuters.com/article/us-india-srilanka-strike-sb/partial-strike-in-india-tamil-nadu-state-on-sri-lanka-idUSTRE51328520090204.

———. 2009b. "Sri Lanka War Politics Shuts Down Tamil Nadu." Reuters, April 23. www.reuters.com/article/us-india-srilanka-sb-idUSTRE53M2BS20090423?mod=related&channelName=worldNews.

Murphy, Ann Marie. 2017. "Great Power Rivalries, Domestic Politics and Southeast Asian Foreign Policy: Exploring the Linkages." *Asian Security* 13, no. 3: 165–82.

Murray, A. J. 1996. "The Moral Politics of Hans Morgenthau." *Review of Politics* 58, no. 1 (Winter): 81–107.

Murthy, Padmaja. 1999. "The Gujral Doctrine and Beyond." *Strategic Analysis* 23, no. 4: 639–52.

———. 2000. "Sri Lanka's 'War Within' and India." *Strategic Analysis* 24, no. 4: 773–95.

Nagal, B. S. 2014a. "Checks and Balances." *Force*, June, 12–17.

———. 2014b. "Perception and Reality." *Force*, October, 8–14.

———. 2015. "Strategic Stability: Conundrum, Challenge and Dilemma—The Case of India, China, and Pakistan." *CLAWS Journal*, Summer, 1–22.

———. 2019. "India's Nuclear Doctrine and Strategy." In *Military Strategy for India in the 21st Century*, edited by A. K. Singh and B. S. Nagal. New Delhi: Knowledge World.

Nakato, Sachio. 2012. "North Korea's Second Nuclear Test: Neoclassical Realism Perspectives." *Pacific Focus* 27, no. 1: 10–35.

Nandy, Ashis. 1972. "The Bomb, the NPT and Indian Elites." *Economic and Political Weekly* 7, nos. 31–33: 1533–40.

Nanjappa, Vicky. 2009. "I Felt There Were More Than Ten Terrorists." Rediff.com, November 24. www.rediff.com/news/interview/anniversary-26-11-exclusive-interview-with-former-nsg-chief-j-k-dutt/20091124.htm.

Narang, Vipin. 2014. *Nuclear Strategy in the Modern Era: Regional Strategy in the Modern Era.* Princeton, NJ: Princeton University Press.

Narang, Vipin, and Paul Staniland. 2018. "Democratic Accountability and Foreign Security Policy: Theory and Evidence from India." *Security Studies* 27, no. 3: 410–47.

Narizny, Kevin. 2017. "On Systemic Paradigms and Domestic Politics: A Critique of the Newest Realism." *International Security* 42, no. 2 (Fall): 155–90.

Narlikar, Amrita. 2013. "India Rising: Responsible to Whom?" *International Affairs* 89, no. 3: 595–614.

Narveson, Jan. 2002. "Collective Responsibility." *Journal of Ethics* 6, no. 2: 179–98.

National Security Advisory Board, India. 1999. "Draft Report of National Security Advisory Board on Indian Nuclear Doctrine." Ministry of External Affairs, Government of India, August 17. https://mea.gov.in/in-focus-article.htm?18916/Draft+Report+of+National+Security+Advisory+Board+on+Indian+Nuclear+Doctrine.

Nau, Henry R., and Deepa Ollapally. 2012. *Worldviews of Aspiring Powers: Domestic Foreign Policy Debates in China, India, Iran, Japan, and Russia.* Oxford: Oxford University Press. DOI: 10.1093/acprof:oso/9780199937479.003.0003.

Naval Technology. No date. "Sukanya Class Offshore Patrol Vessels." www.naval-technology.com/projects/sukanya-class-offshore-patrol-vessels/.

Navlakha, Gautam. 2009. "Lessons from the Mumbai Attack." *Economic and Political Weekly* 44, no. 11: 13–16.

Nayar, Baldev Raj, and T. V. Paul. 2003. *India in the World Order: Searching for Major-Power Status.* Cambridge: Cambridge University Press.

NDTV. 2009. "Govt Turns Down Demands for 26/11 Commission." June 5. www.ndtv.com/india-news/govt-turns-down-demands-for-26-11-commission-395641.

Nebehay, Stephanie, and Alasdair Pal. 2021. "Sri Lanka Faces UN Scrutiny over Civil War Crimes." Reuters, March 23. www.reuters.com/article/sri-lanka-rights-un-idUSKBN2BF1DF.

Nehru, Jawaharlal. 1948. "Letter from Nehru to Blackett." September 26. Archives of the Royal Society, London, document PB/8/27 H53-56.

———. 1957. "Letter from Nehru to Blackett." January 23. Archives of the Royal Society, London, document PB/7/1/2 G5.

Nölke, Andreas, Tobias ten Brink, Simone Claar, and Christian May. 2015. "Domestic Structures, Foreign Economic Policies and Global Economic Order: Implications from the Rise of Large Emerging Economies." *European Journal of International Relations* 21, no. 3: 538–67.

Norris, Robert S., and Hans M. Kristensen. 2013. "Global Nuclear Inventories, 1945–2013." *Bulletin of the Atomic Scientists* 69, no. 5: 75–81.

Nuclear Testing Tally. 2019. Arms Control Association, February. www.armscontrol.org/factsheets/nucleartesttally.

Nye, Joseph S., Jr. 2000. "The US and Europe: Continental Drift?" *International Affairs* 76, no. 1 (January): 51–59.

Nye, Mary Joe, ed. 2004. *Blackett: Physics, War and Politics in the Twentieth Century.* Cambridge, MA: Harvard University Press.

O'Donnell, Francis Dominic. 2015. "India's Nuclear Journey, Nuclear Discourse and Decisions, 1997–2009." PhD thesis, King's College London.

O'Donnell, Frank. 2019. "India's Nuclear Counter-Revolution: Nuclear Learning and the Future of Deterrence." *Nonproliferation Review* 26, nos. 5–6: 407–26.

O'Donnell, Frank, and Yogesh Joshi. 2014. "Lost at Sea: The Arihant in India's Quest for a Grand Strategy." *Comparative Strategy* 33, no. 5: 466–81.

Ogden, Chris. 2017. *China and India: Asia's Emergent Great Powers.* Cambridge: Polity Press.

Ollapally, Deepa M., and Rajesh Rajagopalan. 2012. "India: Foreign Policy Perspectives of an Ambiguous Power." In *Worldviews of Aspiring Powers*, edited by Henry R. Nau and Deepa M. Ollapally. Oxford: Oxford University Press.

Onea, Tudor. 2012. "Putting the 'Classical' in Neoclassical Realism: Neoclassical Realist Theories and US Expansion in the Post–Cold War." *International Relations* 26, no. 2 (June): 139–64.

Onuf, Nicholas G. 1989. *World of Our Making.* Columbia: University of South Carolina Press.

Orjuela, Camilla. 2008. "Distant Warriors, Distant Peace Workers? Multiple Diaspora Roles in Sri Lanka's Violent Conflict." *Global Networks: A Journal of Transnational Affairs* 8, no. 4 (2008): 436–52.

Outlook. 2009. "Govt Dismissive of Scientist's Claim over Pokhran-II." August 27. www.outlookindia.com/newswire/story/govt-dismissive-of-scientists-claims-over-pokhran-ii/665044.

Oxford Living Dictionaries. No date. "Drift." https://en.oxforddictionaries.com/definition/drift.

Palit, Amitendu. 2019. "Domestic Politics Force India's Withdrawal from RCEP and Broader Trade Disengagement." *Asia Pacific Bulletin*, November 26. www.eastwestcenter.org/publications/domestic-politics-force-india%E2%80%99s-withdrawal-rcep-and-broader-trade-disengagement.

Panagariya, Arvind. 2004. "India in the 1980s and 1990s: A Triumph of Reforms." Working paper, International Monetary Fund. www.imf.org/external/pubs/ft/wp/2004/wp0443.pdf.

———. 2008. *India: The Emerging Giant*. New York: Oxford University Press.

Pande, B. N. 1989. *Indira Gandhi*. New Delhi: Ministry of Information and Broadcasting, Government of India.

Pandit, Rajat. 2007. "India Quietly Steps Up Arms Aid to Sri Lanka." *Times of India*, October 15. https://timesofindia.indiatimes.com/india/India-quietly-steps-up-arms-aid-to-Lanka/articleshow/2458421.cms.

———. 2008a. "Complete Overhaul of Coastal Security Needed." *Times of India*, December 4. http://timesofindia.indiatimes.com/india/Complete-overhaul-of-coastal-security-setup-needed/articleshow/3789428.cms.

———. 2008b. "India to Expand Military Ties with Sri Lanka." *Times of India*, June 23. http://timesofindia.indiatimes.com/India_to_expand_military_ties_with_Lanka/articleshow/3154497.cms.

———. 2008c. "India to Train Lankan Soldiers." *Times of India*, July 1. https://timesofindia.indiatimes.com/india/India-to-train-Lankan-soldiers/articleshow/3182598.cms.

———. 2016. "Navy Chief Says They Received No 'Actionable Intelligence.'" *Times of India*, December 3. http://timesofindia.indiatimes.com/india/Navy-chief-says-they-received-no-actionable-intelligence/articleshow/3785611.cms.

Panneerselvan, A. A. 2009. "Metamorphosis of Belief." *Outlook*, May 29. www.outlookindia.com/magazine/story/metamorphosis-of-belief/209464.

Pant, Harsh V. 2008. *Contemporary Debates in Indian and Foreign Security Policy: India Negotiates Its Rise in the International System*. New York: Palgrave Macmillan.

———. 2009. "A Rising India's Search for a Foreign Policy." *Orbis* 53, no. 2 (January): 250–64.

———. 2011. *The US–India Nuclear Pact: Policy, Process, and Great Power Politics*. New Delhi: Oxford University Press.

———. 2019. "The US–India–China 'Strategic Triangle': Theoretical, Historical, and Contemporary Dimensions." *India Review* 18, no. 4: 343–47.

Parashar, Sachin. 2009. "Pokhran-II Not Fully Successful: Scientist." *Economic Times*, August 27. https://economictimes.indiatimes.com/news/politics-and

-nation/pokhran-ii-not-fully-successful-scientist/articleshow/4939162.cms?from=mdr.
———. 2011. "Manmohan Singh, Musharraf Came Close to Striking Kashmir Deal: WikiLeaks." *Times of India*, September 3. https://timesofindia.indiatimes.com/india/Manmohan-Singh-Musharraf-came-close-to-striking-Kashmir-deal-WikiLeaks/articleshow/9841701.cms.
Pardesi, Manjeet S. 2015. "Is India a Great Power? Understanding Great Power Status in Contemporary International Relations." *Asian Security* 11, no. 1: 1–30.
Parthasarthy, G. 2000. "Tamil Nadu and the Sri Lankan Crisis." Rediff.com, July 17. http://m.rediff.com/news/2000/jul/17gp.htm.
Pasternak, Avia. 2011. "The Collective Responsibility of Democratic Publics." *Canadian Journal of Philosophy* 41, no. 1: 99–123.
Pattanaik, Smruti S. 2014. "Federalizing India's Neighborhood Policy: Making the States Stakeholders." *Strategic Analysis* 38, no. 1: 31–48.
Paul, T. V. 1998. "The Systemic Bases of India's Challenge to the Global Nuclear Order." *Nonproliferation Review* 6, no. 1: 1–11.
———. 2005. *The India-Pakistan Conflict: An Enduring Rivalry*. Cambridge: Cambridge University Press.
———, ed. 2010a. *South Asia's Weak States: Understanding the Regional Insecurity Predicament*. Stanford, CA: Stanford University Press.
———. 2010b. "State Capacity and South Asia's Perennial Insecurity Problems." In *South Asia's Weak States: Understanding the Regional Insecurity Predicament*, edited by T. V. Paul. Stanford, CA: Stanford University Press.
———. 2014. *The Warrior State: Pakistan in the Contemporary World*. New York: Oxford University Press.
———, ed. 2018. *The China–India Rivalry in the Globalization Era*. Washington, DC: Georgetown University Press.
Paul, T. V., Deborah Welch Larson, and William C. Wohlforth, eds. 2017. *Status in World Politics*. New York: Cambridge University Press.
Paul, T. V., and Mahesh Shankar. 2017. "Status Accommodation through Institutional Means: India's Rise in the Global Order." In *Status in World Politics*, edited by T. V. Paul, Deborah Welch Larson, and William C. Wohlforth. New York: Cambridge University Press.
Payne, Keith B., and James Schlesinger. 2014. "Minimum Deterrence: Examining the Evidence." *Comparative Strategy* 33, no. 1: 2–103.
Pepinsky, Thomas B. 2012. "The Domestic Politics of Internationalization in the Developing World." *Review of International Political Economy* 20, no. 4: 848–80.
Perkovich, George, 1999. *India's Nuclear Bomb: The Impact on Global Proliferation*. Berkeley: University of California Press.
———. 2003–4. "Is India a Major Power?" *Washington Quarterly* 17, no. 1 (Winter): 129–44.
———. 2005. "Faulty Promises: The US–India Nuclear Deal." Carnegie

Endowment for International Peace, Washington, DC. https://carnegieendowment.org/files/PO21.Perkovich.pdf.

Pfaffenberger, Bryan. 1981. "The Cultural Dimension of Tamil Separatism in Sri Lanka." *Asian Survey* 21, no. 11 (November): 1145–57.

PIPS Policy Brief. 2017. "National Dialogue and Social Contract." April 3. http://pakpips.com/downloads/PB_CVE3_National_Dialogue.pdf.

Plagemann, Johannes, and Sandra Destradi. 2015. "Soft Sovereignty, Rising Powers, and Subnational Foreign Policy-Making: The Case of India." *Globalizations* 12, no. 5: 728–43.

———. 2019. "Populism and Foreign Policy: The Case of India." *Foreign Policy Analysis* 15, no. 2: 283–301.

Poddar, Tushar, and Eva Yi. 2007. *India's Rising Growth Potential.* Economics Paper 152, Goldman Sachs, January. www.goldmansachs.com/our-thinking/archive/archive-pdfs/brics-book/brics-chap-1.pdf.

Posner, Eric A. 2002–3. "Do States Have a Moral Obligation to Obey International Law?" *Stanford Law Review* 55 (May): 1901–19.

Power, Jonathan. 2004. "Talking to the New Prime Minister of India." Transnational Foundation for Peace and Future Research, May 24. www.oldsite.transnational.org/SAJT/forum/power/2004/05.04_IndiaPrimeMinster.htm.

Prakash, Arun. 2012. "9 Minutes to Midnight." *Force*, July, 4–8.

———. 2014. *India's Nuclear Deterrent: The More Things Change . . .* Policy Report. Singapore: S. Rajaratnam School of International Studies, Nanyang Technological University.

———. 2018. "The Significance of Arihant." *Indian Express*, November 7. https://indianexpress.com/article/opinion/columns/the-significance-of-ins-arihant-nuclear-submarine-navy-5436432/.

Price, Gareth. 2005. *Diversity in Donorship: The Changing Landscape of Official Humanitarian Aid—India's Official Aid Programme.* London: Humanitarian Policy Group.

Pritchett, Lant. 2009. "Is India a Flailing State? Detours on the Four-Lane Highway to Modernization." Working paper, Kennedy School of Government, Harvard University. https://dash.harvard.edu/bitstream/handle/1/4449106/Pritchett%20India%20Flailing%20State.pdf?sequence=1.

Putnam, Robert D. 1988. "Diplomacy and Domestic Politics: The Logic of Two-Level Games." *International Organization* 42, no. 3: 427–60.

PwC (PricewaterhouseCoopers). 2017. *The World in 2050.* www.pwc.com/world2050.

———. 2010. "Shift in World Economic Power Means a Decade of Seismic Change." January 21. http://pwc.blogs.com/press_room/2010/01/shift-in-world-economic-power-means-a-decade-of-seismic-change.html.

Rabasa, Angela, Robert D. Blackwill, Peter Chalk, Kim Cragin, C. Christine Fair, Brian A. Jackson, Brian Michael Jenkins, Seth G. Jones, Nathaniel Shestak, and Ashley J. Tellis. 2009. *The Lessons of Mumbai*. Santa Monica, CA: RAND Corporation.

Racine, Jean-Luc. 2009. "Caste and Beyond in Tamil Nadu Politics." In *Rise of the Plebeians? The Changing Face of Indian Legislative Assemblies*, edited by Christophe Jaffrelot and Sanjay Kumar. New Delhi: Routledge.

Raghavan, P. S. 2019. "The Evolution of India's National Security Architecture." *Journal of Defence Studies* 13, no. 3: 33–52.

Raghavan, Srinath. 2018. *The Most Dangerous Place: A History of the United States in South Asia*. Gurgaon: Allen Lane.

———. 2012. "Soldiers, Statesmen, and India's Security Policy." *India Review* 11, no. 2: 116–33.

Raja Mohan, C. 1998. "India Committed to Minimum N-Deterrence." *The Hindu*, December 7. https://global.factiva.com/ga/default.aspx.

———. 2003. *Crossing the Rubicon: The Shaping of India's New Foreign Policy*. New Delhi: Penguin.

———. 2005. "Ending Our Nuclear Winter." *Indian Express*, July 26. http://archive.indianexpress.com/oldStory/75079/.

———. 2006. *Impossible Allies: Nuclear India, United States, and the Global Order*. New Delhi: India Research Press.

———. 2014. "Managing Strategic Partnerships." *Mint*, June 17. www.livemint.com/Opinion/tHfbrRq1SsLcp99satnkqK/Managing-strategic-partnerships.html.

———. 2015. *Modi's World: Expanding India's Sphere of Influence*. Noida: Harper Collins.

Rajagopalan, Rajesh. 2016a. "India and NSG: It's Simply Power Politics." *Indian Foreign Affairs Journal* 11, no. 3: 201–6.

———. 2016b. "India's Nuclear Doctrine Debate." Carnegie Endowment for International Peace, June 30. https://carnegieendowment.org/2016/06/30/india-s-nuclear-doctrine-debate-pub-63950.

Rajagopalan, Rajeswari Pillai, and Arka Biswas. 2016. "India's Membership to the Nuclear Suppliers Group." ORF Issue Brief 41. https://orfonline.org/wp-content/uploads/2016/05/ORF_Issue_Brief_141.pdf.

Ramachandran, R. 2006. "The Complicated World of Nuclear Deals." *The Hindu*, February 9. www.thehindu.com/todays-paper/tp-opinion/the-complicated-world-of-nuclear-deals/article3175865.ece.

Ramakrishnan, Venkitesh. 1998. "Pulls and Pressure." *The Hindu Frontline*, June 20–July 3. https://frontline.thehindu.com/static/html/fl1513/15130340.htm.

Raman, Sunil. 2009. "'Sri Lanka Factor' in Tamil Nadu Poll." BBC News, May 11. http://news.bbc.co.uk/go/pr/fr/-/2/hi/south_asia/8043588.stm.

Ramanna, Anitha. 2004. "Interest Groups and Patent Reform in India." Working paper, Indira Gandhi Institute of Development Research, Mumbai. www.igidr.ac.in/pdf/publication/WP-2003-006.pdf.

Rana, A. P. 1976. *The Imperatives of Non-Alignment: A Conceptual Study of India's Foreign Policy Strategy in the Nehru Period*. New Delhi: Macmillan.

Range, Jackie. 2008. "Chairman of India's Tata Calls for Security Efforts." *Wall Street Journal*, December 1. www.wsj.com/articles/SB122806478088367089.

Ranjan, Amit. 2017. "The Teesta Muddle: Can India and Bangladesh Find a Way Out?" *ISAS Insights*, April 3. www.isas.nus.edu.sg/papers/397-the-teesta-muddle-can-india-and-bangladesh-find-a-way-out/.

Rath, Saroj Kumar. 2014. *Fragile Frontiers: The Secret History of the Mumbai Terrorist Attacks*. New Delhi: Routledge.

Rathbun, Brian. 2008. "A Rose by Any Other Name: Neoclassical Realism as the Logical and Necessary Extension of Structural Realism." *Security Studies* 17: 294–321.

Ravi, N. 2005. "A Persistent Irritant Goes with a Grand Bargain,." *The Hindu*, July 30. www.thehindu.com/2005/07/30/stories/2005073002601000.htm.

Rediff News. 2010. "India Refused to Build Hambantota Port: Rajapaksa." March 18. www.rediff.com/news/report/what-mahinda-rajapaksa-says-about-indo-lanka-ties/20100318.htm.

Rediff India Abroad. 2007. "PM 'Dares' Left to Withdraw Support; Left Mum." August 11. www.rediff.com/news/2007/aug/11ndeal.htm.

———. 2009a. "Chidambaram Chairs First Multi-Agency Centre Meet." January 1. www.rediff.com/news/2009/jan/01mumterror-chidambaram-chairs-first-mac-meet.htm.

———. 2009b. "Pak Claims Key Role in SL Victory over LTTE." May 28. www.rediff.com/news/2009/may/28ltte-pak-claims-key-role-in-lankan-victory.htm.

Reich, Michael R., and B. Bowonder. 1992. "Environmental Policy in India: Strategies for Better Implementation." *Policy Studies Journal* 20, no. 4 (December): 643–61.

Rendall, Matthew. 2006. "Defensive Realism and the Concert of Europe." *Review of International Studies* 32, no. 3 (July): 523–40.

Review. 1949. Untitled. *The Thought*, Delhi, April 16, Archives of the Royal Society, London, document PB/12/3/7 4a.

Rice, Condoleezza. 2011. *No Higher Honor: A Memoir of My Years in Washington*. New York: Crown.

Riedel, Bruce. 2013. *Avoiding Armageddon: America, India, and Pakistan to the Brink and Back*. Washington, DC: Brookings Institution Press.

Ripsman, Norrin, Jeffrey W. Taliaferro, and Steven E. Lobell. 2016. *Neoclassical Realist Theory of International Politics*. New York: Oxford University Press.

Robinson, Thomas W. 1981. "The Sino-Soviet Border Conflict." In *Diplomacy and Power: Soviet Armed Forces as a Political Instrument*, edited by Stephen S. Kaplan. Washington, DC: Brookings Institution Press.

———. 2003. "The Sino-Soviet Border Conflict of 1969: New Evidence Three Decades Later." In *Chinese Warfighting: The PLA Experience*, edited by Mark A. Ryan, David Michael Finkelstein, and Michael A. McDevitt. Armonk, NY: M. E. Sharpe.

Roehrig, Terence. 2006. "Restraining the Hegemon: North Korea, the US, and

Asymmetrical Deterrence." In *The United States and the Korean Peninsula in the 21st Century*, edited by Tae-Hwan Kwak and Seung-Ho Joo. Burlington, VT: Ashgate.

Rosa, Paolo. 2018. *Neoclassical Realism and the Underdevelopment of China's Nuclear Doctrine*. Cham, UK: Palgrave Macmillan.

Rosa, Paolo, and Paolo Foradori. 2017. "Politics Does Not Stop at the 'Nuclear Edge': Neoclassical Realism and the Making of China's Military Doctrine." *Italian Political Science Review* 47, no. 3 (November): 359–84.

Rose, Gideon. 1998. "Neoclassical Realism and Theories of Foreign Policy." *International Security* 42, no. 2 (Fall): 155–90.

Rosecrance, Richard. 1991. "Albert Wohlstetter." In *Makers of Nuclear Strategy*, edited by John Baylis and John Garnett. London: Pinter.

Rotberg, Robert I. 1999. "Sri Lanka's Civil War: From Mayhem toward Diplomatic Resolution." In *Creating Peace in Sri Lanka: Civil War and Reconciliation*, edited by Robert I. Rotberg. Washington, DC: Brookings Institution Press.

Roy, Nobhojit, Vikas Kapil, Italo Subbarao, and Isaac Ashkenazi. 2011. "Mass Casualty Response in the 2008 Mumbai Terrorist Attacks." *Disaster Medicine and Public Health Preparedness* 5, no. 4: 273–79.

Roy-Chaudhury, Rahul. 1999. "Trends in the Delimitation of India's Maritime Boundaries." *Strategic Analysis* 22, no. 10: 1513–24.

Rumer, Eugene B. 2000. *Dangerous Drift: Russia's Middle East Policy*. Policy Paper 4, Washington Institute for Near East Policy, Washington, DC. www.washingtoninstitute.org/uploads/Documents/pubs/PP_54_DANGEROUS_DRIFT.pdf.

Ruparelia, Sanjay. 2005. "Managing the United Progressive Alliance: The Challenges Ahead." *Economic and Political Weekly* 40, no. 24 (June 11–17): 2407–12.

Sagar, Rahul. 2009. "State of Mind: What Kind of Power Will India Become?" *International Affairs* 85, no. 4 (July): 801–16.

Sahadevan, P. 2007. "India and the Peace Process in Sri Lanka." In *Peace Process in Sri Lanka: Challenges and Opportunities*, edited by V. R. Raghavan. Chennai: EastWest Books.

Sajó, András. 1992. "Discipline and the Responsibility Deficit: A Hungarian Heritage." *Capital University Law Review* 21: 1107–23.

Sakhuja, Vijay. 2005. "Indian Naval Diplomacy: Post Tsunami." Institute of Peace and Conflict Studies, New Delhi, February 8. www.ipcs.org/comm_select.php?articleNo=1640.

Saksena, Jyotika. 2006. "Regime Design Matters: The CTBT and India's Nuclear Dilemma." *Comparative Strategy* 25, no. 3 (July): 209–29.

Saltzman, Ilai Z. 2015. "Growing Pains: Neoclassical Realism and Japan's Security Policy Emancipation." *Contemporary Security Policy* 36, no. 3: 498–527.

Samanta, Pranab Dhal. 2008. "Surge in Pak Arms Sale to Sri Lanka Worries India." *Indian Express*, May 11. http://archive.indianexpress.com/news/surge-in-pak-arms-sale-to-sri-lanka-worries-/307986/.

———. 2009. "Only One Taj Master Key, No Hotel Maps, NSG Walked in Hands Tied." *Indian Express*, June 7. www.indianexpress.com/news/only-one-taj-master-key-no-hotel-maps-nsg-walked-in-hands-tied/472633/.

Sambandan, V. S. 2003a. "'Operation Denim' Comes to a Formal End." *The Hindu*, June 6. www.thehindu.com/thehindu/2003/06/06/stories/2003060604511200.htm.

———. 2003b. "Stateless No Longer." *The Hindu Frontline*, October 25–November 7. https://frontline.thehindu.com/static/html/fl2022/stories/20031107001305600.htm.

———. 2004. "India, Sri Lanka Carry out Naval Exercise." *The Hindu*, December 17. www.thehindu.com/2004/12/17/stories/2004121705511200.htm.

———. 2005a. "India Should Be Involved in Peace Process." *The Hindu*, December 22. www.thehindu.com/2005/12/22/stories/2005122207991100.htm.

———. 2005b. "India–Sri Lanka Naval Exercise Ends." *The Hindu*, December 15. www.thehindu.com/2005/12/15/stories/2005121506261300.htm.

———. 2005c. "Moratorium on Sri Lankan Debt." *The Hindu*, May 4. www.thehindu.com/2005/05/04/stories/2005050415091700.htm.

———. 2006. "An Air of Apprehension," *The Hindu Frontline*, January 27, https://frontline.thehindu.com/world-affairs/article30208049.ece.

Santhanam. K. 2005. "Indo-US Nuclear Treaty: A Good Deal." Rediff.com, July 25. www.rediff.com/news/2005/jul/25guest1.htm.

Saran, Shyam. 2013a. "Is India's Nuclear Deterrent Credible?" *Arms Control Wonk*, April 24. www.armscontrolwonk.com/files/2013/05/Final-Is-Indias-Nuclear-Deterrent-Credible-rev1-2-1-3.pdf.

———. 2013b. "Weapon that Has More Than Symbolic Value." *The Hindu*, May 4. www.thehindu.com/opinion/lead/Weapon-that-has-more-than-symbolic-value/article12121573.ece.

———. 2014. "The Dangers of Nuclear Revisionism." *Business Standard*, April 22. www.business-standard.com/article/opinion/shyam-saran-the-dangers-of-nuclear-revisionism-114042201335_1.html.

———. 2015. *The Indo-US Civil Nuclear Agreement: Ten Years After*. New Delhi: India Habitat Centre.

———. 2017. *How India Sees the World: Kautilya to the 21st Century*. New Delhi: Juggernaut Books.

Sarkar, Jayita. 2015. "The Making of a Non-Aligned Nuclear Power: India's Proliferation Drift, 1964–68." *International History Review* 37, no. 5: 933–50.

Sasikumar, Karthika, and Gilles Verniers. 2013. "The India–US Nuclear Cooperation Agreement: Explaining the Contentious Debate." *Asian Survey* 53, no. 4 (July–August): 679–702.

Schaffer, Teresita C. 2009. *India and the United States in the 21st Century: Reinventing Partnership*. New Delhi: India Research Press.

Schaffer, Teresita C., and Howard B. Schaffer. 2016. *India at the Global High Table:*

The Quest for Regional Primacy and Strategic Autonomy. Washington, DC: Brookings Institution Press.

Schmidt, Johannes Dragsbaek. 2017. "The Internal and External Constraints on Foreign Policy in India: Exploring Culture and Ethnic Sensitivities." *Third World Quarterly* 38, no. 17: 1894–1908.

Schneider, Mark. 2014. "Minimum Deterrence and Russian and Chinese Threat Developments." *Comparative Strategy* 33, no. 1: 193–201.

Schultz, Kenneth. 2013. "Domestic Politics and International Relations." In *Handbook of International Relations*, edited by Walter Carlsnaes, Thomas Risse, and Beth Simmons. London: Sage.

Schweller, Randall L. 2006. *Unanswered Threats: Political Constraints on the Balance of Power*. Princeton, NJ: Princeton University Press.

Scott, David. 2009. "India's 'Extended Neighborhood' Concept: Power Projection for a Rising Power." *India Review* 8, no. 2: 107–43.

Scott-Clark, Cathy, and Adrian Levy. 2013. *The Siege: 68 Hours Inside the Taj Hotel*. New York: Penguin.

Sears, Nathan Alexander. 2017. "The Neoclassical Realist Research Program: Between Progressive Promise and Degenerative Dangers." *International Politics Reviews* 5, no. 1: 21–31.

Sechser, Todd S., and Matthew Fuhrmann. 2017. *Nuclear Weapons and Coercive Diplomacy*. New York: Cambridge University Press.

Sen Gupta, Bhabani. 1983. "Carnage in Sri Lanka Spawns Indian Doctrine of Regional Security." *India Today*, August 31 (updated June 18, 2014). www.indiatoday.in/magazine/cover-story/story/19830831-carnage-in-sri-lanka-spawns-indian-doctrine-of-regional-security-770977-2013-07-20.

Senadhira, Sugeeswara P. 2000. "Sri Lankan Security: Internal and External Factors." In *Security in Europe and South Asia: Challenges and Options for the Twenty-First Century*, edited by Naveed Ahmad Tahir. Karachi: University of Karachi; and Islamabad: Hanns Seidel Foundation.

Shamsi, Aamir Firoz, Iqbal A. Panhwar, Badar Iqbal, and Khizar Cheema. 2014. "India as an Emerging Economy." *Transnational Corporations Review* 6: no. 1: 15–25.

Shankar, Mahesh. 2018. "Territory and the China–India Competition." In *The China–India Rivalry in the Globalization Era*, edited by T. V. Paul. Washington, DC: Georgetown University Press.

Shanker, Thom, and David E. Sanger. 2003. "North Korea Hides New Nuclear Sites, Evidence Suggests." *New York Times*, July 20.

Sharma, Dhirendra. 1983. *India's Nuclear Estate*. New Delhi: Lancer International.

Sharma, Kalpana. 1998. "The Hindu Bomb." *Bulletin of the. Atomic Scientists* 54, no. 4: 30–33.

Sharma, Prachi, M. K. Unnikrishnan, and Abhishek Sharma. 2015. "Sexual Violence in India: Addressing Gaps between Policy and Implementation." *Health Policy and Planning* 30, no. 5 (June 1): 656–59.

Shekhar, Kumar Shakti. 2020. "Rajya Sabha Polls: BJP Won More Seats but

Opposition May Have Upper Hand." *Times of India*, June 23. https://timesofindia.indiatimes.com/india/rajya-sabha-polls-bjp-won-more-seats-but-opposition-may-have-upper-hand/articleshow/76528176.cms.

Shourie, Arun. 2008. "Surprised?" *Indian Express*, December 1. http://archive.indianexpress.com/news/surprised-/392625/.

Shidore, Sarang. 2015. "India's Strategic Culture and Strategic Stability on the Subcontinent." In *Deterrence Instability and Nuclear Weapons in South Asia*, edited by Michael Krepon, Joshua T. White, Julia Thompson, and Shane Mason. Washington, DC: Henry L. Stimson Center.

Siddiqa, Ayesha. 2011. "Pakistan's Counterterrorism Strategy: Separating Friends from Enemies." *Washington Quarterly* 34, no. 1: 149–62.

Siddiqui, Imran Ahmed, and G. S. Mudur. 2019. "No-First-Use Not Cast in Stone, Says Rajnath Singh." *Telegraph*, August 17. www.telegraphindia.com/india/no-first-use-not-cast-in-stone-says-rajnath-singh/cid/1698270.

Sikri, Rajiv. 2009. *Challenge and Strategy: Rethinking India's Foreign Policy*. New Delhi: Sage.

Singer, J. David. 1961. "The Level of Analysis Problem in International Relations." *World Politics* 14, no. 1 (October): 77–92.

Singh, Jasjit. 2005. "Do We Need the Nuclear Deal with the US?" Rediff.com, July 26. www.rediff.com/news/2005/jul/26guest.htm.

Singh, Prakash. 2001. *Kohima to Kashmir: On the Terrorist Trail*. New Delhi: Rupa.

Singh, Rahul. 2009. "Black Cats Could Have Cut Terror Short." In *26/11: The Attack on Mumbai by Hindustan Times*. New Delhi: Penguin.

Singh, Rashmi. 2018. "India's Experience with Terrorism." In *The Oxford Handbook of India's National Security*, edited by Sumit Ganguly, Nicolas Blarel, and Manjeet S. Pardesi. New Delhi: Oxford University Press.

Singh, Sinderpal. 2013. *India in South Asia: Domestic Identity Politics and Foreign Policy from Nehru to the BJP*. New York: Routledge.

Singh, Surendra, and Satish Misra. 2012. *Federalism in India: Time for a Relook?* Issue Brief 40, Observer Research Foundation, New Delhi. http://cf.orfonline.org/wp-content/uploads/2012/07/IssueBrief_40.pdf.

Singh, Sushant. 2016a. "Manohar Parrikar Questions India's No-First-Use Nuclear Policy, Adds 'My Thinking.'" *Indian Express*, November 11. https://indianexpress.com/article/india/india-news-india/manohar-parrikar-questions-no-first-use-nuclear-policy-adds-my-thinking-4369062/.

———. 2016b. *Operation Cactus: Mission Impossible in the Maldives* New Delhi: Juggernaut.

Sinha, Amitabh. 2009. "What We Learnt from Mumbai: US Agencies to Senate." *Indian Express*, January 20. http://indianexpress.com/article/news-archive/web/what-we-learnt-from-mumbai-us-agencies-to-senate/.

SIPRI (Stockholm International Peace Research Institute). 2018. "World Nuclear Forces." www.sipri.org/yearbook/2018/06.

———. 2021. "Global Nuclear Arsenals Grow as States Continue to Modernize."

https://sipri.org/media/press-release/2021/global-nuclear-arsenals-grow-states-continue-modernize-new-sipri-yearbook-out-now.

Sirohi, Seema. 1987. "Indian Ships Retreat after Tense Standoff with Sri Lankan Vessels." Associated Press, June 4. https://apnews.com/e2a9336ea76a6180be768c1ef8f972de.

Sivarajah, A. 1990. "Indo-Sri Lanka Relations and Sri Lanka's Ethnic Crisis: The Tamil Nadu Factor." In *South Asian Strategic Issues: Sri Lankan Perspectives*, edited by Shelton U. Kodikara. New Delhi: Sage.

Smith, Chris. 1994. *India's Ad Hoc Arsenal: Direction or Drift in Defence Policy?* Oxford: Oxford University Press.

Smith, Elliot. 2020. "UK Enters Recession after GDP Plunged by a Record 20.4% in the Second Quarter." CNBC, August 12. www.cnbc.com/2020/08/12/uk-gdp-plunged-by-a-record-20point4percent-in-the-second-quarter.html.

Snyder, Glenn H. 1965. "The Balance of Power and the Balance of Terror." In *The Balance of Power*, edited by Paul Seabury. San Francisco: Chandler.

———. 2002. "Mearsheimer's World: Offensive Realism and the Struggle for Security." *International Security* 27, no. 1 (Summer): 149–73.

Snyder, Jack, and Keir A. Lieber. 2008. "Correspondence: Defensive Realism and the 'New' History of World War I." *International Security* 33, no. 1 (Summer): 174–94.

Sokov, Nikolai. 2007. "Second Thoughts about a First Strike." *Nonproliferation Review* 14, no. 1: 139–47.

Solingen, Etel. 2014. "Domestic Coalitions, Internationalization, and War: Then and Now." *International Security* 39, no. 1 (Summer): 44–70.

Sood, Vikram. 2015. "The Indian Intelligence System: Meeting the Challenges of a New World." In *Handbook of Indian Defence Policy: Themes, Structures and Doctrines*, edited by Harsh V. Pant. New Delhi: Routledge.

Sooriyanarayan, K. 2002. "Indo–Sri Lanka Relations in the Present Context." *Journal of the Association of Retired Flag Rank Officers*, January 5, 90–99. http://arfro.org/publications/2002/2002.pdf.

Sørensen, Camilla. 2013. "Is China Becoming More Aggressive? A Neoclassical Realist Analysis." *Asian Perspective* 37, no. 3 (July–September): 363–85.

South Asia Terrorism Portal. No date–a. "Cumulative Fatalities by Conflict Theatres: 2005–2019." www.satp.org/satporgtp/countries/india/database/Cumulative_Fatalities.htm/india.

———. No date–b. "Datasheet India: Yearly Fatalities." www.satp.org/datasheet-terrorist-attack/fatalities/india.

———. No date–c. "Fatalities in Terrorist Violence 1988–2019." www.satp.org/satporgtp/countries/india/states/jandk/data_sheets/annual_casualties.htm.

———. No date–d. "India: Terrorist, Insurgent and Extremist Groups." www.satp.org/terrorist-groups/india.

———. No date–e. "Terrorist Attacks in Mumbai since 1993." www.satp.org/satporgtp/countries/india/database/mumbai_blast.htm.

Sri Lanka Guardian. 2008. "GoSL Orders Emergency Military Supplies." April 4. www.slguardian.org/gosl-orders-emergency-pak-military-supplies/.

Sridharan, E. 2004. "Electoral Coalitions in 2004 General Elections: Theory and Evidence." *Economic and Political Weekly* 39, no. 51 (December 18-24): 5418–25.

———. 2013. "Drift and Confusion Reign in Indian Politics." *Current History* 112, no. 753 (April): 123–29.

———. 2016. "Indo–Sri Lanka Relations: Geopolitics, Domestic Politics, or Something More Complex?" In *Engaging the World: Indian Foreign Policy since 1947*, edited by Sumit Ganguly. New Delhi: Oxford University Press.

———. 2018. "Coalition Congruence in India's Federal System." In *Coalition Politics and Federalism*, edited by Adrián Albala and Josep Maria Reniu. Cham: Springer International.

Srinivas, M. N. 1966. *Social Change in Modern India*. Berkeley: University of California Press.

Srinivasan, M. R. 2006a. "India May Lose Control of Its Nuclear Future." *The Hindu*, December 14. www.thehindu.com/todays-paper/tp-opinion/india-may-lose-control-of-its-nuclear-future/article3033310.ece.

———. 2006b. "Remember Lessons from Tarapur." *The Hindu*, December 27. www.thehindu.com/todays-paper/tp-opinion/remember-lessons-from-tarapur/article18510623.ece.

———. 2007. "The India–US Nuclear Stalemate. *The Hindu*, May 31. www.thehindu.com/todays-paper/tp-opinion/The-India-U.S.-nuclear-stalemate/article14770963.ece.

Staniland, Paul. 2018. "Internal Security Strategy in India." *India Review* 17, no. 1: 142–58.

"Statement to Parliament by Prime Minister Vajpayee, 27 May." 1998. www.acronym.org.uk/old/archive/spind.htm.

Stein, Arthur A. 2006. "Constraints and Determinants: Structure, Purpose, and Process in the Analysis of Foreign Policy." In *Approaches, Levels, and Methods of Analysis in International Politics: Crossing Boundaries*, edited by Harvey Starr. New York: Palgrave Macmillan.

Sterling-Folker, Jennifer. 2009. "Forward Is as Forward Does: Assessing Neoclassical Realism from a Traditions Perspective." In *Rethinking International Relations: Between Traditions and Innovation*, edited by Annette Freyberg-Inan, Ewan Harrison, and Patrick James. Baltimore: Johns Hopkins University Press.

Stoessinger, John G. 1994. *Nations at Dawn: China, Russia and America*. New York: McGraw Hill.

Strange, Susan. 1988. *States and Markets*. London: Pinter.

Subrahmanyam, K. 2004a. "Narasimha Rao and the Bomb." *Strategic Analysis* 28, no. 4: 593–95.

———. 2004b. "Politics of Security: When Vajpayee Said 'No' to Going Nuclear." *Times of India*, April 10. http://articles.timesofindia.indiatimes.com/2004-04

-10/edit-page/28347582_1_nuclear-weapon-weapons-programme-peaceful-nuclear-explosions.

———. 2005. "The Great Nuclear Handshake." *Times of India*, August 15. https://timesofindia.indiatimes.com/edit-page/The-great-nuclear-handshake/articleshow/1201022.cms.

———. 2018. "Indian Nuclear Policy—1964–98 (a Personal Recollection)." *Strategic Analysis* 42, no. 3: 293–311.

Subramaniam, Arjun. 2012. "Challenges of Protecting India from Terrorism." *Terrorism and Political Violence* 24, no. 3: 396–414.

Subramanian, Nirupama. 2000. "We Cannot Let Down the People of Jaffna: Chandrika." *The Hindu*, May 24. www.thehindu.com/thehindu/2000/05/24/stories/01240004.htm.

———. 2005. "India and Sri Lanka: So Near and Yet So Far." *The Hindu*, December 28. www.thehindu.com/2005/12/28/stories/2005122801741000.htm.

———. 2011. "How India Kept Pressure Off Sri Lanka." *The Hindu*, March 16 (updated October 1, 2016). www.thehindu.com/opinion/lead/How-India-kept-pressure-off-Sri-Lanka/article14950828.ece.

Subramanian, R. R. 2015. "India's Nuclear Situation: Where To?" *Strategic Analysis* 39, no. 5: 610–23.

Subramanian, T. S. 1999. "Chronicle of Murders." *The Hindu Frontline*, August 14–27. https://frontline.thehindu.com/static/html/fl1617/16171020.htm.

———. 2005a. "Identifying a Civilian Nuclear Facility Is India's Decision" (interview). *The Hindu*, August 12. www.thehindu.com/2005/08/12/stories/2005081204521100.htm.

———. 2005b. "No Sanctity About Bush Promise: Nuclear Experts." *The Hindu*, July 21. www.thehindu.com/2005/07/21/stories/2005072106301200.htm.

Suchitra, J. Y. 2005. "N-Energy Not the Best Option." *Times of India*, November 17. https://timesofindia.indiatimes.com/edit-page/N-energy-not-the-best-option/articleshow/1297921.cms.

Sundaram, Kumar, and Ramana, M. V. 2018. "India and the Policy of No First Use of Nuclear Weapons." *Journal for Peace and Nuclear Disarmament*, no. 1: 152–68.

Sunday Island. No date. "India to Keep Distance from LTTE." www.island.lk/2005/05/22/news14.html.

Suryanarayan, Pavithra. 2021. "State Capacity: A Useful Concept or Meaningless Pablum?" *Broadstreet*, April 12.

Suryanarayan, V. 2009. "Sri Lankan Crisis: Influence of Tamil Nadu in India's Sri Lanka Policy." *Sri Lanka Guardian*, August 12. www.slguardian.org/sri-lankan-crisis-influence-of-tamil-nadu-in-indias-sri-lanka-policy/.

Suryanarayana, P. S. 1988. *The Peace Trap: An Indo–Sri Lankan Political Crisis*. New Delhi: Affiliated East-West Press.

Swami, Praveen. 2008. "India's Strategic Deafness and the Massacre in Mumbai." *The Hindu*, November 29. www.thehindu.com/todays-paper/tp-opinion/indias-strategic-deafness-the-massacre-in-mumbai/article1385240.ece.

———. 2009. "Where Style Has Trumped Substance." *The Hindu*, November 27. www.thehindu.com/opinion/op-ed/where-style-has-trumped-substance/article55402.ece.

Talbott, Strobe. 2004. *Engaging India: Diplomacy, Democracy, and the Bomb*. Washington, DC: Brookings Institution Press.

Taliaferro, Jeffrey W. 2001–2. "Security Seeking under Anarchy: Defensive Realism Revisited." *International Security* 25, no. 3 (Winter 2001–2): 128–61.

———. 2006. "State Building for Future Wars: Neoclassical Realism and the Resource-Extractive State." *Security Studies* 15, no. 3 (July–September): 464–95.

Taneja, Pradeep, and Azad Singh Bali. 2021. "India's Domestic and Foreign Policy Responses to COVID-19." *Round Table* 110, no. 1: 46–61.

Tang, Shiping. 2008. "From Offensive to Defensive Realism: A Social Evolutionary Interpretation of China's Security Strategy." In *China's Ascent: Power, Security, and the Future of International Politics*, edited by Robert S. Ross and Zhu Feng. Ithaca, NY: Cornell University Press.

———. 2009. "Taking Stock of Neoclassical Realism." *International Studies Review* 11, no. 4 (December): 799–803.

———. 2010. *A Theory of Security Strategy for Our Time: Defensive Realism*. New York: Palgrave Macmillan.

Tellis, Ashley. 2013. "The Transforming US–Indian Relationship and Its Significance for American Interests." In *India's Foreign Policy: A Reader*, edited by Kanti P. Bajpai and Harsh V. Pant. New Delhi: Oxford University Press.

———. 2016. *India as a Leading Power*. Washington, DC: Carnegie Endowment for International Peace. http://carnegieendowment.org/files/CP_268_Tellis_India_final1.pdf.

———. 2019. *A Troubled Transition: Emerging Nuclear Forces in India and Pakistan*. Stanford, CA: Hoover Institution. www.hoover.org/research/troubled-transition-emerging-nuclear-forces-india-and-pakistan.

Thakur, Pradeep. 2008. "Maharashtra Callous towards Maritime Security: CAG Report." *Times of India*, December 2. https://timesofindia.indiatimes.com/india/Maharashtra-callous-towards-maritime-security-CAG-report/articleshow/3781321.cms.

Thakur, Ramesh. 2003. "Why India Said 'No' to US." *Japan Times*, July 17. www.japantimes.co.jp/opinion/2003/07/17/commentary/world-commentary/why-india-said-no-to-u-s/.

Thevar, Steffy. 2018. "More Than 100 Mumbai Firemen Were Involved in the Rescue Operations on 26/11." *Hindustan Times*, November 23. www.hindustantimes.com/mumbai-news/more-than-100-mumbai-firemen-were-involved-in-the-rescue-operations-on-26-11/story-G5xYxIyAZYMAXm47zYWXuJ.html.

Thomas, C. Joshua. 1995. *Sri Lanka's Turmoil and Indian Government: A Study of Ethnic Conflict*. New Delhi: Omsons.

Thompson, William R. 2018. "Indian National Security and State Capacity." In *The*

Oxford Handbook of India's National Security, edited by Sumit Ganguly, Nicolas Blarel, and Manjeet S. Pardesi. New Delhi: Oxford University Press.

Tickner, J. Ann. 1987. *Self-Reliance Versus Power Politics: The American and Indian Experience in Building Nation States*. New York: Columbia University Press.

Times of India. 2006a. "CPM Objects to Several Clauses in N-Deal Bill." June 29. https://timesofindia.indiatimes.com/india/CPM-objects-to-several-clauses-in-N-deal-Bill/articleshow/1689047.cms.

———. 2006b. "US Wants to Block India's Indigenous Nuclear-Programme." February 9. https://timesofindia.indiatimes.com/india/US-wants-to-block-Indias-indigenous-nuclear-programme/articleshow/1408499.cms.

———. 2008a. "China Woos Lanka with $1B in Aid." March 11. http://timesofindia.indiatimes.com/China_woos_Lanka_with_1b_in_aid/articleshow/2853174.cms.

———. 2008b. "Chronology of the Indo-US Nuclear Deal." October 9. https://timesofindia.indiatimes.com/Chronology_of_the_Indo-US_nulear_deal/articleshow/3575350.cms.

———. 2008c. "We Have to Ensure India's Pre-eminent Position: NSA." March 26. https://timesofindia.indiatimes.com/india/we-have-to-ensure-indias-pre-eminent-position-nsa/articleshow/2902544.cms.

———. 2009. "I Would Have Resigned If Nuke Deal Had Fallen Through: PM." April 11. https://timesofindia.indiatimes.com/india/I-would-have-resigned-if-nuke-deal-had-fallen-through-PM/articleshow/4386584.cms.

———. 2013. "UPA Suffering from 'Policy Paralysis': Nitish." April 5. https://timesofindia.indiatimes.com/india/UPA-suffering-from-policy-paralysis-Nitish/articleshow/19398936.cms.

Tremblay, Reeta Chowdhari, and Ashok Kapur. 2017. *Modi's Foreign Policy*. New Delhi: Sage.

Treverton, Gregory F. 1989. "From No Cities to Stable Vulnerability." In *US Nuclear Strategy: A Reader*, edited by Philip Bobbitt, Lawrence Freedman, and Gregory F. Treverton. Basingstoke: Macmillan.

Tribune. 2020. "Dysfunctional CCTV Cameras, Outdated Radio Communication among CAG Red Flags on Delhi Police." September 24. www.tribuneindia.com/news/nation/dysfunctional-cctv-cameras-outdated-radio-communication-among-cag-red-flags-on-delhi-police-145830.

Trofimov, Yaroslav, Geeta Anand, Peter Wonacott, and Matthew Rosenberg. 2008. "India Security Faulted as Survivors Tell of Terror." *Wall Street Journal*, December 1. www.wsj.com/articles/SB122809281744967785.

Tuke, Victoria. 2011. "Japan's Foreign Policy towards India: A Neoclassical Realist Analysis of the Policymaking Process." PhD thesis, University of Warwick. http://webcat.warwick.ac.uk:80/record=b2581463~S1.

Tummala, Krishna K. 2009. "Coalition Politics in India, 2004–2009." *Asian Journal of Political Science* 17, no. 3 (December): 323–48.

UNCTAD (United Nations Conference on Trade and Development). No date.

"Bilateral FDI Statistics." https://unctad.org/Sections/dite_fdistat/docs/webdiaeia2014d3_LKA.pdf.

United Nations. 2011. "Report of the Secretary-General's Panel of Experts on Accountability in Sri Lanka, March 31." www.un.org/News/dh/infocus/Sri_Lanka/POE_Report_Full.pdf.

Unnithan, Sandeep. 2007. "Sri Lanka: A Call for Arms." *India Today*, September 2. http://indiatoday.intoday.in/site/Story/1439/International/Sri+Lanka:+A+call+for+arms.html.

———. 2014. *Black Tornado: The Three Sieges of Mumbai 26/11*. Noida: HarperCollins.

Van de Wetering, Carina. 2016. *Changing US Foreign Policy toward India: US–India Relations since the Cold War*. New York: Palgrave Macmillan.

Van der Heijden, Jeroen. 2010. "A Short History of Studying Incremental Institutional Change: Does Explaining Institutional Change Provide Any New Explanations?" *Regulation and Governance* 4, no. 2: 230–43.

Varadarajan, Siddharth. 2005. "Nuclear Bargain May Prove Costly in Long Run." *The Hindu*, July 20. www.thehindu.com/2005/07/20/stories/2005072007791500.htm.

———. 2006a. "IAEA Inspections Will Compromise Breeder Research." *The Hindu*, January 21. www.thehindu.com/todays-paper/tp-national/iaea-inspections-will-compromise-breeder-research/article18391976.ece.

———. 2006b. "Indo-US Nuclear Deal: Safeguards for Breeder Reactors a Key Obstacle." *The Hindu*, January 21. https://svaradarajan.com/2006/01/21/indo-u-s-nuclear-deal-safeguards-for-breeder-reactors-a-key-obstacle/.

———. 2007. "Questions Arise over Reprocessing Restrictions." *The Hindu*, July 28. www.thehindu.com/todays-paper/tp-opinion/questions-arise-on-reprocessing-restrictions/article18464279.ece.

———. 2016. "Menon: The Policy of No First Use of Nuclear Weapons Has Served India's Purpose" (interview). *The Wire*, December 16. https://thewire.in/diplomacy/menon-india-nuclear-weapons-nfu-nsa.

Vargas, Manuel. 2010. "Responsibility in a World of Causes." *Philosophic Exchange* 40, no. 1. http://digitalcommons.brockport.edu/cgi/viewcontent.cgi?article=1012&context=phil_ex.

Varshney, Ashutosh. 1991. "India, Pakistan, and Kashmir: Antinomies of Nationalism." *Asian Survey* 3, no. 11: 997–1019.

Verma, Raj. 2017. *India and China: A Comparative Perspective of the Oil Industry*. New York: Routledge.

———. 2020. "The Regional Comprehensive Economic Partnership and India: A Test Case of Narendra Modi's Statesmanship." *Australian Journal of International Affairs* 74, no. 5: 479–85.

Vickery, Raymond E. Jr. 2011. *The Eagle and the Elephant: Strategic Aspects of US–India Economic Engagement*. New Delhi: Oxford University Press.

Vikraman, Shaji. 2017. "In Fact: How Govts Pledged Gold to Pull Economy Back from the Brink." *Indian Express*, April 5. https://indianexpress.com/article/explained/in-fact-how-govts-pledged-gold-to-pull-economy-back-from-the-brink/.

Virmani, Arvind. 2006. "World Economy, Geopolitics and Global Strategy: Indo-US Relations in the 21st Century." *Economic and Political Weekly* 41, nos. 43–44 (November 4): 4601–12.

Viswanathan. 2000. "Double Speak in Tamil Nadu." *The Hindu Frontline*, June 24–July 7. https://frontline.thehindu.com/static/html/fl1713/17130330.htm.

Volgy, Thomas J., Renato Corbetta, Keith A. Grant, and Ryan G. Baird, eds. 2011a. *Major Powers and the Quest for Status in International Politics: Global and Regional Perspectives.* New York: Palgrave Macmillan.

———. 2011b. "Major Power Status in International Politics." In *Major Powers and the Quest for Status in International Politics: Global and Regional Perspectives*, edited by Thomas J. Volgy, Renato Corbetta, Keith A. Grant, and Ryan G. Baird. New York: Palgrave Macmillan.

Voo, Julia, Irfan Hemani, Simon Jones, Winnona De Sombre, Daniel Cassidy, and Anina Schwarzenbach. 2020. *National Cyber Power Index 2020*. Belfer Center for Science and International Affairs, Harvard University, Cambridge, MA. www.belfercenter.org/sites/default/files/2020-09/NCPI_2020.pdf.

Vyas, Neena. 2007. "123 Agreement an Assault on Nuclear Sovereignty: BJP." *The Hindu*, August 5. www.thehindu.com/todays-paper/123-agreement-an-assault-on-nuclear-sovereignty-BJP/article14810272.ece.

Wagner, Christian. 2005. *From Hard Power to Soft Power? Ideas, Interaction, Institutions, and Images in India's South Asia Policy*. Working Paper 26, Heidelberg Papers on South Asian and Comparative Politics. Heidelberg: University of Heidelberg. http://archiv.ub.uni-heidelberg.de/volltextserver/5436/1/hpsacp26.pdf.

Walt, Stephen M. 2020. "The Realist's Guide to the Coronavirus Outbreak." *Foreign Policy*, March 9. https://foreignpolicy.com/2020/03/09/coronavirus-econ omy -globalization-virus-icu-realism/.

Waltz, Kenneth N. 1959. *Man, the State and War: A Theoretical Analysis*. New York: Columbia University Press.

———. 1979. *Theory of International Politics*. Reading, MA: Addison-Wesley.

Walton, Douglas. 1974. "Control." *Behaviorism* 2, no. 2: 162–71.

Ward, Steven Michael. 2017. "Lost in Translation: Social Identity Theory and the Study of Status in World Politics." *International Studies Quarterly* 61, no. 4: 821–34.

Wariavwalla, Bharat. 1989. "India in 1988: Drift, Disarray, or Pattern?" *Asian Survey* 29, no. 2 (February): 189–98.

Warren, Mark E. 2014. "Accountability and Democracy." In *The Oxford Handbook of Accountability*, edited by Mark Bovens, Robert E. Goodin, and Thomas Schillemans. Oxford: Oxford University Press. DOI: 10.1093/oxfordhb/9780199641253.013.0028.

Weigold, Auriol. 2016. *India, China, the United States and the NSG Impasse: Competing Objectives or Just a Distraction?* Nedlands, Australia: Future Directions International. https://core.ac.uk/reader/51343010.

Weisman, Steven R. 1987. "India Airlifts Aid to Tamil Rebels." *New York Times*, June 5. www.nytimes.com/1987/06/05/world/india-airlifts-aid-to-tamil-rebels.html.

Weiss, Leonard. 2006. "Power Points." *Bulletin of the Atomic Scientists* 62, no. 3 (May–June): 21, 63.

Weiss, Linda. 2018. *The Myth of the Powerless State*. Ithaca, NY: Cornell University Press.

Wendt, Alexander. 1987. "The Agent–Structure Problem in International Relations Theory." *International Organization* 41, no. 3: 335–70.

———. 1992. "Anarchy Is What States Make of It: The Social Construction of Power Politics." *International Organization* 46, no. 2: 391–425.

———. 1999. *Social Theory of International Politics*. Cambridge: Cambridge University Press.

Wernick, David A., and Mary Ann von Glinow. 2012. "Reflections on the Evolving Terrorist Threat to Luxury Hotels: A Case Study on Marriott International Hotels." *Thunderbird International Business Review* 54, no. 5 (September–October): 729–46.

Westcott, Stephen P. 2021. "Seizing a Window of Opportunity? The Causes and Consequences of the 2020 Sino-Indian Border Stand-Off." *Journal of Asian Security and International Affairs*, February 22. https://doi.org/10.1177/2347797021992527.

White House. 2005a. "Background Briefing by Administration Officials on US–South Asia Relations," March 25. https://2001-2009.state.gov/r/pa/prs/ps/2005/43853.htm.

———. 2005b. "Joint Statement by President George W. Bush and Prime Minister Manmohan Singh, July 18." https://2001-2009.state.gov/p/sca/rls/pr/2005/49763.htm.

Wickramasinghe, Nira. 2014. *Sri Lanka in the Modern Age: A History*. Oxford: Oxford University Press.

Wight, Colin. 2006. *Agents, Structures and International Relations: Politics as Ontology*. Cambridge: Cambridge University Press.

Wikileaks. No date. "The BJP Attacks UPA Foreign Policy." https://wikileaks.org/plusd/cables/05NEWDELHI9761_a.html.

Williams, Michael C. 2004. "Why Ideas Matter in International Relations: Hans Morgenthau, Classical Realism, and the Moral Construction of Power Politics." *International Organization* 58, no. 4 (October): 633–65.

———. 2005. *The Realist Tradition and the Limits of International Relations*. Cambridge: Cambridge University Press.

The Wire. 2019. "Total Recall: Ten Things That Went Wrong during the 26/11 Attacks." November 26. https://thewire.in/security/26-11-mumbai-terror-attacks.

Wivel, Anders. 2005. "Explaining Why State X Made a Certain Move Last Tuesday: The Promise and Limitations of Realist Foreign Policy Analysis." *Journal of International Relations and Development* 8, no. 4, 355–80.

Wojczewski, Thorsten. 2020. "Populism, Hindu Nationalism, and Foreign Policy in India: The Politics of Representing 'the People.'" *International Studies Review* 22, no. 3: 396–422.

Wohlstetter, Albert. 1958. *The Delicate Balance of Terror*, revised. Document P-1472. Santa Monica, CA: RAND Corporation.

———. 1959. "The Delicate Balance of Terror." *Foreign Affairs* 37, no. 2: 211–34.

———. 1961. "Nuclear Sharing: NATO and the N+1 Country." *Foreign Affairs* 39, no. 3: 355–87.

Wohlstetter, Roberta. 1962. *Pearl Harbor: Warning and Decision*. Stanford, CA: Stanford University Press, 1962.

World Bank. No date–a. "Data." https://data.worldbank.org/indicator/NY.GDP.MKTP.KD?end=1991&locations=IN-CN&start=1966.

World Bank. No date–b. "Data." https://data.worldbank.org/indicator/NY.GDP.MKTP.CD.

World Bank. No date–c. "GDP (Constant 2010 US$): India." https://data.worldbank.org/indicator/NY.GDP.MKTP.KD?end=2019&locations=IN&start=1991&year_low_desc=true.

World Bank. No date–d. "Military Expenditure (Current USD): India." https://data.worldbank.org/indicator/MS.MIL.XPND.CD?end=2018&locations=IN&start=1991.

Wyatt, Andrew. 2013. "Populism and Politics in Contemporary Tamil Nadu." *Contemporary South Asia* 21, no. 4: 365–81.

Yang Sheng, Chen Qingqing, and Liu Xuanzun. 2021. "Honoring Martyrs Shows Nationwide Support to PLA, Sincerity of Easing Tensions." *Global Times*, February 22. www.81.cn/jwywpd/2021-02/22/content_9989896.htm.

Yechury, Sitaram. 2006. "Uncle Sam Kneads You." *Debating India*, February 8. http://india.eu.org/spip.php?article4112.

Yeşilyurt, Nuri. 2017. "Explaining Miscalculation and Maladaptation in Turkish Foreign Policy towards the Middle East during the Arab Uprisings: A Neoclassical Realist Perspective." *All Azimuth* 6, no. 2: 65–83.

Yoo, Hyon Joo. 2012. "Domestic Hurdles for System-Driven Behavior: Neoclassical Realism and Missile Defense Policies in Japan and South Korea." *International Relations of the Asia-Pacific* 12, no. 2 (May): 317–48.

Zakaria, Fareed. 2008. *From Wealth to Power: The Unusual Origins of America's World Role*. Princeton, NJ: Princeton University Press.

Zarate, Robert, and Henry Sokolski, eds. 2009. *Nuclear Heuristics: Selected Writings of Albert and Roberta Wohlstetter*. Carlisle, PA: Strategic Studies Institute, US Army War College. https://publications.armywarcollege.edu/pubs/1985.pdf.

Zee News. 2009. "MARCOS Out of Depth during Mumbai Operation: Ex-NSG DG." November 23. https://zeenews.india.com/news/maharashtra/marcos-out-of-depth-during-mumbai-operation-ex-nsg-dg_581519.html.

Zhai Qiang. 1998. "Reassessing China's Role in the Vietnam War: Some Mysteries Explored." In *China and the United States: A New Cold War History*, edited by Xiaobing Li and Hongshan Li. Lanham, MD: University Press of America.

INDEX

Note: Information in tables is indicated by *t*.

ABOUT THE AUTHOR

Rajesh Basrur is a senior fellow in the South Asia Program at the S. Rajaratnam School of International Studies in the Nanyang Technological University in Singapore. Concurrently, he is a research associate with the Contemporary South Asian Studies Program at the Oxford School of Global and Area Studies in the University of Oxford. Previously he was professor of international relations at the Rajaratnam School; taught at the University of Mumbai; and held numerous visiting positions, including at the University of Oxford, Stanford University, and the Brookings Institution. He is the author (with Kate Sullivan de Estrada) of *Rising India: Status and Power* (Routledge, 2017); *South Asia's Cold War* (Routledge, 2008); and *Minimum Deterrence and India's Nuclear Security* (Stanford University Press, 2006).